MERIDIANS
Sources in World History

S0-BZM-916

Pearson Learning Solutions

New York   Boston   San Francisco
London   Toronto   Sydney   Tokyo   Singapore   Madrid
Mexico City   Munich   Paris   Cape Town   Hong Kong   Montreal

Senior Vice President, Editorial and Marketing: Patrick F. Boles
Senior Sponsoring Editor: Natalie Danner
Development Editor: Katherine R. Gehan and Mary Kate Paris
Editorial Assistant: Jill Johnson
Marketing Manager: Brian T. Berkeley
Operations Manager: Eric M. Kenney
Production Manager: Jennifer Berry
Rights Manager: Jillian Santos
Art Director and Cover Designer: Renée Sartell

Cover Art: Courtesy of the Stapleton Collection/CORBIS.

Please visit our website at *www.pearsoncustom.com.*

Attention bookstores: For permission to return any unsold stock, contact us at *pe-uscustomreturns@pearson.com.*

Pearson Learning Solutions, 501 Boylston Street, Suite 900, Boston, MA 02116
A Pearson Education Company
www.pearsoned.com

1 2 3 4 5 6 7 8 9 10 XXXX 14 13 12 11 10 09

ISBN 10: 0-558-28635-6
ISBN 13: 978-0-558-28635-4

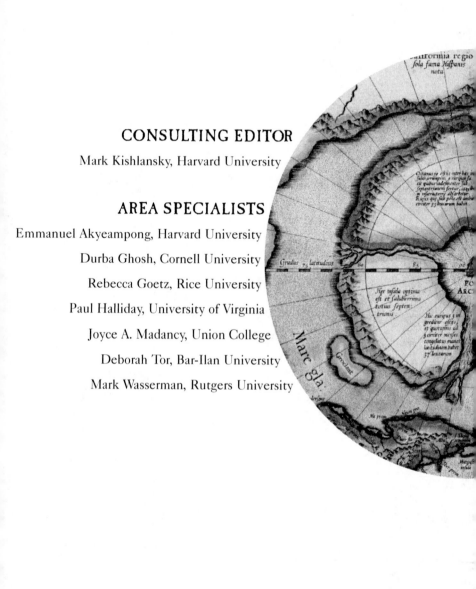

CONSULTING EDITOR
Mark Kishlansky, Harvard University

AREA SPECIALISTS
Emmanuel Akyeampong, Harvard University
Durba Ghosh, Cornell University
Rebecca Goetz, Rice University
Paul Halliday, University of Virginia
Joyce A. Madancy, Union College
Deborah Tor, Bar-Ilan University
Mark Wasserman, Rutgers University

Contents

JOURNAL OF THE FIRST VOYAGE OF VASCO DA GAMA, 1497–1499

Vasco da Gama was born in 1469, just as Portugal's maritime empire began to flourish. As a young man he earned a name for himself protecting the Portuguese trading stations along the west coast of Africa. In 1497, the king of Portugal charged him with finding a sea route from Europe to India. Over the next two years, da Gama and his crew rounded the Cape of Good Hope, claimed Mozambique for Portugal, visited cities along the Swahili Coast and ultimately reached the Indian trading centers of Goa and Calicut.

It remains unclear precisely who authored the Journal of the First Voyage of Vasco da Gama, *but the specificity of details and accuracy of navigational information suggests that the writer did travel with da Gama. If that is the case, he would have been one of only fifty-four men, out of an original crew of 170, to return to Europe with the explorer. His account reflects not only his perspective as a relatively well-traveled sailor but also the cosmopolitan nature of society along the Swahili Coast.*

On Saturday (7 April) we cast anchor off Mombasa, but did not enter the port. No sooner had we been perceived than a *zavra* [small boat] manned by Moors came out to us: in front of the city there lay numerous vessels all dressed in flags. And we, anxious not to be outdone, also dressed our ships, and we actually surpassed their show, for we wanted in nothing but men, even a few whom we had being very ill. We anchored here with much pleasure, for we confidently hoped that on the following day we might go on land and hear mass jointly with the Christians reported to live there under their own *alcaide* in a quarter separate from that of the Moors.

The pilots who had come with us told us there resided both Moors and Christians in this city; that these latter lived apart under their own lords, and that on our arrival they would receive us with much honour and take us to their houses. But they said this for a purpose of their own, for it was not true. At midnight there approached us a *zavra* with about 100 men, all armed with cutlasses and bucklers. When they came to the vessel of the captain-major they attempted to board her, armed as they were, but this was not permitted, only four or five of the most distinguished men among them being allowed on board. They remained about a couple of hours, and it seemed to us that they paid us this visit merely to find out whether they might not capture one or the other of our vessels.

On Palm Sunday (8 April) the King of Mombasa sent the captain-major a sheep and large quantities of oranges, lemons and sugar-cane, together with a ring, as a pledge of safety, letting him know that in case of his entering the port he would be supplied with all he stood in need of. This present was conveyed to us by two men, almost white, who said they were Christians, which appeared to be the fact. The captain-major sent the king a string of coral-beads as a return present, and let him know that he purposed entering the port on the following day. On the same day the captain-major's vessel was visited by four Moors of distinction.

Two men were sent by the captain-major to the king, still further to confirm these peaceful assurances. When these landed they were followed by a crowd as far as the gates of the palace. Before reaching the king they passed through four doors, each guarded by a doorkeeper with a drawn cutlass. The king received them hospitably, and ordered that they should be shown over the city. They stopped on their way at the house of two Christian merchants, who showed them a paper, an object of their adoration, on which was a sketch of the Holy Ghost. When they had seen all, the king sent them back with samples of cloves, pepper and corn, with which articles he would allow us to load our ships.

On Tuesday (10 April), when weighing anchor to enter the port, the captain-major's vessel would not pay off, and struck the vessel which followed astern. We therefore again cast anchor. When the Moors who were in our ship saw that we did not go on, they scrambled into a *zavra* attached to our stern; whilst the two pilots whom we had brought from Mozambique jumped into the water, and were picked up by the men in the *zavra*. At night the captain-major questioned two Moors (from Mozambique) whom we had on board, by dropping boiling oil upon their skin, so that they might confess any treachery intended against us. They said that orders had been given to capture us as soon as we entered the port, and thus to avenge what we had done at Mozambique. And when the torture was being applied a second time, one of the Moors, although his hands were tied, threw himself into the sea, whilst the other did so during the morning watch.

About midnight two *almadias*, with many men in them, approached. The *almadias* stood off whilst the men entered the water, some swimming in the direction of the *Berrio,* others in that of the *Raphael.* Those who swam to the *Berrio* began to cut the cable. The men on watch thought at first that they were tunny fish, but when they perceived their mistake they shouted to the other vessels. The other swimmers had already got hold of the rigging of the mizzen-mast. Seeing themselves discovered, they silently slipped down and fled. These and other wicked tricks were practised upon us by these dogs, but our Lord did not allow them to succeed, because they were unbelievers.

Mombasa is a large city seated upon an eminence washed by the sea. Its port is entered daily by numerous vessels. At its entrance stands a pillar, and by the sea a low-lying fortress. Those who had gone on shore told us that in the town they had seen many men in irons; and it seemed to us that these must be Christians, as the Christians in that country are at war with the Moors.

The Christian merchants in the town are only temporary residents, and are held in much subjection, they not being allowed to do anything except by the order of the Moorish king.

It pleased God in his mercy that on arriving at this city all our sick recovered their health, for the climate of this place is very good.

After the malice and treachery planned by these dogs had been discovered, we still remained on Wednesday and Thursday (11 and 12 April).

We left in the morning (13 April), the wind being light, and anchored about eight leagues from Mombasa, close to the shore. At the break of day

3

(14 April) we saw two boats about three leagues to the leeward, in the open sea, and at once gave chase, with the intention of capturing them, for we wanted to secure a pilot who would guide us to where we wanted to go. At vesper-time we came up with one of them, and captured it, the other escaping towards the land. In the one we took we found seventeen men, besides gold, silver, and an abundance of maize and other provisions; as also a young woman, who was the wife of an old Moor of distinction, who was a passenger. When we came up with the boat they all threw themselves into the water, but we picked them up from our boats.

That same day (14 April) at sunset, we cast anchor off a place called Milinde,[1] which is thirty leagues from Mombasa. The following places are between Mombasa and Milinde, viz. Benapa, Toca, and Nuguoquioniete.[2]

On Easter Sunday (15 April) the Moors whom we had taken in the boat told us that there were at this city of Melinde four vessels belonging to Christians from India, and that if it pleased us to take them there, they would provide us, instead of them, Christian pilots and all we stood in need of, including water, wood and other things. The captain-major much desired to have pilots from the country, and having discussed the matter with his Moorish prisoners, he cast anchor off the town, at a distance of about half a league from the mainland. The inhabitants of the town did not venture to come aboard our ships, for they had already learnt that we had captured a vessel and made her occupants prisoners.

On Monday morning (16 April) the captain-major had the old Moor taken to a sandbank in front of the town, where he was picked up by an *almadia*. The Moor explained to the king the wishes of the captain-major, and how much he desired to make peace with him. After dinner the Moor came back in a *zavra*, accompanied by one of the king's cavaliers and a Sharif: he also brought three sheep. These messengers told the captain-general that the king would rejoice to make peace with him, and to enter into friendly relations; that he would willingly grant to the captain-major all his country afforded, whether pilots or anything else. The captain-major upon this sent word that he proposed to enter the port on the following day, and forwarded by the king's messengers a present consisting of a *balandrau* [a tunic worn by the Brothers of Mercy in Portugal], two strings of coral, three wash-hand basins, a hat, little bells and two pieces of lambel [striped cotton stuff].

4

Consequently, on Tuesday (17 April) we approached nearer to the town. The king sent the captain-major six sheep, besides quantities of cloves, cumin, ginger, nutmeg, and pepper, as also a message, telling him that if he desired to have an interview with him he (the king) would come out in his *zavra*, when the captain-major could meet him in a boat.

On Wednesday (18 April), after dinner, when the king came up close to the ships in a *zavra*, the captain-major at once entered one of his boats, which had been well furnished, and many friendly words were exchanged when they lay side by side. The king having invited the captain-major to come to his house to rest, after which he (the king) would visit him on board his ship, the captain-major said that he was not permitted by his master to go on land, and if he were to do so a bad report would be given of him. The king wanted to know what would be said of himself by his people if he were to visit the ships, and what account could he render them? He then asked for the name of our king, which was written down for him, and said that on our return he would send an ambassador with us, or a letter.

When both had said all they desired, the captain-major sent for the Moors whom he had taken prisoner, and surrendered them all. This gave much satisfaction to the king, who said he valued this act more highly than if he had been presented with a town. And the king, much pleased, made the circuit of our ships, the bombards of which fired a salute. About three hours were spent in this way. When the king went away he left in the ship one of his sons and a Sharif, and took two of us away with him, to whom he desired to show his palace. He, moreover, told the captain that as he would not go ashore he would himself return on the following day to the beach, and would order his horsemen to go through some exercises.

The king wore a robe (royal cloak) of damask trimmed with green satin, and a rich *touca* (turban). He was seated on two cushioned chairs of bronze, beneath a round sunshade of crimson satin attached to a pole. An old man, who attended him as a page, carried a short sword in a silver sheath. There were many players on *anafils*, and two trumpets of ivory, richly carved, and of the size of a man, which were blown from a hole in the side, and made sweet harmony with the *anafils*.

On Thursday (19 April) the captain-major and Nicolau Coelho rowed along the front of the town, bombards having been placed in the poops of their long-boats. Many people were along the shore, and among them two horsemen, who appeared to take much delight in a sham fight. The king was carried in a palanquin from the stone steps of his palace to the side of the captain-major's boats. He again begged the captain to come ashore, as he had a helpless father who wanted to see him, and that he and his sons would go on board the ships as hostages. The captain, however, excused himself.

END NOTES

1. sc. Malindi.
2. Probably Mtwapa, Takaungu, and Kioni, near Kilifi.

QUESTIONS

1. What landmarks distinguish the entrance to Mombasa?
2. Why does da Gama's crew chase the two boats on April 14?
3. How does the author's description of individuals reflect his own background?
4. The relationship between the king and the captain-general seems polite and even friendly, while at the same time there is an undercurrent of violence between the Portuguese and the Africans. What does this apparent contradiction suggest about cross-cultural relations in the late fifteenth century?

DOCUMENT

JOURNAL OF THE FIRST VOYAGE

Christopher Columbus

Christopher Columbus was born in Genoa, Italy, in 1451. His father was a weaver and wool merchant and the Genoese were a seafaring people who lived by trade. By his early twenties, Christopher had become a sailor in the Portuguese merchant marine, as well as an amateur cartographer. He became involved in the West African gold trade and made a number of voyages along the African coast under the Portuguese flag. It was during these years that he conceived his idea of reaching the spice-rich Indies by sailing directly west across the Atlantic rather than east around Africa to Asia. By 1486 he was in Spain attempting to interest Queen Isabella of Castille in his project, and bargaining hard for a portion of the riches he was sure would be the result of his voyage. In 1492, with royal backing, he set out with three small ships to test his plan. Columbus had grossly underestimated the size of the globe and when he reached land on October 12, 1492, it was in the Caribbean near Cuba rather than in the Pacific near Japan. Columbus made four voyages to the New World, proving his outstanding navigational abilities even if he never could be persuaded that he had found a new continent rather than a passage to the Indies. He was rewarded with the title of Admiral of the Ocean Seas and his family reaped the benefits of his fame. He died in 1506.

During his outward journey Columbus kept a daily log in which he recorded the progress made by his expedition, along with any remarkable events that occurred. The logbook, which has disappeared, was edited for publication by Bartolomé de las Casas, the great Spanish priest who wrote a history of the founding and settlement of the Indies.

DIGEST[1] OF COLUMBUS'S LOG-BOOK ON HIS FIRST VOYAGE MADE BY BARTOLOMÉ DE LAS CASAS

On 2 January in the year 1492, when your Highnesses had concluded their war with the Moors who reigned in Europe, I saw your Highnesses' banners victoriously raised on the towers of the Alhambra, the citadel of that city, and the Moorish king come out of the city gates and kiss the hands of your Highnesses and the prince, My Lord. And later in that same month, on the grounds of information I had given your royal Highnesses concerning the lands of India and a prince who is called the Great Khan—which means in Spanish 'King of Kings'—and of his and his ancestors' frequent and vain applications to Rome for men learned in the holy faith who should instruct them in it, your Highnesses decided to send me, Christopher Columbus, to see these parts of India and the princes and peoples of those lands and consider the best means for their conversion. For, by the neglect of the Popes to send instructors, many nations had fallen to idolatory and adopted doctrines of perdition, and your Highnesses as Catholic princes and devoted propagators of the holy Christian faith have always been enemies of the sect of Mahomet and of all idolatries and heresies.

Your Highnesses ordained that I should not go eastward by land in the usual manner but by the western way which no one about whom we have positive information has ever followed. Therefore having expelled all the Jews[2] from your dominions in that same month of January, your Highnesses commanded me to go with an adequate fleet to those parts of India. In return you granted me great favours bestowing on me the titles of Don and High Admiral of the Ocean Sea and Viceroy and perpetual governor of such islands and mainland as I should discover and win or should in future be discovered and won in the Ocean Sea, and that these rights should be inherited by my eldest son and so on from generation to generation.

I departed from the city of Granada on Saturday, 12 May, and went to the seaport of Palos, where I prepared three ships very suitable for such a voyage and set out from that port well supplied both with provisions and seamen. Half an hour before sunrise on Friday, 3 August, I departed on a course for the Canary Islands, from which possession of your Highnesses I intended to set out and sail until I reached the Indies, there to deliver your Highnesses' letters to their princes and to fulfil your other commands. I decided therefore to make this careful daily report of my voyage and of everything I should do, see or experience. In addition to a report of the day's events recorded each night, and of the night's sailing recorded each morning, I decided to make a new chart for navigation, giving the correct disposition according to their bearings of the land and water in the ocean sea. I intended also to compile a book which would contain everything mapped by latitude measured from the Equator and by longitude from the west. Though all these things will be a great labour it is essential that I should neglect sleep and carefully watch my course.

. . .

THURSDAY, 11 OCTOBER. He sailed west-south-west. They ran into rougher seas than any they had met with on the voyage. They saw petrels and a green reed near the ship. The men of the *Pinta* saw a cane and a stick and picked up another small stick, apparently shaped with an iron tool; also a piece of cane and some land-grasses and a small board. Those on the caravel *Niña* saw other indications of land and a stick covered with barnacles. At these signs, all breathed again and were rejoiced. That day they went twenty-seven leagues before sunset and after sunset he resumed his original western course. They made twelve miles an hour and up to two hours before midnight had gone ninety miles, which are twenty-two leagues and a half. The caravel *Pinta,* being swifter and sailing ahead of the Admiral, now sighted land and gave the signals which the Admiral had commanded.

The first man to sight land was a sailor called Rodrigo[3] from Triana, who afterwards vainly claimed the reward, which was pocketed by Columbus. The Admiral, however, when on the sterncastle at ten o'clock in the night, had seen a light, though it was so indistinct he would not affirm that it was land. He called Pero Gutierrez,[4] butler of the King's table, and told him that there seemed to be a light and asked him to look. He did so and saw it. He said the same to Rodrigo Sanchez of Segovia, whom the King and Queen had sent in the fleet as accountant,[5] and he saw nothing because he was not in a position from which anything could be seen. After the Admiral spoke this light was seen once or twice and it was like a wax candle that went up and down. Very few thought that this was a sign of land, but the Admiral was quite certain that they were near land. Accordingly, after the recitation of the *Salve* in the usual manner by the assembled sailors, the Admiral most seriously urged them to keep a good lookout from the forecastle and to watch carefully for land. He promised to give a silk doublet to the first sailor who should report it. And he would be entitled also to the reward promised by the sovereigns, which was an annual payment of ten thousand *maravedis*.[6]

Two hours after midnight land appeared, some two leagues away. They took in all sail, leaving only the mainsail, which is the great sail without bonnets, and lay close-hauled waiting for day. This was Friday, on which they reached a small island of the Lucayos, called in the Indian language Guanahani.[7] Immediately some naked people appeared and the Admiral went ashore in the armed boat, as did Martin Alonso Pinzón and Vicente Yanez his brother, captain of the *Niña*. The Admiral raised the royal standard and the captains carried two banners with the green cross which were flown by the Admiral on all his ships. On each side of the cross was a crown surmounting the letters F and Y[8] (for Ferdinand and Isabela). On landing they saw very green trees and much water and fruit of various kinds. The Admiral called the two captains and the others who had landed and Rodrigo Escobedo, recorder of the whole fleet, and Rodrigo Sanchez de Segovia, and demanded that they should bear faithful witness that he had taken possession of the island—which he did—for his sovereigns and masters the King and Queen. He further made the required declarations, which are recorded at greater length in the evidence there set down in writing. Soon many people of the island came up to them. What follows are the Admiral's actual words in his account of his first voyage and the discovery of these Indies.

'In order to win their friendship, since I knew they were a people to be converted and won to our holy faith by love and friendship rather than by force, I gave some of them red caps and glass beads which they hung round their necks, also many other trifles. These things pleased them greatly and they became marvellously friendly to us. They afterwards swam out to the ship's boats in which we were sitting, bringing us parrots and balls of cotton thread and spears and many other things, which they exchanged with us for such objects as glass beads, hawks and bells. In fact, they very willingly traded everything they had. But they seemed to me a people very short of everything. They all go naked as their mothers bore them, including the women, although I saw only one very young girl.

'All the men I saw were young. I did not see one over the age of thirty. They were very well built with fine bodies and handsome faces. Their hair is coarse, almost like that of a horse's tail and short; they wear it down over their eyebrows except for a few strands at the back, which they wear long and never cut. They are the colour of the Canary Islanders (neither black nor white). Some of them paint themselves black, others white or any colour they can find. Some paint their faces, some their whole bodies, some only the eyes, some only the nose. They do not carry arms or know them. For when I showed them swords, they took them by the edge and cut themselves out of ignorance. They have no iron. Their spears are made of cane. Some instead of an iron tip have a fish's tooth and others have points of different kinds. They are fairly tall on the whole, with fine limbs and good proportions. I saw some who had wound scars on their bodies and I asked them by signs how they got these and they indicated to me that people came from other islands near by who tried to capture them and they defended themselves. I supposed and still suppose that they come from the mainland to capture them for slaves. They should be good servants and very intelligent, for I have observed that they soon repeat anything that is said to them, and I believe that they would easily be made Christians, for they appeared to me to have no religion. God willing, when I make my departure I will bring half a dozen of them back to their Majesties, so that they can learn to speak. I saw no animals of any kind on this island except parrots.' These are the Admiral's own words.

SATURDAY, 13 OCTOBER. At daybreak many of these men came to the shore—all young, as I have said, and all of a good height—a very fine people. Their hair is not curly but straight and as coarse as horse hair. All have very broad brows and heads, broader than those of any people I have seen before. Their eyes are very fine and not small. They are not at all black, but the colour of Canary Islanders, as could be expected, since this is in the same latitude as the island of Hierro in the Canaries. They have very straight legs and no bellies, but well-formed bodies.[9] They came to the ship in boats which are made from tree-trunks, like a long boat all cut out of a single log. They are marvellously carved in the native style and they are so big that forty or fifty-five men came in them. There are others smaller, so small that some carried only a single man. They row them with a paddle like a baker's shovel and they go wonderfully fast. If one capsizes they all start swimming and right it. They bale it out with gourds which they carry with them. They brought balls of cotton thread and parrots and spears and other things which it would be tedious to mention, and exchanged them for anything that was given them. I watched carefully to discover whether they had gold and saw that some of them carried a small piece hanging from a hole pierced in the nose. I was able to understand from their signs that to the south, either inland or along the coast, there was a king who had large vessels made of it and possessed a great deal. I tried hard to make them go there but saw in the end that they had no intention of doing so. I decided to remain till the afternoon of the next day and then to sail south-west, for according to the signs which many of them made there was land to the south, south-west and north-west. They indicated that men from the north-west often came to attack them. So I resolved to go south-west to seek the gold and precious stones.

This island is fairly large and very flat. It has very green trees and much water. It has a very large lake in the middle and no mountains and all is delightfully green. The people are very gentle and anxious to have the things we bring. Thinking that nothing will be given them, however, unless they give something in exchange, and having nothing to give, they take anything they can, jump into the water and swim away. But they will give all that they do possess for anything that is given to them, exchanging things even for bits of broken crockery or broken glass cups. I saw one give sixteen balls of cotton for three Portuguese *ceotis,* the equivalent of the Castilian *blanca,*[10] and in these balls there was more than an *aroba*[11] of cotton thread.

I should like to forbid this and let no one take any cotton except at my command; then if there were any quantity I would order it all to be taken for your Majesties. It grows here on this island, but owing to shortage of time I can give no exact account of it. And here too the gold is found that they wear hanging from their noses. But in order not to waste time I wish to go and see if I can strike the island of Chipangu.

Now when night fell they all went ashore in their boats.

SUNDAY, 14 OCTOBER. At dawn I ordered the ship's boat and the boats of the caravels to be made ready, and coasted the island in a north-easterly direction in order to see the other and eastward part and to look for villages. I saw two or three, whose people all came down to the beach calling to us and offering thanks to God. Some brought us water, others various sorts of food, and others, when they saw that I did not intend to land, jumped into the sea and swam out. We understood them to be asking us if we came from the sky. One old man got into the boat, and all the others, men and women alike, shouted, 'Come and see the men who have come from the skies; and bring them food and drink.' Many men and women came, each bringing something and offering thanks to God; they threw themselves on the ground and raised their hands to the sky and then called out to us, asking us to land. But I was afraid to do so, seeing a great reef of rocks which encircled the whole island. Inside there is deep water which would give sufficient anchorage for all the ships in Christendom. But the entrance is very narrow. It is true that there are some shoals within this reef, but the sea is as still as well water.

I went to view all this this morning, in order to give an account to your Majesties and to decide where a fort could be built. I saw a piece of land which is much like an island, though it is not one, on which there were six huts. It could be made into an island in two days, though I see no necessity to do so since these people are very unskilled in arms, as your Majesties will discover from seven whom I caused to be taken and brought aboard so that they may learn our language and return. However, should your Highnesses command it all the inhabitants could be taken away to Castile or held as slaves on the island, for with fifty men we could subjugate them all and make them do whatever we wish. Moreover, near the small island I have described there are groves of the loveliest trees I have seen, all green with leaves like our trees in Castile in April and May, and much water.

. . .

MONDAY, 15 OCTOBER. I stood off that night, fearing to approach land before morning because I did not know if the coast was free from shoals. At daybreak I hoisted sail. As the island was more than five leagues away— indeed more like seven—and the tide was against me, it was midday when I reached this island. I found that the coast which faces San Salvador runs north and south for some five leagues, and the other coast which I followed runs east and west for more than ten leagues. And as from this island I saw another larger one to the west, I hoisted sail to run all that day till night, since I should otherwise not have been able to reach its western point. I named this island Santa Maria de la Concepción.[12] And it was almost sunset when I reached this point. I wished to learn whether there was gold there, because the men I had taken aboard at the island at San Salvador told me that here they wore very large gold bracelets round their legs and arms. I thought that this tale was probably a lie told in the hope of getting away. Generally it was my wish to pass no island without taking possession of it. Though having annexed one it might be said that we had annexed all. I anchored and stayed there until today, Tuesday, when at daybreak I approached the shore with the armed boats and landed.

There were many people all naked and like those of San Salvador. They let us go about the island and gave us all that we asked for. But as the wind was blowing from the south-east I did not wish to delay and went back to the ship. A large canoe happening to lie alongside the *Niña*, a little before midnight one of the men from San Salvador who was in the caravel jumped overboard and went off in it. A few minutes later another threw himself overboard also and swam after the canoe, which went so fast that no boat could overtake it, for it had a considerable start.[13]

So they came to land and left the canoe. Several members of my crew went ashore after them and they ran off like frightened hens. We took the canoe they had abandoned aboard the caravel *Niña;* it was approached by another small canoe with a man who had come to barter a ball of cotton. Since he would not board the caravel some sailors jumped down and seized him. Having seen all this from the forecastle where I was standing, I sent for him and gave him a red cap and some green glass beads which I put on his arm and two hawk's bells which I put in his ears. I told the sailors to give him back his canoe which they had taken on to the ship's boat, and sent him ashore. I then raised sail for the other large island which I saw to the west and ordered that the second canoe which the *Niña* was towing astern should be set adrift. Shortly afterwards I saw the man to whom I had given these gifts come ashore.

I had not taken the ball of cotton from him, although he wished to give it to me. The people gathered round him and he appeared astonished. It seemed to him that we were good people and that the man who had escaped in the canoe must have wronged us or we should not have carried him off.[14]

It was to create this impression that I had him set free and gave him presents. I was anxious that they should think well of us so that they may not be unfriendly when your Majesties send a second expedition here. All I gave him was worth less than four *maravedis.*

So I set sail for the other island at about ten o'clock with a south-east wind which veered southerly. It is very large and, according to the signs made by the men we had brought from San Salvador, contains much gold, which they wear as bracelets on their arms and legs and in their ears and noses and round their necks. This other island was about nine leagues west of Santa Maria, and this part of its coast apparently runs from north-west to south-east, for upwards of twenty-eight leagues.

Like San Salvador and Santa Maria it is very flat with no mountains. All the beaches are free from rocks, although all have submerged reefs near the shore, for which reason it is necessary to look carefully before anchoring and not to anchor too near land. The water, however, is always very clear and you can see bottom. A couple of lombard shots off land the water is so deep around all these islands that it cannot be sounded. They are all very green and fertile and subject to gentle breezes. They may contain many things of which I do not know because I did not care to land and explore them, being anxious to find gold; and since these islands show signs of containing it—for the natives wear it round their arms and legs, and it is certainly gold, because I showed them some pieces which I have—I cannot fail, with God's help, to find out where it comes from.

When I was in mid-channel, between Santa Maria and this other island which I have named Fernandina,[15] I found a man alone in a canoe crossing from the one to the other. He was carrying a lump of their bread, about the size of a fist, and a gourd of water and a bit of red earth which had been powdered and then kneaded; also some dried leaves which they must value very highly since they gave me a present of them. He also carried a native basket containing some glass beads and two *blancas,* by which I knew that he had come from San Salvador to Santa Maria and was now on

15

his way to Fernandina. He came alongside and I let him come aboard as he asked. I had his canoe hauled aboard also and all that he carried kept safe. I ordered that he should be given bread and honey and something to drink. I shall carry him to Fernandina and restore all his possessions to him so that he may give a good account of us. Then when, God willing, your Highnesses send others here, we shall be favourably received and the natives may give us of all they possess.

TUESDAY, 16 OCTOBER. Having left the islands of Santa Maria de la Concepción[16] at about mid-day for Fernandina, which appeared very large in the west, I sailed for the rest of the day in a calm and could not reach it in time to anchor, for the water was not clear enough for me to see bottom and one has to take great care not to lose the anchors. So I lay off all that night and in the morning saw a village off which I anchored. This was the native village of the man I had found on the previous day with his canoe in mid-channel. He had given such a good account of us that canoes swarmed round the ship all that night. They brought us water and some-thing of all they had. I ordered presents to be given to all of them, that is to say, strings of ten or a dozen small glass beads and some brass clappers of a kind that are worth a *maravedi* each in Castile and some leather tags, all of which they value very highly, and when they came aboard I had them given molasses to eat. And afterwards at nine in the morning I sent a ship's boat ashore for water and they most gladly showed our men where it could be found and themselves carried the full casks back to the boat. They were delighted to give us pleasure.

This island is very large and I decided to sail round it because as I understand, in it or near it, there is a goldfield. The island is eight leagues west of Santa Maria and from the cape where I touched, the coast runs north-north-west and south-south-east; I saw quite twenty leagues of it and it still continued. As I write this I have set sail with a south wind intending to push on round the island until I come to Samoet, which is the island or city where the gold is, for all who have come aboard the ship have said so. Both the people of San Salvador and Santa Maria told us so.

The people here are like the people of those islands; both in language and customs, though here they seem to me rather more civilized, more tractable and more intelligent, for I see they are better able to bargain for the cotton and other trifles which they have brought to the ship than were the other peoples. And I saw on this island cotton cloths made like shawls. The people are more friendly and the women wear a small piece of cotton in front which just hides their private parts.

This island is very green, flat and fertile and I have no doubt that they sow and reap Indian corn and other crops throughout the year. I saw many trees very unlike ours. Many of them had several branches of different kinds coming from one root. One branch may be of one kind and another of another and the variation is quite marvellous. They are so extremely different, that, for example, one branch may have leaves like those of the cane and another like those of a mastic tree, and thus on a single tree there are five or six different kinds, all distinct from one another. They are not grafted, though they might be supposed to be the result of grafting; on the contrary they are wild and these people do not cultivate them.

They have no religion and I think that they would be very quickly Christianized, for they have a very ready understanding.

The fish here are surprisingly unlike ours. There are some of the shape of dories and of the finest colours in the world, blue, yellow, red and every other hue and others variously flecked. The colours are so marvellous that everybody wondered and took pleasure in the sight. There are also whales. But I saw no kind of land animal at all except parrots and lizards. A ship's boy told me that he had seen a large snake. I saw no sheep or goats nor any other animals at all. But I was there only for a very short time; for it is now midday. If there had been any, however, I could not have failed to see some. I will describe the circuit of this island when I have made it.

WEDNESDAY, 17 OCTOBER. At midday I set sail from the village off which I had anchored and where I had landed and taken water to make a circuit of this island of Fernandina. The wind was south-west and south. It was my intention to follow the coast of this island from where I was to the south-east, since it runs as a whole from north-north-west to south-south-east. I wanted to take my course to the south-south-east, because all the Indians whom I have aboard and others from whom I inquired tell me that southwards from here lies the island they call Samoet, where the gold is. Martin

17

Alonso Pinzón, captain of the *Pinta,* in which I had placed three of these Indians, came to me and said that one of them had very explicitly given him to understand that the island could be rounded more quickly in a north-north-westerly direction.

I saw that the wind would not help me on the course I wished to steer and that it favoured the other course, so I steered north-north-west, and when I was about two leagues from the island's[17] cape I saw a marvellous harbour with an entrance, or rather two entrances, since there is an islet in the middle. Both entrances are very narrow, but it would have been large enough to provide anchorage for a hundred ships if it had been deep and free of rocks and the entrance channels had been deep also. I thought fit to examine it closely and take soundings; therefore I anchored outside and went in with all the ships' boats and we found that it was shallow. When I first saw it I thought it was the mouth of a river, so I had ordered casks to be brought to take water. On land I saw eight or ten men who quickly came up to us and pointed to a nearby village, where I sent my men for water, which they took, some going armed and others carrying the casks. As the village was some distance away I had to remain there for two hours.

During that time I walked among the trees, which were the loveliest sight I had yet seen. They were green as those of Andalusia in the month of May. But all these trees are as different from ours as day from night and so are the fruit and plants and stones, and everything else. It is true that some trees were of species that can be found in Castile, yet there was a great difference; but there are many other varieties which no one could say are like those of Castile or could compare with them. The people were all of the same kind as those already described; their condition was the same; they were naked and of the same height. They gave whatever they possessed for whatever we gave them and here I saw some ships' boys exchanging small bits of broken crockery or glass for spears.

The men who had gone for water told me that they had entered their houses and that they were very clean and well swept and that their beds and blankets are like cotton nets. These houses are like large tents. They are high and have good chimneys. But of all the villages I saw none consisted of more than a dozen or fifteen houses. Here they found that married women wear cotton drawers, but girls do not, until they reach the age of eighteen. Here there were mastiffs and small dogs and here they met

18

one man who wore in his nose a piece of gold about half the size of a *castellano* on which they saw letters. I was angry with them because they had not bargained for it and given as much as they were asked, so that we could examine it and see where the coin came from. They answered that they did not dare to bargain for it.

After taking the water I returned to the ship, raised sail and followed a north-westerly course along the shore to the point where the coast turns east-west. Later all the Indians insisted that this island was smaller than Samoet and that it would be better to turn back in order to reach that island sooner. Then the wind fell and began to blow west-north-west, which was unfavourable to the course we had been following. I therefore turned back and sailed all that night in an east-south-easterly direction, sometimes due east and sometimes south-east in order to keep clear of land, because the clouds were very thick and the weather very heavy. The wind was slight and I could not make land to anchor. In the night heavy rain fell from after midnight almost till daybreak and it is still cloudy with more rain to come.

We are now at the south-east tip of the island, where I hope to anchor until the weather clears, and I can see the other islands to which I am going. It has rained practically every day since I have been in these Indies. Your Highnesses must believe me that these islands are the most fertile, and temperate and flat and good in the whole world.

. . .

SUNDAY, 21 OCTOBER. At ten o'clock I reached this Cabo del Isleo and anchored, as did the caravels. After eating a meal I went ashore, but there was no village—only one house in which I found nobody. I think they had all run away from fright, for all their things were there.

I wouldn't allow anything to be touched but went with the captains and men to examine the island. Though all the others we had seen were beautiful, green and fertile, this was even more so. It has large and very green trees, and great lagoons, around which these trees stand in marvellous groves. Here and throughout the island the trees and plants are as green as in Andalusia in April. The singing of small birds is so sweet that no one could ever wish to leave this place. Flocks of parrots darken the sun and there is a marvellous variety of large and small birds very different from our own; the trees are of many kinds, each with its own fruit, and all have a marvellous scent. It grieves me extremely that I cannot identify them, for I am quite certain that they are all valuable and I am bringing samples of them and of the plants also.

As I was walking beside one of the lagoons I saw a snake, which we killed. I am bringing the skin to our Highnesses. As soon as we saw it, it swam into the lagoon and we followed it, for the water was not very deep, and we killed it with spears. It is almost five foot long and I believe there are many of them in this lagoon. Here I recognized aloe, and tomorrow I intend to have half a ton brought aboard, for they tell me it's very valuable. Also when we were looking for good water we found a village near by, half a league from where I am anchored.

As soon as the inhabitants saw us they ran away, leaving their houses. They hid their clothing and all that they had in the undergrowth. I allowed nothing to be taken, not even to the value of a pin. Afterwards a few of the men approached us and one of them came quite close. I gave him hawk's bells and some small glass beads, and he was very pleased and happy. In order to foster this friendship and ask for something from them, I asked them for water, and after I had returned to the ship they came down to the beach with their gourds full and gave it to us with delight. I ordered that they should be given another string of little glass beads and they said they would return the next day.

I decided to have all the vessels on board filled with water. Therefore if the weather allows I will presently set out to coast this island until I have speech with this king and see whether I can get the gold that I hear he wears. After this I shall set out for another large island which, according to the indications given me by the Indians whom I have aboard, must be Chipangu. They however call it Colba[18] and say that there are many large ships and sailors there. From here I shall go to another island, which they call Bohio[19] and say is also very large. In passing I shall see the others that lie between and according to whether I find a quantity of gold or spices I shall decide what to do next. But I am still determined to go to the city of Quinsay,[20] to deliver your Highnesses' letters to the Grand Khan and request his answer which I shall bring back.

MONDAY, 22 OCTOBER. I have waited here all night on the chance that the king of this place or other persons may bring me gold or other valuables.

Many people came who were like the people in the other islands, all naked and painted white, red, black and in many different ways. They carried spears and some of them brought balls of cotton to barter. These they exchanged with some of the sailors for bits of glass from broken bowls and fragments of earthenware. Some of them wore pieces of gold hanging from their noses, which they happily exchanged for little bells, for bells of the kind made for the feet of a sparrow-hawk and for glass beads, but the amount was a mere trifle. Indeed, however small the things we give them, they still consider our coming a great marvel. I think they believe that we have come from the sky. We are taking water for the ships from the lagoon which lies near Cabo del Isleo, as I named it; and here Martin Alonso Pinzón, of the *Pinta,* killed another snake about five foot long and like that of yesterday. I had as much aloe collected as was to be found.

TUESDAY, 23 OCTOBER. I should like to depart today for the island of Colba, which I believe according to the indications of its size and riches given us by these people must be Chipangu. I shall not stay here any longer, to round this island or go to the village as I had intended, to have speech with the king or lord. I do not wish to delay long, since I see that there is no goldfield here and to round these islands one needs many changes of wind and the wind doesn't blow as one wishes. It is best to go where there is much to be done and so it is right not to stay here but to continue on our course, discovering many lands until we find one that is truly profitable. I think, however, that this place is very rich in spices. I am extremely sorry that I cannot recognize them, for I see a very great number of trees each bearing its own kind of fruit, and they are as green now as trees in Spain in the months of May and June. There are a thousand kinds of plants also, all in flower. But the only one I recognize is this aloe, which I ordered to be taken aboard yesterday and brought for your Highnesses.

I have not set out and I am not setting out for Colba, since there is no wind, but dead calm and much rain. It rained heavily yesterday but was not at all cold. On the contrary the days are warm and the nights mild as in May in Andalusia.

END NOTES

1. This digest was made by the historian Bartolomé de las Casas from the log-book of the Admiral, which has since disappeared. The frequent quotation of the Admiral's actual phrases makes it the prime authority for the voyage itself, and it is used here up to the landfall on Cuba, from which point the narrative is taken up by Columbus's report written on his homeward voyage, copies of which he sent to various important persons. Where the narrative is in the first person Las Casas is using the Admiral's words. Where it is in the third he is giving his own rendering.
2. After the fall of Granada the sovereigns gave their Jewish subjects the choice of conversion or exile.
3. This was probably Juan Rodriguez Bermeo.
4. Pero Gutierrez was actually a steward, not a butler in the literal sense.
5. Rodrigo Sanchez de Segovia was a high official whose duties as accountant or *veedor* were to keep count of the gold, treasure or spices, and see that the sovereigns got their share.
6. A small copper coin.
7. This is generally assumed to be Watling Island in the Bahamas.
8. The contemporary spelling was Ysabela.
9. Las Casas appears to have quoted from two parallel accounts of the landing—the first being the Admiral's lost 'Book' which he perhaps found in the library of his son Hernando and the second from the log-book (also lost).
10. A small copper coin worth perhaps a farthing.
11. About 25 lb.
12. Rum Kay.
13. The text is obscure at this point, but this appears to be the meaning.
14. Here the text speaks of one man only but, as far as can be seen from the defective manuscript, two men escaped.
15. Long Island.
16. There were in fact two islands close together.
17. Long Island.
18. Cuba.
19. Hispaniola.
20. This was Hangchow—the capital of the Grand Khan—described by Marco Polo. Columbus's information about Cathay was based on the stories of old travellers, so he did not know that there had been no Grand Khan since the thirteenth century.

QUESTIONS

1. Why did Columbus make his voyage? What did he hope to accomplish?
2. What are Columbus's first impressions of the people he meets in the Indies? What details about their society concern him most?
3. What does Columbus do to give the natives a good impression of himself and his own people? Why does he take these actions?
4. What kinds of plants, animals, or land and water features interest Columbus? Why do they interest him?

THE SECOND LETTER: A CONQUISTADOR DESCRIBES THE CAPITAL OF MEXICO

Hernán Cortés

Hernán Cortés (1485–1547), the greatest of the conquistadores, was born to a decaying noble family in Estradura, Spain. He was sent to law school but escaped to Hispaniola where he fought under the command of Diego Velásquez and took part in the conquest of Cuba. After that he was sent by Velásquez to reconnoitre the Mexican mainland, but instead he embarked, without permission, on an independent campaign of conquest. With six hundred men, thirteen muskets, seven cannons, and sixteen horses—and a strategic alliance with the Mayans of Tlaxcala—he succeeded in conquering the Aztec Empire, which ruled over five million souls. He was helped initially by the fact that the Aztec ruler, Moctezuma, briefly confused him with the Aztec god Quetzalcoatl. Subsequent successes were ensured by the divisions among the Aztecs and by Spanish technical superiority in armament—though their steel swords and armor turned out to be of more help than their muskets and cannons. Still, the conquest of Mexico was a remarkable feat of arms that has excited wonder among historians and military men down to the present day.

The passage excerpted here, from Cortés's second report to the Emperor of New Spain, was first published in 1522. It was a document partly intended to exculpate himself from the charge of mutiny against Governor Velásquez, and it is not great literature. But it is still an invaluable eyewitness account of

---

Reprinted from Hernán Cortés' *Second Letter to the Emperor of New Spain*, first published in 1522.

the conquest of Mexico from the point of view of the chief actor. The present selection is today's best description of the great city of the Aztecs, Tenochtitlán, before the city was destroyed and rebuilt by the Spaniards as Mexico City.

⸺

But before beginning to relate the wonders of this city and people, their rights and government, I should perhaps for a better understanding say something of the state of Mexico itself which contains this city and the others of which I have spoken, and is the principal seat of Moctezuma. The province is roughly circular in shape and entirely surrounded by very lofty and rocky mountains, the level part in the middle being some seventy leagues in circumference and containing two lakes which occupy it almost entirely, for canoes travel over fifty leagues in making a circuit of them. One of the lakes is of fresh water, the other and larger one of salt. A narrow but very lofty range of mountains cuts across the valley and divides the lakes almost completely save for the western end where they are joined by a narrow strait no wider than a sling's throw which runs between the mountains. Commerce is carried on between the two lakes and the cities on their banks by means of canoes, so that land traffic is avoided. Moreover, since the salt lake rises and falls with the tide sea water pours from it at high tide into the fresh water lake with the rapidity of a mountain torrent, and likewise at low tide flows back from the fresh to the salt.

The great city of Tenochtitlán is built in the midst of this salt lake, and it is two leagues from the heart of the city to any point on the mainland. Four causeways lead to it, all made by hand and some twelve feet wide. The city itself is as large as Seville or Córdova. The principal streets are very broad and straight, the majority of them being of beaten earth, but a few and at least half the smaller thoroughfares are waterways along which they pass in their canoes. Moreover, even the principal streets have openings at regular distances so that the water can freely pass from one to another, and these openings which are very broad are spanned by great bridges of huge beams, very stoutly put together, so firm indeed that over many of them ten horsemen can ride at once. Seeing that if the natives intended any treachery against us they would have every opportunity from the way in which the city is built, for by removing the bridges from the entrances and exits they could leave us to die of hunger with no possibility of getting to the mainland, I immediately set to work as soon as we entered the city on the building of four brigs, and in a short space of time had them finished, so that we could ship three hundred men and the horses to the mainland whenever we so desired.

The city has many open squares in which markets are continuously held and the general business of buying and selling proceeds. One square in particular is twice as big as that of Salamanca and completely surrounded by arcades where there are daily more than sixty thousand folk buying and selling. Every kind of merchandise such as may be met with in every land is for sale there, whether of food and victuals, or ornaments of gold and silver, or lead, brass, copper, tin, precious stones, bones, shells, snails and feathers; limestone for building is likewise sold there, stone both rough and polished, bricks burnt and unburnt, wood of all kinds and in all stages of preparation. There is a street of game where they sell all manner of birds that are to be found in their country, including hens, partridges, quails, wild duck, fly-catchers, widgeon, turtle doves, pigeons, little birds in round nests made of grass, parrots, owls, eagles, vulcans, sparrow-hawks and kestrels; and of some of these birds of prey they sell the skins complete with feathers, head, bill and claws. They also sell rabbits, hares, deer and small dogs which they breed especially for eating. There is a street of herb-sellers where there are all manner of roots and medicinal plants that are found in the land. There are houses as it were of apothecaries where they sell medicines made from these herbs, both for drinking and for use as ointments and salves. There are barbers' shops where you may have your hair washed and cut. There are other shops where you may obtain food and drink. There are street porters such as we have in Spain to carry packages. There is a great quantity of wood, charcoal, braziers made of clay and mats of all sorts, some for beds and others more finely woven for seats, still others for furnishing halls and private apartments. All kinds of vegetables may be found there, in particular onions, leeks, garlic, cresses, watercress, borage, sorrel, artichokes, and golden thistles. There are many different sorts of fruits including cherries and plums very similar to those found in Spain. They sell honey obtained from bees, as also the honeycomb and that obtained from maize plants which are as sweet as sugar canes; they also obtain honey from plants

25

which are known both here and in other parts as *maguey,* which is preferable to grape juice; from *maguey* in addition they make both sugar and a kind of wine, which are sold in their markets. All kinds of cotton thread in various colours may be bought in skeins, very much in the same way as in the great silk exchange of Granada, except that the quantities are far less. They have colours for painting of as good quality as any in Spain, and of as pure shades as may be found anywhere. There are leathers of deer both skinned and in their natural state, and either bleached or dyed in various colours. A great deal of chinaware is sold of very good quality and including earthen jars of all sizes for holding liquids, pitchers, pots, tiles and an infinite variety of earthenware all made of very special clay and almost all decorated and painted in some way. Maize is sold both as grain and in the form of bread and is vastly superior both in the size of the ear and in taste to that of all the other islands or the mainland. Pasties made from game and fish pies may be seen on sale, and there are large quantities of fresh and salt water fish both in their natural state and cooked ready for eating. Eggs from fowls, geese and all the other birds I have described may be had, and likewise omelettes ready made. There is nothing to be found in all the land which is not sold in these markets, for over and above what I have mentioned there are so many and such various other things that on account of their very number and the fact that I do not know their names, I cannot now detail them. Each kind of merchandise is sold in its own particular street and no other kind may be sold there: this rule is very well enforced. All is sold by number and measure, but up till now no weighing by balance has been observed. A very fine building in the great square serves as a kind of audience chamber where ten or a dozen persons are always seated, as judges, who deliberate on all cases arising in the market and pass sentence on evildoers. In the square itself there are officials who continually walk amongst the people inspecting goods exposed for sale and the measures by which they are sold, and on certain occasions have seen them destroy measures which were false.

There are a very large number of mosques or dwelling places for their idols throughout the various districts of this great city, all fine buildings, in the chief of which their priests live continuously, so that in addition to the actual temples containing idols there are sumptuous lodgings. These pagan priests are all dressed in black and go habitually with their hair uncut; they do not even comb it from the day they enter the order to that on which they leave. Chief men's sons, both nobles and distinguished citizens, enter these orders at the age of six or seven and only leave when they are of an age to marry, and this occurs more frequently to the first-born who will inherit their father's estates than to others. They are denied all access to women, and no woman is ever allowed to enter one of the religious houses. Certain foods they abstain from and more so at certain periods of the year than at others. Among these temples there is one chief one in particular whose size and magnificence no human tongue could describe. For it is so big that within the lofty wall which entirely circles it one could set a town of fifteen thousand inhabitants.

Immediately inside this wall and throughout its entire length are some admirable buildings containing large halls and corridors where the priests who live in this temple are housed. There are forty towers at the least, all of stout construction and very lofty, the largest of which has fifty steps leading up to its base: this chief one is indeed higher than the great church of Seville. The workmanship both in wood and stone could not be bettered anywhere, for all the stonework within the actual temples where they keep their idols is cut into ornamental borders of flowers, birds, fishes and the like, or trellis-work, and the woodwork is likewise all in relief highly decorated with monsters of very various device. The towers all serve as burying places for their nobles, and the little temples which they contain are all dedicated to a different idol to whom they pay their devotions.

There are three large halls in the great mosque where the principal idols are to be found, all of immense size and height and richly decorated with sculptured figures both in wood and stone, and within these halls are other smaller temples branching off from them and entered by doors so small that no daylight ever reaches them. Certain of the priests but not all are permitted to enter, and within are the great heads and figures of idols, although as I have said there are also many outside. The greatest of these idols and those in which they placed most faith and trust I ordered to be dragged from their places and flung down the stairs, which done I had the temples which they occupy cleansed for they were full of the blood of human victims who had been sacrificed, and placed in them the image of Our Lady and other saints, all of which made no small impression upon Moctezuma and the inhabitants. They are first remonstrated with me, for should it be known, they said, by the people of the country they would rise against me, believing as they did that to these idols were due all temporal goods, and that should they allow them to be ill used they would be wroth against them and would give them nothing, denying them the fruits of the earth, and thus the people would die of starvation. I instructed them by my interpreters how mistaken they were in putting their trust in idols made by their own hands from unclean things, and that they must know that there was but one God, Lord of all, Who created the sky, the earth and all things, Who made both them and ourselves, Who was without beginning and immortal, Whom alone they had to adore and to believe in, and not in any created thing whatsoever: I told them moreover all things else that I knew of touching this matter in order to lead them from their idolatry and bring them to the knowledge of Our Lord: and all, especially Moctezuma, replied that they had already told me that they were not natives of this land but had come to it long time since, and that therefore they were well pre-pared to believe that they had erred somewhat from the true faith during the long time since they had left their native land, and I as more lately come would know more surely the things that it was right for them to hold and believe than they themselves: and that hence if I would instruct them they would do whatever I declared to be best. Upon this Moctezuma and many of the chief men of the city went with me to remove the idols, cleanse the chapels, and place images of the saints therein, and all with cheerful faces. I forbade them moreover to make human sacrifice to the idols as was their wont, because besides being an abomination in the sight of God it is prohibited by your Majesty's laws which declare that he who kills shall be killed. From this time henceforth they departed from it, and during the whole time that I was in the city not a single living soul was known to be killed and sacrificed.

The images of the idols in which these people believed are many times greater than the body of a large man. They are made from pulp of all the cereals and greenstuffs which they eat, mixed and pounded together. This mass they moisten with blood from the hearts of human beings which they tear from their breasts while still alive, and thus make sufficient quantity of the pulp to mould into their huge statues: and after the idols have been set up still they offer them more living hearts which they sacrifice in like manner and anoint their faces with the blood. Each department of human affairs has its particular idol after the manner of the ancients who thus honoured their gods: so that there is one idol from whom they beg success in war, another for crops, and so on for all their needs.

The city contains many large and fine houses, and for this reason. All the nobles of the land owing allegiance to Moctezuma have their houses in the city and reside there for a certain portion of the year; and in addition there are a large number of rich citizens who likewise have very fine houses. All possess in addition to large and elegant apartments very delightful flower gardens of every kind, both on the ground level as on the upper storeys.

Along one of the causeways connecting this great city with the mainland two pipes are constructed of masonry, each two paces broad and about as high as a man, one of which conveys a stream of water very clear and fresh and about the thickness of a man's body right to the centre of the city, which all can use for drinking and other purposes. The other pipe which is empty is used when it is desired to clean the former. Moreover, on coming to the breaks in the causeway spanned by bridges under which the salt water flows through, the fresh water flows into a kind of trough as thick as an ox which occupies the whole width of the bridge, and thus the whole city is served. The water is sold from canoes in all the streets, the manner of their taking it from the pipes being in this wise: the canoes place themselves under the bridges where the troughs are to be found, and from above the canoes are filled by men who are especially paid for this work.

At all the entrances to the city and at those parts where canoes are unloaded, which is where the greatest amount of provisions enters the city, certain huts have been built, where there are official guards to exact so much on everything that enters. I know not whether this goes to the lord or to the city itself, and have not yet been able to ascertain, but I think that it is to the ruler, since in the markets of several other towns we have seen such a tax exacted on behalf of the ruler. Every day in all the markets and public places of the city there are a number of workmen and masters of all manner of crafts waiting to be hired by the day. The people of this city are nicer in their dress and manners than those of any other city or province, for since Moctezuma always holds his residence here and his vassals visit the city for lengthy periods, greater culture and politeness of manners in all things has been encouraged.

29

Finally, to avoid prolixity in telling all the wonders of this city, I will simply say that the manner of living among the people is very similar to that in Spain, and considering that this is a barbarous nation shut off from a knowledge of the true God or communication with enlightened nations, one may well marvel at the orderliness and good government which is everywhere maintained.

The actual service of Moctezuma and those things which call for admiration by their greatness and state would take so long to describe that I assure your Majesty I do not know where to begin with any hope of ending. For as I have already said, what could there be more astonishing than that a barbarous monarch such as he should have reproductions made in gold, silver, precious stones, and feathers of all things to be found in his land, and so perfectly reproduced that there is no goldsmith or silversmith in the world who could better them, nor can one understand what instrument could have been used for fashioning the jewels; as for the featherwork its like is not to be seen in either wax or embroidery, it is so marvellously delicate.

I was unable to find out exactly the extent of Moctezuma's kingdom, for in no part where he sent his messengers (even as much as two hundred leagues in either direction from this city) were his orders disobeyed; although it is true there were certain provinces in the middle of this region with whom he was at war. But so far as I could understand his kingdom was almost as large as Spain. Most of the lords of these various provinces resided, as I have said, for the greater part of the year in the capital, and the majority of them had their eldest sons in Moctezuma's service. The king had fortresses in all these provinces armed with his own men, and also overseers and tax-collectors to see to the services and rent which each province owed him, and which was inscribed in written characters and pictures on a kind of paper they have, by which they can make themselves understood. The manner of service rendered differed for each province according to the quality of its land, in such manner that every kind of produce that grew in the various parts of the country came to the royal hand. He was feared by all both present and distant more than was any other monarch in the world. He possessed many houses of recreation both within and without the city, each with its own special pastime, built in the most ingenious manner as was fitting for such a mighty prince: of which I will say no more than that there is not their like in all Spain. Another palace of his (not quite so fine as the one we were lodged in) had a magnificent garden with balconies overhanging it, the pillars and flagstones of which were all jasper beautifully worked. In this palace there was room to lodge two powerful princes with all their retinue. There were also ten pools of water in which were kept every kind of waterfowl known in these parts, fresh water being provided for the river birds, salt for those of the sea, and the water itself being frequently changed to keep it pure: every species of bird, moreover, was provided with its own natural food, whether fish, worms, maize or the smaller cereals. And I can vouch for it to your Majesty that those birds who ate fish alone and nothing else received some two hundred and fifty pounds of it every day, which was caught in the salt lake. It was the whole task of three hundred men to look after these birds. Others likewise were employed in ministering to those who were ill. Each pool was overhung by balconies cunningly arranged, from which Moctezuma would delight to watch the birds. In one room of this palace he kept men, women and children, who had been white since their birth, face, body, hair, eyebrows and eyelashes. He had also another very beautiful house in which there was a large courtyard, paved very prettily with flagstones in the manner of a chessboard. In this palace there were cages some nine feet high and six yards round: each of these was half covered with tiles and the other half by a wooden trellis skilfully made. They contained birds of prey, and there was an example of every one that is known in Spain, from kestrel to eagle, and many others which were new to us. Of each species there were many examples. In the covered part of every cage there was a stake on which the bird could perch and another under the wooden grating, so that the birds could go inside at nighttime and when it was raining and in the daytime come out into the sun and air. They were fed daily on chickens as their sole fare. Other large rooms on the ground floor were full of cages made of stout wood very firmly put together and containing large numbers of lions, tigers, wolves, foxes and wild cats of various kinds; these also were given as many chickens as they wanted. There were likewise another three hundred men to look after these animals and birds. In another palace he had men and women monsters, among them dwarfs, hunchbacks and others deformed in various ways, each manner of monster being kept in a separate apartment, and likewise with guards charged with looking after them.

His personal service was equally magnificent. Every morning at dawn there were over six hundred nobles and chief men present in his palace, some of whom were seated, others walking about the rooms and corridors, others amusing themselves in talk and other diversions, but none entering the actual apartment where he lay. The servants of these nobles filled two or three large courtyards and overflowed into the street, which was very large. They remained there all day, not quitting the palace until nightfall: at the time when the king took his meals food was served to them with equal profusion and rations were likewise dispensed to their servants and followers. His larders and wine cellars were open daily to all who wished to eat and drink. The meal was served by some three or four hundred youths. The dishes were innumerable since on every occasion that the king ate or drank every manner of dish was served to him, whether it were meat, fish, fruit, or herbs of whatever kind was found in the land. Since the climate is cold every plate and dish had under it a little brazier filled with lighted coals that it might not get cold. All the dishes were placed in a large hall in which he took his meals. It was almost entirely filled but kept ever fresh and clean, the King himself being seated on a small delicately fashioned leather cushion. While he ate some five or six ancient nobles stood a little way off to whom he gave morsels from his own dish. One of the youthful servitors remained on foot to place the dishes before him and remove them, and he requested from others who were further off anything which was lacking. Both at the beginning and end of the meal he was always given water with which to wash his hands, and the towel on which he dried his hands was never used again, nor likewise were the plates and dishes on which the food was brought ever used twice and the same with the little braziers which were also new for every meal. Every day he changed his garments four times, always putting on new clothes which were never worn more than once. The nobles always entered his palace barefoot, and those who were bidden to present themselves before him did so with bowed head and eyes fixed on the ground, their whole bearing expressing reverence; nor would they when speaking to him lift their eyes to his face, all of which was done to show their profound humiliation and respect. That such was the motive I am certain because certain of the nobles rebuked the Spanish soldiers for speaking to me without due shame in that they looked me full in the face, which seemed to them the height of disrespect. When Moctezuma went abroad, which was seldom, all who were with him or whom he met in the street turned away their faces and avoided looking at him, some of them prostrating themselves on the ground until he had passed. One of the nobles always preceded him bearing three long thin rods, for the purpose, as I think, of intimating the royal presence. For on his descending from the litter he bore one in his hand and carried it with him wherever he went. In short the various ceremonies which this ruler observed were so many and curious that there is not space here to recount them, and I think that not even the sultans themselves or other eastern potentates were surrounded by such pomp and display.

In this great city I was now busied in providing such things as seemed profitable to your Majesty's service, pacifying and subduing many provinces containing great numbers of large cities, towns and fortresses, discovering mines, and finding out and enquiring many secrets of these lands under the rule of Moctezuma, as also of others bordering on them of which he knew, which are so extensive and marvelous that their existence is almost incredible: all this with the goodwill and pleasure of Moctezuma and all the natives of these lands as if they had recognized from the beginning your Majesty as their natural lord and governor, and now did with no less goodwill all these things which they were bidden in your Majesty's royal name.

QUESTIONS

1. What is the physical setting of Tenochtitlán? How does this setting shape life there?
2. How does Cortés describe Aztec commerce and urban life? What does he think of the Aztecs in comparison to his own countrymen?
3. What does Cortés say about Aztec religious belief? Why, according to Cortés, do the Aztecs accept his religious instruction?
4. Why do the Aztecs not gaze directly on Moctezuma? What is the relationship of Aztecs to their ruler? What do the Aztecs think of Cortés' relationship with his own followers?

DOCUMENT

BROKEN SPEARS

The Aztec Account of the Conquest of Mexico

In April 1519 the Spanish adventurer Hernán Cortés (1484–1547) landed at what now is Veracruz, Mexico on a mission of trade and evangelization. Over the course of the next twenty-eight months Cortés and his small army, starting with only 508 soldiers, endured considerable hardship, nearly suffered catastrophic defeat, and finally overcame the vast empire of the Aztecs, ultimately conquering the magnificent capital of the Aztecs, Tenochtitlán, in August 1521. Cortés won his great victories as a result of his acquisition of crucial allies among the native peoples who despised the Aztecs and who provided hundreds of thousands of soldiers, and the debilitating effects of European diseases, such as smallpox, that ravaged the population and killed off a series of important indigenous leaders, and the superiority of weaponry at the Spaniards' disposal.

On the night of June 30, 1520, Cortés nearly suffered a decisive defeat, during what is now known as "La Noche Triste," the "Night of Sorrows." Trapped in the center of Tenochtitlán with 1,100, the Spaniards were surrounded by tens of thousands of Aztecs. Cortés tried to sneak out during the night, but the Aztecs discovered their retreat and attacked in enormous force trapping the Spaniards on the causeways out of the city. The Spaniards lost about half their soldiers.

This selection describes the Spanish defeat on the Night of Sorrows from the Aztec perspective.

Reprinted from *The Broken Speaks: The Aztec Account of the Conquest of Mexico*, by permission of Beacon Press. Copyright © 1962, 1990, 1992 by Migeul Lon-Portilla.

34

THE SPANIARDS ABANDON THE CITY

At midnight the Spaniards and Tlaxcaltecas came out in closed ranks, the Spaniards going first and the Tlaxcaltecas following. The allies kept very close behind, as if they were crowding up against a wall. The sky was overcast and rain fell all night in the darkness, but it was a gentle rain, more like a drizzle or a heavy dew.

The Spaniards carried portable wooden bridges to cross the canals. They set them in place, crossed over and raised them again. They were able to pass the first three canals—the Tecpantzinco, the Tzapotlan and the Atenchicalco—without being seen. But when they reached the fourth, the Mixcoatechialtitlan, their retreat was discovered.

THE BATTLE BEGINS

The first alarm was raised by a woman who was drawing water at the edge of the canal. She cried: "Mexicanos, come running! They are crossing the canal! Our enemies are escaping!"

Then a priest of Huitzilopochtli shouted the call to arms from the temple pyramid. His voice rang out over the city: "Captains, warriors, Mexicanos! Our enemies are escaping! Follow them in your boats. Cut them off, and destroy them!"

When they heard this cry, the warriors leaped into the boats and set outr in pursuit. These boats were from the garrisons of Tenochtitlan and Tlatelolco, and were protected by the warriors' shields. The boatmen paddled with all their might; they lashed the water of the lake until it boiled.

Other warriors set out on foot, racing to Nonohualco and then to Tlacopan to cut off the retreat.

The boats converged on the Spaniards from both sides of the causeway, and the warriors loosed a storm of arrows at the fleeing army. But the Spaniards also turned to shoot at the Aztecs; they fired their crossbows and their arquebuses. The Spaniards and Tlaxcaltecas suffered many casualties, but many of the Aztec warriors were also killed or wounded.

35

THE MASSACRE AT THE CANAL OF THE TOLTECS

When the Spaniards reached the Canal of the Toltecs, in Tlaltecayohua-can, they hurled themselves headlong into the water, as if they were leaping from a cliff. The Tlaxcaltecas, the allies from Tliliuhquitepec, the Spanish foot soldiers and horsemen, the few women who accompanied the army—all came to the brink and plunged over it.

The canal was soon choked with the bodies of men and horses; they filled the gap in the causeway with their own drowned bodies. Those who followed crossed to the other side by walking on the corpses.

When they reached Petlalco, where there was another canal, they crossed over on their portable bridge without being attacked by the Aztecs. They stopped and rested there for a short while, and began to feel more like men again. Then they marched on to Popotla.

Dawn was breaking as they entered the village. Their hearts were cheered by the brightening light of this new day: they thought the horrors of the retreat by night were all behind them. But suddenly they heard war cries and the Aztecs swarmed through the streets and surrounded them. They had come to capture Tlaxcaltecas for their sacrifices. They also wanted to complete their revenge against the Spaniards.

The Aztecs harried the army all the way to Tlacopan. Chimalpopoca, the son of Motecuhzoma, was killed in the action at Tlilyuhcan by an arrow from the crossbows. Tlatecatzin, the Tepanec prince, was wounded in the same action and died shortly after. He had served the Spaniards as a guide and advisor, pointing out the best roads and short cuts.

QUESTIONS

1. Why did the Spaniards abandon Tenochtitlán?
2. How were the Aztecs able to trap the Spaniards?
3. What happened to the captured Spaniards?
4. Why was the Spanish technological superiority negated on this night?

DOCUMENT

THE DISCOVERY AND CONQUEST OF MEXICO, 1517–1521

Bernal Díaz del Castillo

In April 1519 the Spanish adventurer Hernán Cortés (1484–1547) landed at what now is Veracruz, Mexico on a mission of trade and evangelization. Over the course of the next twenty-eight months Cortés and his small army, starting with only 508 soldiers, endured considerable hardship, nearly suffered catastrophic defeat, and finally overcame the vast empire of the Aztecs, ultimately conquering the magnificent capital of the Aztecs, Tenochtitlán, in August 1521. Cortés won his great victories as a result of his acquisition of crucial allies among the indigenous peoples who despised the Aztecs and who provided hundreds of thousands of soldiers; the debilitating effects of European diseases, such as smallpox, that ravaged the native populations and killed off a series of important indigenous leaders; and the superiority of weaponry at the Spaniards' disposal.

The so-called conquest was, however, by no means complete. Cortés, himself, embarked on another campaign toward present-day Central America. Other explorers went north. Many of the indigenous peoples, notably the Maya of Yucatán and Guatemala and the Yaqui of Sonora never succumbed to the Europeans.

Bernal Díaz del Castillo (1495–1584) accompanied Hernán Cortés on all his adventures. Probably more than any other account his chronicle puts forth the Spanish view of the conquest of the Aztecs and other Indian peoples. He apparently began to write when he was an old man of sixty years, three decades after the events he described occurred, and continued to revise over the course of the next thirty years. Given the lapse in time, the inevitable dulling of his memory, and his obvious aim to glorify both himself and Cortés, its strict accuracy is highly doubtful. Nonetheless, it remains a valuable source. Historians have proven particularly adept at reading between the lines.

Now we saw our forces diminishing every day and those of the Mexicans increasing, and many of our men were dead and all the rest wounded, and although we fought like brave men we could not drive back nor even get free from the many squadrons which attacked us both by day and night, and the powder was giving out, and the same was happening with the food and water, and the great Montezuma being dead, they were unwilling to grant the peace and truce which we had sent to demand of them. In fact we were staring death in the face, and the bridges had been raised. It was therefore decided by Cortés and all of us captains and soldiers that we should set out during the night. That very afternoon we sent to tell them, through one of their priests whom we held prisoner and who was a man of great importance among them, that they should let us go in peace within eight days and we would give up to them all the gold; and this was done to put them off their guard so that we might get out that night.

The order was given to make a bridge of very strong beams and planks, so that we could carry it with us and place it where the bridges were broken. Four hundred Tlaxcalan Indians and one hundred and fifty soldiers were told off to carry this bridge and place it in position and guard the passage until the army and all the baggage had crossed. Two hundred Tlaxcalan Indians and fifty soldiers were told off to carry the cannon, and Gonzalo de Sandoval, Diego de Ordás, Francisco de Sauzedo, Francisco de Lugo and a company of one hundred young and active soldiers were selected to go in the van to do the fighting. It was agreed that Cortés himself, Alonzo de Ávila, Cristóbal de Olid, and other Captains should go in the middle and support the party that most needed help in fighting. Pedro de Alvarado and Juan Velásquez de Leon were with the rearguard, and placed in the middle between them and the preceding section were two captains and the soldiers of Narvaez, and three hundred Tlaxcalans and thirty soldiers were told off to take charge of the prisoners and of Doña Marina and Doña Luisa; by the time this arrangement was made, it was already night.

In order to bring out the gold and divide it up and carry it, Cortés ordered his steward named Cristóbal de Guzman and other soldiers who were his servants to bring out all the gold and jewels and silver, and he gave them many Tlaxcalan Indians for the purpose, and they placed it in the Hall. . . .

After we had learnt the plans that Cortés had made about the way in which we were to escape that night and get to the bridges, as it was somewhat dark and cloudy and rainy, we began before midnight to bring along the baggage, and the horses and mare began their march, and the Tlaxcalans who were laden with the gold. Then the bridge was quickly put in place, and Cortés and the others whom he took with him in the first detachment and many of the horsemen, crossed over it. While this was happening, the voices, trumpets, cries and whistles of the Mexicans began to sound and they called out in their language to the people of Tlaltelolco, "Come out at once with your canoes for the Teules are leaving; cut them off so that not one of them may be left alive." When I least expected it, we saw so many squadrons of warriors bearing down on us, and the lake so crowded with canoes that we could not defend ourselves. Many of our soldiers had already crossed the bridge, and while we were in this position, a great multitude of Mexicans charged down on us with the intention of removing the bridge and wounding and killing our men who were unable to assist each other; and as fortune is perverse at such times, one mischance followed another, and as it was raining, two of the horses slipped and fell into the lake. When I and others of Cortés' Company saw that, we got safely to the other side of the bridge, and so many warriors charged on us, that despite all our good fighting, no further use could be made of the bridge, so that the passage or water opening was soon filled up with dead horses, Indian men and women, servants, baggage and boxes.

Fearing that they would not fail to kill us, we thrust ourselves ahead along the causeway, and we met many squadrons armed with long lances waiting for us, and they used abusive words to us, and among them they cried: "Oh! villains, are you still alive?"—and with the cuts and thrusts we gave them, we got through, although they then wounded six of those who were going along with me. Then if there was some sort of plan such as we had agreed upon it was an accursed one; for Cortés and the captains and soldiers who passed first on horseback, so as to save themselves and reach dry land and make sure of their lives, spurred on along the causeway, and they did not fail to attain their object, and the horses with the gold and the Tlaxcalans also got out in safety. I assert that if we had waited (the horsemen and the soldiers one for the other) at the bridges, we should all have been put an end to, and not one of us would have been left alive; the reason was this, that as we went along the causeway, charging the Mexican squadrons, on one side of us was water and on the other azoteas,[1] and the lake was full of canoes so that we could do nothing. Moreover the muskets and crossbows were all left behind at the bridge, and as it was night time, what could we do beyond what we accomplished? which was to charge and give some sword-thrusts to those who tried to lay hands on us, and to march and get on ahead so as to get off the causeway.

Had it been in the day-time, it would have been far worse, and we who escaped did so only by the Grace of God. To one who saw the hosts of warriors who fell on us that night and the canoes full of them coming along to carry off our soldiers, it was terrifying. So we went ahead along the causeway in order to get to the town of Tacuba where Cortés was already stationed with all the Captains. Gonzalo de Sandoval, Cristóbal de Olid and others of those horsemen who had gone on ahead were crying out: "Señor Captain, let us halt, for they say that we are fleeing and leaving them to die at the bridges; let us go back and help them, if any of them survive"; but not one of them came out or escaped. Cortés' reply was that it was a miracle that any of us escaped. However, he promptly went back with the horsemen and the soldiers who were unwounded, but they did not march far, for Pedro de Alvarado soon met them, badly wounded, holding a spear in his hand, and on foot, for the enemy had already killed his sorrel mare, and he brought with him four soldiers as badly wounded as he was himself, and eight Tlaxcalans, all of them with blood flowing from many wounds.

While Cortés was on the causeway with the rest of the Captains, we repaired to the courtyard in Tacuba. Many squadrons had already arrived from Mexico, shouting out orders to Tacuba and to the other town named Atzcapotzalco, and they began to hurl darts, stones and arrows and attack with their long lances. We made some charges and both attacked them and defended ourselves.

Let us go back to Pedro de Alvarado. When Cortés and the other Captains met him in that way, and saw that no more soldiers were coming along the causeway, tears sprang to his eyes. Pedro de Alvarado said that Juan Velásquez de Leon lay dead with many other gentlemen both of our own company and that of Narvaez, and that more than eighty of them were at the bridge; that he and the four soldiers whom he brought with him, after their horses had been killed, crossed the bridge in great peril, over the dead bodies, horses and boxes with which that passage at the bridge was choked. Moreover, he said that all the bridges and causeways were crowded with warriors. At the bridge of sorrow, which they afterwards called "Alvarado's leap," I assert that at the time not a single soldier stopped to see if he leaped much or little, for we could hardly save our own lives, as we were in great danger of death on account of the multitude of Mexicans charging down on us. I never heard of this leap of Alvarado until after Mexico was captured, and it was in some satirical verses made by a certain Gonzalo de Ocampo, which, as they were somewhat nasty, I will not fully quote here, except that he says: "Thou shouldst remember the leap that thou tookest from the bridge"; but I will not dwell on this subject.

Let us go on and I will relate how, when we were waiting in Tacuba, many Mexican warriors came together from all those towns and they killed three of our soldiers, so we agreed to get out of that town as quickly as we could, and five Tlaxcalan Indians, who found out a way towards Tlaxcala without following the main road, guided us with great precaution until we reached some small houses placed on a hill, and near to them a Cue or Oratory built like a fort, where we halted.

As we marched along we were followed by the Mexicans who hurled arrows and darts at us and stones from their slings, and the way in which they surrounded us and continually attacked us, was terrifying, as I have already said many times and am tired of repeating it.

We defended ourselves in that Cue and fortress, where we lodged and attended to the wounded and made many fires, but as for anything to eat, there was no thought of it. At that Cue or Oratory, after the great city of

Mexico was captured, we built a church, which is called "Nuestra Señora de los Remedios," and is very much visited, and many of the inhabitants and ladies from Mexico now go there on pilgrimages and to hold *novenas.*[2]

It was pitiable to see our wounds being dressed and bound up with cotton cloths, and as they were chilled and swollen they were very painful. However what was more to be wept over was the loss of the gentlemen and brave soldiers who were missing, namely, Juan Velásquez de Leon, Francisco de Sauzedo, Francisco de Morla, Lares the good horseman and many others of us followers of Cortés. I name these few only because it would be a long business to write the names of the great number of our companions who were missing. Of the followers of Narvaez, the greater number were left at the bridges weighed down with gold.

Let us go on to say how there were left dead at the bridges the sons and daughters of Montezuma as well as the prisoners we were bringing with us, also Cacamatzin the Lord of Texcoco and other kings of provinces. Let us stop relating all these hardships and say how we were thinking of what we had in front of us, for we were all wounded, and only twenty-three horses escaped; then of the cannon and artillery and powder, we saved nothing; the crossbows were few in number and we promptly mended their cords and made arrows but the worst of all was that we did not know what we should find the disposition of our friends the Tlaxcalans would be towards us. In addition to this, always surrounded by Mexicans who fell on us with yells, we determined to get out of that place at midnight with the Tlaxcalans in front as guides, taking every precaution. We marched with the wounded in the middle and the lame supported with staffs, and some, who were very bad and could not walk, on the croups of the horses that were lame and were not fit for fighting. Those horsemen who were not wounded went in front or were divided some on one side, some on the other, and marching in this manner all of us who were most free from wounds kept our faces towards the enemy. The wounded Tlaxcalans went in the body of our squadron and the rest of them who were sufficiently sound faced the enemy in company with us. The Mexicans were always harassing us with loud cries, yells and whistles, shouting out, "You are going where not one of you will be left alive," and we did not understand why they said so, but it will be seen later on. But I have forgotten to write down how happy we were to see Doña Marina still

42

alive, and Doña Luisa the daughter of Xicotenga, whose escape at the bridges was due to some Tlaxcalans, and also a woman named Maria de Estrada, who was the only Spanish woman in Mexico. Those who escaped and got away first from the bridges were some sons of Xicotenga, the brothers of Doña Luisa.

END NOTES

1. The flat roofs of the houses.
2. *Novenas:* religious exercises extending over nine days.

QUESTIONS

1. Who were Cortés's primary indigenous allies?
2. What was "Alvarado's leap"?
3. Why do we refer to the Spanish retreat from Tenochtitlán as the "Sad Night" or "Noche Triste"?
4. How do you think history would have changed if Cortés and his men had perished in the retreat from Tenochtitlán?

43

POTOSÍ, A MINING TOWN IN THE SEVENTEENTH CENTURY

Acarete du Biscay

The Spanish and Portuguese invaders in the Americas were soon transfixed by the lure of precious metals. Mining became the core of the economies of the viceroyalties of New Spain and Peru, and intermittently important in Brazil.

As for all of the colonial economies in the Americas, the greatest problem facing the mining industry was acquiring a stable labor force. Mining was dangerous work. Because of this, few indigenous people willingly chose to mine. In Peru, the Spaniards obtained forced labor through the mita, *a system in which indigenous communities had to send one-seventh of their adult male population to Potosí, the viceroyalty's most important mining town, where they worked for one full year. In the seventeenth century an estimated fourteen thousand mita workers were in Potosí at any time. The miners toiled one week in the mines and then had two weeks for other tasks. The mine owners paid the miners wages, but they were seldom sufficient to cover the high cost of living in the mining camps. As the Indian population rapidly decreased, the victims of European diseases, the Spaniards found it more and more difficult to obtain labor. Many Andean men fled their mita obligations. At the beginning of the seventeenth century there were at least thirty thousand Indian miners in*

Reprinted from *Colonial Travelers in Latin America*, (1972), Alfred A. Knopf.

Potosí. Ten thousand more from neighboring areas supplied the town with food and other materials.

A DESCRIPTION OF THE CITY OF POTOSÍ AND THE MINES THERE

But before we go any farther 'tis convenient I should give some description of the city of Potosí, as I have done of others. The Spaniards call it the Imperial City, but nobody could ever tell me for what reason. 'Tis situate at the foot of a mountain called Arazassou [Aranzazú], and divided in the midst by a river, which comes from a lake inclosed with walls, which lies about a quarter of a league above the city, and is a kind of reserver [reservoir] to hold the water that is necessary for the work-houses of that part of the city, which is on this side of the river over against the mountain, [and] is raised upon a little hill, and is the largest and most inhabited part. As for that part of the city which is on the side of the mountain, there's scarce anything but engines and the houses of those that work in them. The city has neither walls, ditches, nor forts for its defense. There are reckoned to be 4,000 houses well built of good stone, with several floors, after the manner of the buildings in Spain. The churches are well made, and all richly adorned with plate, tapestry, and other ornaments, and above all those of the monks and Nuns, of whom there are several convents of different orders, which are very well furnished. This is not the least populous city of Peru, with Spaniards, mestizos, strangers, and natives (which last the Spaniards call *Indios*), with mulattoes and Negroes. They count there are between 3,000 and 4,000 natural Spaniards bearing arms, who have the reputation of being very stout men and good soldiers. The number of the mestizos is not much less, nor are they less expert at a weapon, but the greatest part of them are idle, apt to quarrel and treacherous. Therefore they commonly wear three or four buff-waistcoats one upon another, which are proof against the point of a sword, to secure themselves from private stabs.

The strangers there are but few; there are some Dutch, Irish, and Genoese, and some French, most of whom are of St. Malo, Provence, or Bayonne, and pass for people of Navarre and Biscaye. As for the Indians, they are reckoned to amount to near 10,000 besides the mulattoes and the

45

blacks; but they are not permitted to wear either swords or firearms, nor [are] their *curacas* and *caciques,* tho' they may all aspire to any degree of knighthood, and to benefices, to which they are often raised for their laudable actions and good services. They are also forbidden to wear the Spanish habit, but are obliged to clothe themselves in a different manner, in a close-coat without sleeves, which they wear next their shirts, to which their band and laced cuffs are fastened. Their breeches are wide at bottom after the French fashion, their legs and feet naked. The blacks and mulattoes, being in the service of the Spaniards, are habited after the Spanish mode and may bear arms, and all the Indian slaves after ten years service are set at liberty, and have the same privileges with the others.

The government of this city is very exact, by the care which is taken by twenty-four magistrates, who are constantly observing that good order be kept in it, besides the *corregidor* and President of Las Charcas, who directs officers after the manner of Spain. It is to be observed that, excepting these two principal officers, as well as Potosí as everywhere else in the Indies, all the people, whether knights, gentlemen, officers or others, are concerned in commerce, of which some of them make so great an advantage that in the city of Potosí there are some reckoned to be worth two, some three, and some four millions of crowns; and a great many worth two, three, or four hundred thousand crowns. The common people, too, live much at their ease, but are all proud and haughty, and always go very fine, either in cloth of gold and silver, or in scarlet, or silk trimmed with a great deal of gold and silver-lace.

The furniture of their houses is very rich, for they are generally served in plate. The wives, both of gentlemen and citizens, are kept very close to a decree beyond what they are in Spain; they never go abroad, unless it be to go to mass, or to make some visit, or to some public feast, and that but rarely. The women here are generally addicted to excess in taking coca. This is a plant that comes from the side of Cuzco, which, when it is made up in rowls [rolls] and dried, they chew as some do tobacco. They are so heated, and sometimes absolutely fuddled by it, that they have no command of themselves at all. 'Tis likewise often used by the men, and has the same effects upon them. They are otherwise very temperate in eating and drinking, tho' they have before dwelt in places well stored with all sort of provisions, as beef, mutton, fowls, venison, raw and preserved fruits, corn

46

and wine, which are brought hither from other parts, and some from a great distance, which makes these commodities dear, so that the meaner sort of people, especially those that have very little beforehand, would find it hard enough to live there, if money were not very plenty, and easy to be got by them that are willing to work.

The best and finest silver in all the Indies is that of the mines of Potosí, the principal of which are found in the mountain of Aranzazú, where, besides the prodigious quantities of silver that have been taken out of veins, in which the metal evidently appeared and which are now exhausted, there is almost as great quantities of it found in places where they had not digged before. Nay, from some of the earth which they threw aside formerly when they opened the mines and made pits and cross-ways in the mountains, they have taken silver and have found by this that the silver has been formed since that time, which shows how proper the quality of this ground is for the production of that metal. But indeed this earth does not yield so much as the mines that are found by veins among the rocks. . . .

The King of Spain does not cause any of these mines to be wrought on his account, but leaves them to those persons that make the discovery of them, who remain masters of them after the *corregidor* has visited them and declared them proprietors, on the accustomed conditions and privileges. The same *corregidor* describes and marks out the superfices of the ground, in which they are allowed to open the mine on the outside; which does not, for all that, limit or restrain their work underground, every man having liberty to follow the vein he has found, the extent and depth of it reaching never so far, tho' it should cross that which another has digged near it. All that the King reserves for himself, besides the duties we shall hereafter speak of, is to give a general direction by his officers for all the work of the mines, and to order the number of savages to be employed in them, to prevent the disorders that would arise if every proprietor of the mines should have liberty to set as many of them to work as he pleased; which would frequently give occasion to those that are most powerful and rich to engross and have so great a number of 'em [savages], that few or none would remain for others to employ to keep their work going forward. For this would be contrary to the King's interest, which is to make provision that there be a sufficient number of slaves for all the mines that are opened. For this end he obliges all the *curacas*, or chiefs of the savages,

47

to furnish every one a certain number, which they must always keep complete, or else are forced to give twice as much money as would have been paid in wages to those that are wanting, [lacking] if they had been present.

Those that are destined for the mines of Potosí don't amount to above two thousand and two or three hundred. These are brought and put into a great enclosure which is at the foot of the mountain, where the *corregidor* makes a distribution of them to the conductors of the mines, according to the number they want. And, after six days constant work, the conductor brings them back the Saturday following to the same place, where the *corregidor* causes a review to be made of them, to make the owners of the mines give them the wages that are appointed them, and to see how many of them are dead, that the *curacas* may be obliged to supply the number that is wanting—for there's no week passes but some of them die, either by divers accidents that occur, as the tumbling down of great quantities of earth and falling of stones, or by sickness and other casualties.

They are sometimes very much incommoded by winds that are shut up in the mines; the coldness of which, joined to that of some parts of the earth, chills them so excessively that, unless they chewed coca, which heats and fuddles them, it would be intolerable to them. Another great hardship which they suffer is that in other places the sulphurous and mineral vapors are so great that it strangely dries them up, so that it hinders them from free respiration. For this they have no other remedy than the drink which is made with the herb of Paraguay, of which they prepare a great quantity to refresh and moisten them when they come out of the mines at the times appointed for eating or sleeping. This drink serves them also for physic to make them vomit and cast up whatever incommodes their stomachs.

Among these savages they ordinarily choose the best workmen to break up the ore between the rocks. This they do with iron bars [crowbars], which the Spaniards call *palancas,* and other instruments of iron; others serve to carry what they dig in little baskets to the entrance of the mine; others to put it in sacks and load it upon a sort of great sheep [llamas], which they call *carneros de la tierra.* They are taller than asses and commonly carry two hundred pound weight; these serve to carry it to the work-houses, which are in the town along the river, which comes from the lake I have spoken of before. In these work-houses, which are a hundred and twenty in number, the ore is refined, of which take the following account:

They first beat it well upon anvils with certain great hammers, which a mill continually keeps at work. When it is pretty well reduced to powder, they pass it thro' a fine sieve and spread it upon the ground about half a foot thick in a square place that is very smooth, prepared for the purpose. Then they cast a great deal of water upon it, after which they, with a sieve, spread upon it a certain quantity of quick-silver, which is proportioned by the officers of the mint, and also a liquid substance of iron, which is prepared by two millstones, one of which is fixed, and the other is continually turning. Between these they put an old anvil, or some other massy piece of iron, which is worn away and consumed with water by the turning millstone, so that 'tis reduced to a certain liquid matter. The ore, being thus prepared, they stir it about and mix it, as men do when they make mortar, for a fortnight together, every day tempering it with water. After this, they several times put it into a tub, wherein there is a little mill which, by its motion, separates from it all the earth with the water, and casts them off together, so that nothing but the metallic matter remains at the bottom, which is afterward put into the fire in crucibles to separate the quick-silver from it, which is done by evaporation. As for the iron substance, that does not evaporate, but remains mixed with the silver, which is the reason that there is always in eight ounces (for example's sake) three-quarters of an ounce or thereabouts of false alloy.

The silver, when thus refined, is carried to the mint, where they make an essay [assay] of it whether it be of the right alloy, after which it is melted into bars or ingots, which are weighed, and the fifth part of them deducted, which belongs to the King, and are stamped with his mark. The rest appertain to the merchant who, in like manner, applies his mark to them and takes them away from thence when he pleases in bars, or else converts them into reals and other money. This fifth part is the only profit the King has from the mines, which yet are esteemed to amount to several millions. But besides this, he draws considerable sums by the ordinary impositions upon goods, without reckoning what he raises upon quick-silver, both that which is taken out of the mines of Huancavelica, which are situated between Lima and Cuzco, and that which is brought from Spain, with which two vessels are loaded every year, because that which is taken out of these mines is not sufficient for all the Indies.

They use divers ways of carriage to transport all the silver that is annually made about Potosí for Spain. First they load it upon mules that carry it to Arica, which is a port on the South-Sea [Pacific], from whence they transport it in small vessels to the fort of Lima, or Los Reyes, which is a fort upon the same sea, two leagues from Lima. Here they embark it with all that comes from other parts of Peru in two great gallions that belong to his Catholic Majesty, each of which carry 1,000 tons and are armed each with fifty or sixty pieces of canon. These are commonly accompanied with a great many small merchant ships as richly loaded, which have no guns but a few *petareroes*[1] to give salutes and take their course toward Panama, taking care always to send a little pinnace 8 or 10 leagues before to make discoveries. They might make this way in a fortnight's time, having always the help of the south-wind, which reigns alone in this sea. Yet they never make it less than a month's voyage, because by this delay the commander of the gallions makes a great advantage in furnishing those with cards that have a mind to play on ship-board during the voyage, which amounts to a very considerable sum, both because the tribute he receives is ten patagons for every pack of cards, and because there is a prodigious quantity of them consumed, they being continually at play, and there being scarce anybody aboard but is concerned for very considerable sums. . . .

FIESTA AT POTOSÍ

Three weeks after my arrival at Potosí, there were great rejoicings made for the birth of the Prince of Spain, which lasted for a fortnight together, during which time all work ceased throughout the city, in the mines, and in the adjacent places. And all the people great and small, whether Spaniards, foreigners, Indians, or blacks, minded nothing else but to do something extraordinary for the solemnizing of this festival. It began with a cavalcade made by the *corregidor,* the twenty-four magistrates of the city, the other officers, the principal of the nobility and gentry, and the most eminent merchants of the city, all richly clothed; all the rest of the people, and particularly the ladies, being at the windows and casting down abundance of perfumed waters, and great quantities of dry sweetmeats. The following days they had several plays, some of which they call *Juegos de Toros,* other *Juegos de Cannas,* [Cañas] several sorts of masquerades, comedies, balls, with vocal and instrumental music, and other divertisements, which were carried on one day by the gentlemen, another day by the citizens; one while by the goldsmiths, another while by the miners; some by the people of divers nations, others by the Indians, and all with great magnificence and a prodigious expense.

The rejoicings of the Indians deserve a particular remark, for, besides that they were richly clothed, and after a different manner, and that comical enough, with their bows and arrows, they, in one night and morning, in the chief public place of the city, prepared a garden in the form of a labyrinth, the plats of which were adorned with fountains spouting out waters, furnished with all sorts of trees and flowers, full of birds, and all sorts of wild beasts, as lions, tigers and other kinds, in the midst of which they expressed their joy a thousand different ways, with extraordinary ceremonies.

The last day save one surpassed all the rest, and that was a race at the ring, which was performed at the charge of the city with very surprising machines. First there appeared a ship towed along by savages of the bulk and burden of a 100 tons, with her guns and equipage of men clothed in curious habit, her anchors, ropes, and sails swelling with the wind, which very luckily blew along the street through which they drew her to the great public place, where, as soon as she arrived, she saluted the company by the discharge of all her canon. At the same time, a Spanish lord, representing an emperor of the East coming to congratulate the birth of the prince, came out of the vessel attended with six gentlemen and a very fine train of servants that led their horses, which they mounted, and so went to salute the President of Los Charcas. And, while they were making their compliment to him, their horses kneeled down and kept in that posture, having been taught this trick before. They afterward went to salute the *corregidor* and the judges of the field, from whom, when they had received permission to run at the ring against the defendants, they acquitted themselves with great gallantry, and received very fine prizes distributed by the hands of the ladies.

The race at the ring being finished, the ship and a great many other small barks that were brought thither advanced to attack a great castle wherein Cromwell the Protector, who was then in war with the King of Spain, was feigned to be shut up; and, after a pretty long combat of fireworks, the fire took hold of the ship, the small barks, and the castle and all

51

was consumed together. After this a great many pieces of gold and silver were distributed and thrown among the people in the name of his Catholic Majesty. And there were some particular persons that had the prodigality to throw away two or three thousand crowns a man among the mob.

The day following, these rejoicings were concluded by a procession made from the great Church to that of the Recollects, in which the Holy Sacrament was carried, attended with all the clergy and laity. And, because the way from one of these churches to the other had been unpaved for the celebration of the other rejoicings, they repaired it for this procession with bars of silver, with which all the way was entirely covered. The altar where the Host was to be lodged in the Church of the Recollects was so furnished with figures, vessels, and plates of gold and silver, adorned with pearls, diamonds, and other precious stones that scarce ever could anything be seen more rich, for the citizens brought thither all the rarest jewels they had. The extraordinary charge of this whole time of rejoicing, was reckoned to amount to above 500,000 crowns. . . .

END NOTE

1. A *petarero* is a small explosive device which shoots or fires small charges—*I. A. L.*

QUESTIONS

1. What were mulattoes and blacks forbidden to wear? Why?
2. What differences were there in the dress of blacks and Indians?
3. How did the Crown regulate the mines?
4. Describe the life of a miner in Potosí.

A JESUIT MISSIONARY GIVES HIS FIRST IMPRESSIONS OF JAPAN

St. Francis Xavier

St. Francis Xavier (1506–52) was perhaps the most extraordinary missionary in the history of the Christian religion. A Basque of noble family, he was one of the original six companions of Ignatius of Loyola who formed the nucleus of the Jesuit Order, founded in 1540. In 1541, at the invitation of King John III of Portugal, he sailed for the East on a mission to convert the whole of Asia to Christianity. Landing first in Goa, where he tried to reform the Portuguese traders and soldiers who had lapsed from their vows, he then proceeded to Ceylon (Sri Lanka), Mylapore (near Madras), and Malacca in India, and went as far as the Moluccas (or Spice Islands) in Indonesia.

In 1549 he traveled to Japan, the "Cipangu" of travelers' legends, and so was among the first Westerners to visit that land. He worked as a missionary for over two years, and made nearly 800 converts to Christianity. His success was in large part due to the cooperation of the local lords who may have allowed him freedom of action in the desire to get access to Portuguese trade and firearms. Eventually some 300,000 Japanese converted to Christianity before the religion was suppressed by the emperor in 1614.

The selection given here is from a letter written in 1549 by Francis to the Jesuits in Goa, which conveys his (extremely positive) first impressions of Japan and his hopes of converting the land to Christianity. Later letters were

Reprinted by permission from *The Christian Century in Japan, 1549–1650*, translated by C.R. Boxer. Copyright © 1951 by Carcarnet Press Limited.

more appreciative of the obstacles presented by the entrenched Buddhist beliefs of most of Japan's rulers and people.

By the experience which we have of this land of Japan, I can inform you thereof as follows. Firstly, the people whom we have met so far, are the best who have yet been discovered, and it seems to me that we shall never find among heathens another race to equal the Japanese. It is a people of very good manners, good in general, and not malicious; they are men of honor to a marvel, and prize honor above all else in the world. They are a poor people in general; but their poverty, whether among the gentry or those who are not so, is not considered as a shame. They have one quality which I cannot recall in any people of Christendom; this is that their gentry howsoever poor they may be, and the commoners howsoever rich they may be, render as much honor to a poor gentleman as if he were passing rich. On no account would a poverty-stricken gentleman marry with someone outside the gentry, even if he were given great sums to do so; and this they do because they consider that they would lose their honor by marrying into a lower class. Whence it can clearly be seen that they esteem honor more than riches. They are very courteous in their dealings with another; they highly regard arms and trust much in them; always carrying sword and dagger, both high and low alike, from the age of fourteen onwards. They are a people who will not submit to any insults or contemptuous words. Those who are not of gentle birth give much honor to the gentry, who in their turn pride themselves on faithfully serving their feudal lord, to whom they are very obedient. It seems to me that they act thus rather because they think that they would lose their honor if they acted contrarily, than for fear of the punishment they would receive if disobedient. They are small eaters albeit somewhat heavy drinkers, and they drink rice wine since there are no ordinary wines in these parts. They are men who never gamble, because they consider it a great dishonor, since those who gamble desire what is not theirs and hence tend to become thieves. They swear but little, and when they do it is by the Sun. There are many persons who can read and write, which is a great help to their learning quickly prayers and religious matters. It is a land where there are but few thieves in some kingdoms, and this by the strict justice which is executed against those that are, for their lives are never spared. They abhor beyond measure this vice of theft. They are a people of very good will, very sociable and very desirous of knowledge; they are very fond of hearing about things of God, chiefly when they understand them. Of all the lands which I have seen in my life, whether those of Christians or of heathens, never yet did I see a people so honest in not thieving. Most of them believe in the men of old, who were (so far as I understand) persons who lived like philosophers; many of them adore the Sun and others the Moon. They like to hear things propounded according to reason; and granted that there are sins and vices among them, when one reasons with them pointing out that what they do is evil, they are convinced by this reasoning. I discerned fewer sins in the laity and found them more obedient to reason, than those whom they regard as fathers and priests, whom they call Bonzes.

Two things have astonished me greatly about this country. The first, to see how lightly they regard great sins; and the reason is because their forebears were accustomed to live in them, from whom those of the present generation take their example; see how continuation in vices which are against nature corrupts the people, in the same manner as continual disregard of imperfections undermines and destroys perfection. The second point is to see that the laity live better in their state than the Bonzes in theirs; and withal this is so manifest, it is astonishing in what esteem the former hold the latter. There are many other errors and evils among these Bonzes, and the more learned are the worst sinners. I spoke many times with some of the wiser, chiefly with one who is highly regarded by all in these parts, both for his letters, life, and dignity, as for his great age, he being eighty years old, and called Ningit [Ninjitsu], which is to say in Japanese "truthful heart"; he is as a bishop amongst them, and if the term could be applied to him, might well be called "blessed." In many talks which I had with him, I found him doubtful, and unable to decide whether our soul is immortal, or whether it dies with the body; sometimes he told me yes, at others no, and I fear that the other learned are alike. This Ningit is so great a friend of mine, that it is a marvel to see. All, both laity and Bonzes like us very much, and are greatly astonished to see how we have come from such distant lands as from Portugal to Japan, which is more than six thousand leagues, only to speak of the things of God, and how people can save their souls by belief in Jesus Christ; saying that our coming to these lands is the work of God. One thing I tell you, for which you may give many thanks to God Our Lord, that this land of Japan is very fit for our holy faith greatly to increase therein; and if we knew how to speak the language, I have no doubt whatsoever that we would make many Christians. May it please Our Lord that we may learn it soon, for already we begin to appreciate it, and we learned to repeat the ten commandments in the space of forty days which we applied ourselves thereto.

In the place of Paulo de Santa Fé,[1] our good and true friend, we were received by the local Captain and by the Alcayde, with much benignity and love, and likewise by all the people; everyone marveling to see Fathers from the land of the Portuguese. They were not in the least surprised at Paul having become a Christian, but rather are pleased and delighted thereat, both his relatives as those who are not so, since he has been in India and seen things which they here have never seen. And the Duke [Daimyo] of this land is well affected to him, and renders him much honor, and asked many questions concerning the customs, worth, and authority of the Portuguese and of their Empire in India; and Paulo gave him a very full account of everything, whereat the Duke was greatly contented.

Here they are not now surprised at people becoming Christians, and as a great part of them can read and write, they very soon learn the prayers; may it please God to give us tongue whereby we can speak to them of the things of God, for then we would reap much more fruit with His aid, grace, and favor. Now we are like so many statues among them, for they speak and talk to us about many things, whilst we, not understanding the language, hold our peace. And now we have to be like little children learning the language; God grant that we may likewise imitate them in true simplicity and purity of soul, striving by all means to become like them, both as regards learning the language as in showing the simplicity of children devoid of malice. And in this did God grant us great and notable favors in bringing us to these infidel lands, so that we should not neglect ourselves, since this land is wholly of idolators and enemies of Christ, and we have none in whom we can confide or trust, save only in God, for here we have neither relatives nor friends nor acquaintances, nor even some Christian piety, but only foes of Him who made the heaven and earth; and for this cause are we forced to place all our faith, hope, and trust in Christ

Our Lord, and not in any living creature, since, through unbelief, all are enemies of God.

Likewise it is necessary that we should give you an account of other favors which God hath granted us, teaching us through His mercy, so that you may help us in rendering thanks to God always for them. This is, that elsewhere the abundance of bodily provisions is often the reason whereby disordered appetites are given free rein, frequently despising the virtue of abstinence, which leads to the no little detriment of men's souls and bodies. This is the origin of the majority of corporal ills, and even spiritual, and men have much difficulty in finding a means of relief, and many find that the days of their life are shortened before obtaining it, suffering all kinds of bodily pains and torments, taking physic to cure themselves which gives them more distaste to swallow than enjoyment they received from the dainties which they ate and drank. God granted us a signal favor in bringing us to these lands which lack such abundancies, so that even if we wished to minister to our bodies with these superfluities, the country does not allow of it. They neither kill nor eat anything which they rear. Sometimes they eat fish; there is rice and corn, albeit little; there are numerous herbs, on which they live, and some fruit but not much. This people live wonderfully healthy lives and there are many aged. The Japanese are a convincing proof of how our nature can subsist on little, even if it is not a pleasing sustenance. We live in this land very healthy in body, God grant that we may be likewise in our souls. A great part of the Japanese are Bonzes, and these are strictly obeyed in the places where they are, even if their sins are manifest to all; and it seems to me that the reason why they are held in such esteem is because of their rigorous abstinence, for they never eat meat, nor fish, but only herbs, fruit, and rice, and this once a day and very strictly, and they are never given wine. There are many Bonzes and their temples are of but little revenue. By reason of their continual abstinence and because they have no intercourse with women (especially those who go dressed in black like clergy) on pain of death, and because they know how to relate some histories or rather fables of the things in which they believe, it seems to me they are held in great veneration. And it may well happen that since they and we feel so differently about God and the method of salvation, that we may be persecuted by them with something stronger than words. What we in these parts endeavor to do, is to bring people to the knowledge of their Creator and Saviour, Jesus Christ Our Lord. We live with great hope and trust in Him to give us strength, grace, help, and favor to prosecute this work. It does not seem to me that the laity will oppose or persecute us of their own volition, but only if they are importuned by the Bonzes. We do not seek to quarrel with them, neither for fear of them will we cease to speak of the glory of God, and of the salvation of souls. They cannot do us more harm than God permits, and what harm comes to us through them is a mercy of God; if through them for His love, service, and zeal for souls, He sees good to shorten the days of our life, in order to end this continual death in which we live, our desires will be speedily fulfilled and we will go to reign forever with Christ. Our intentions are to proclaim and maintain the truth, however much they may contradict us, since God compels us to seek rather the salvation of our future than the safety of our present lives; we endeavoring with the grace and favor of Our Lord to fulfil this precept, He giving us internal strength to manifest the same before the innumerable idolatries which there are in Japan.

It is well that we should give you an account of our stay in Cangoxima [Kagoshima]. We arrived here at a season when the winds were contrary for going to Miaco, [Kyoto] which is the chief city of Japan, where the King and the greatest lords of the Kingdom reside. And there is no wind that will serve us to go thither, save only five months from now, and then we will go with the help of Our Lord. It is three hundred leagues from here to Miaco, according to what they tell us, and we are likewise told great things of that city, which is said to contain more than ninety thousand houses; there is also a great university frequented by students therein, which has six principal colleges and more than two hundred houses of Bonzes, and of others like friars who are called Ieguixu [Zenshu], and of nuns who are called Hamacata [Amakata]. Besides this university of Miaco, there are five other chief universities whose names are these, Coya [Koya], Nenguru [Negoro], Feizan [Hieizen], Taninomine [Tamu no mine]. These are in the neighborhood of Miaco, and it is said that there are more than 3,500 students in each one of them. There is another university, a great way off, which is called Bandou [Bando, the Ashikaga Gakko] which is the best and biggest in Japan, and more frequented by students than any other. Bandou is a great lordship where there are six dukes, and a chief one among them, whom the others obey. This chief owes allegiance to the King of Japan who is the great King of Miaco. They tell us such things of the greatness of these lands and universities, that we would prefer to see them before affirming and writing them; and if things be as they tell us, then we will write of our experiences in detail. In addition to these principal universities, they say that there are many other smaller ones throughout the kingdom. During the year 1551, we hope to write you at length concerning the disposition that there is in Miaco and its universities for the knowledge of Jesus Christ Our Lord to be spread therein. This year two Bonzes are going to India who have studied in the universities of Bandou and Miaco, and with them many other Japanese to learn the things of our law.

On St. Michael's day we spoke with the duke of this land, who gave us great honor, saying that we should keep well the books in which was written the law of the Christians, and that if it was the true and good law of Jesus Christ, it would be troublesome to the Devil. A few days afterwards he gave leave to all his vassals that those who might wish to become Christians could do so. This good news I write at the end of the letter for your consolation, and that you may give thanks unto God our Lord. It seems to me that this winter we must occupy ourselves in making a declaration concerning the Articles of Faith in Japanese, somewhat copiously, for it to be printed (because all the principal persons here know how to read and write) so that our holy faith may be understood and spread throughout many parts, since we cannot go to all. Our dearest brother Paulo will translate faithfully into his own tongue everything which is necessary for the salvation of souls.

From Cangoxima, fifth of November of the year 1549.

Your most loving brother wholly in Christ.

END NOTE

1. Yajiro

QUESTIONS

1. Why is Xavier impressed by the Japanese emphasis on honor? How does honor shape Japanese social life?

2. What qualities, according to Xavier, make the Japanese ready and able to learn about Christianity?

3. What has Xavier learned about his own society and his own beliefs by observing the Japanese?

4. What habits of the Japanese and other aspects of Japanese life make it easier for Xavier to live according to his own Christian beliefs?

DOCUMENT

AKBARNAMA

Abu al-Fazl ibn Mubarak

The emperor Akbar, whose long reign lasted from 1556–1605, firmly cemented the authority of the Mughal emperors over most of north India and is often regarded as the one of the greatest of Indian rulers. His fame springs from his success in battle, his administrative skills, and his eclectic style of rule.

Akbar's court attracted some of the greatest artists and writers of the day, not least among them Abu al-Fazl ibn Mubarak (1551–1602) the son of a famous scholar and mystic. Abu al-Fazl rose to become Akbar's closest adviser and confidant, and was instrumental in developing a new imperial ideology that emphasized the divinely inspired nature of Akbar and his ancestors. In two massive works, the Akbarnama *or "Biography of Akbar," and the* Ain-I Akbari *or "Institutes of Akbar," Abu al-Fazl elaborated his theory of divinely illumined kingship, drawing on Shiite Muslim ideas of the "just Imam" and also on Greek neo-platonist philosophy interpreted by Muslim sages. Abu al-Fazl eventually aroused the jealousy of Akbar's son, Prince Salim (later the emperor Jahangir), who murdered him in 1602.*

This passage from the Akbarnama *describes Akbar's visit to Agra in 1560, his return to Delhi in 1564, and the building of the Agra fort in 1565. Shahinshah was the term used for the Mughal emperors to denote that they were the kings of kings, or that they ruled over the minor kings who ruled India. As was common in the sixteenth century, Mughal emperors traveled with their nobles, their wives, concubines, servants, slaves, and an entourage of animals from one capital to another. The Mughals had four capitals, Delhi, Lahore, Agra, and Fatehpur Sikri, between which they traveled every few years. This peripatetic lifestyle was a way of making themselves visible to their subjects, as was building forts, palaces, and tombs to showcase their political authority.*

MARCH OF THE S̲H̲ĀHINS̲H̲ĀH FROM THE PANJAB TO AGRA, HIS CASTING THE SHADOW OF FORTUNE OVER DELHI, AND FROM THENCE PROCEEDING BY WATER TO THE CAPITAL.

When H.M. the S̲h̲āhins̲h̲āh had by the might of soaring fortune removed one screen from the face of his actions and had set before himself the management of political and financial affairs, when the shops of the short-sighted and ill-fated had been overset, and each one of them had retired to a corner, ashamed and downcast, and when the holy soul was by heavenly aids freed from these affairs, he turned his rein towards the capital. His object was that by increasing his attention to the administration of justice, new vigour might be given to the perturbed universe, and that certain regulations should be established which should be codes for the use of administrators, present and future. As the standards of fortune were pitched at Sihrind the order was issued that the camp should proceed by the direct road to Delhi, while his own cavalcade should, for the purpose of hunting, proceed towards His̲ār Fīrūza. When His̲ār Fīrūza became the seat of the standards, the huntsmen represented that there were in the neighbourhood jungles containing *yūz,* which in Hindī are called *cīta,* and that the method of catching that ravening animal was one of the most remarkable of the arts of hunting. Accordingly the sacred heart, which is a decorated mansion of sports, mental and physical, turned its attention towards this charming spectacle. An order was given for making the necessary arrangement. In a short time all the apparatus was got ready, and sundry pits, which in Hindi are called *odī*[1] were dug according to a special plan (of Akbar's, see Blochmann 286). Several heads of *cīta*[2] were caught there and then a *Akbar* cavalcade moved towards Delhi. Though before this many *cīta* had been collected for the royal establishment, this was the first time that H.M. hunted them in person. On 11 Āz̲ar; Divine month corresponding to Saturday 4 Rabi'al-awal 968, 24th November, 1560, the standards were Set up in Delhi, and mortals attained the, materials of tranquillity.

. . .

In short, H.M. the S̲h̲āhins̲h̲āh after passing some days in Delhi proceeded on the day of Āzar 9 Dai, Divine month, corresponding to Friday 2 Rabī'-as-sānī, 21st December, to Agra, and he made the journey by water. The nobles and pillars of the empire accompanied him, while the

62

great camp proceeded in the same direction by land. H.M. arrived at Agra on the day of Farwardin 19 Dai, Divine month, corresponding to Monday 12 Rabī-aṣ-ṣanī, 31st December. The gardens of the hopes of the sincere bloomed. The wounded ones of the age obtained healing plasters. The market of justice grew brisk. Fortune embraced the truthful, and a time of joy came to the good. The sapling of fortune shot up. The bud of prestige began to expand. The world-adorning mind of the Shāhinshāh gave its attention to the education of the spiritual and temporal world under the guise of inattention. He took up his abode in the fort, which is the beat building in the city. The foundations of delightful dwellings were laid. The house of Bairām Khān was given to Mun'im Khār Khān-Khānan. All the other courtiers and servants commenced to build pleasant houses on both banks of the Jamna, and so the city became adorned. In the interval Mun'im Khān Khān-Khānan gave a royal feast and begged that H.M. would honour it by his presence. His prayer was granted, and his mansion received celestial glory by the radiance of H.M. the Shāhinshāh's advent. The Khan-Khanan tendered rare and exquisite presents and stood ready to sacrifice his life for H.M. (*lit.* stood with the coin of life in his palm).

MARCH OF THE SHĀHINSHĀH'S CORTÉGE TO DELHI, AND THE CASTING THE SHADE OF THE UMRELLA OF AUSPCIOUS-NESS OVER THAT CITY : THE ENTRY OF THE THORN INTO THE ROSE-LEAD ELEMENTS OF THE SHĀHINSHĀH AND OF ITS CHANGING INTO AN ERA OF AUSPICIOUSNESS, AND OR HIS PROXIMITY TO THE DIVINE PROTECTION.

As in all his ways, the peace of the world, and the repose of mortals are kept in view by the inspired soul of H.M. the Shāhinshāh, and his true intent in miscellaneous matters, such as hunting, etc., is to acquaint himself with the condition of the people without the intermediary of interested persons and hypocrites, and to take proper measures for the protection of mankind he, upon hearing of Shāh Abu-l-m'aālī's commotion, proceeded towards Delhi on the day of Āsmān, the 27th Dai, Divine month; corresponding to Saturday 23 Jamādā-al-awala. On the day of Marisfand the 29th Dai, corresponding to 25 Jamādā-al-awala, 8 January, 1564, that city was illumined by the advent of the Shāhinshāh Abū-l-m'aālī could not, on account of the glory of the Sh̲āhin̲s̲h̲āh, and the sublime dynasty, abide longer in India, and carried the burden of destruction to Kābul. Sedition which had awoke with bleared eyes went into a profound slumber, and mankind stretched their hands to heaven in supplication for the permanency of daily-increasing dominion. As the squint-eyed world lies in wait and searches for opportunities for promoting the cause of the wicked, wounds are continually being inflicted on the good and pure, but they are preserved by the Divine protection from the calamity thereof, and acquire eternal felicity in spite of the ill-intentioned. The Divine decree too has issued that whenever unstinted joys and lofty blessings are to be bestowed on anyone, he is in the first place to be made the recipient of griefs and pains, so that he may the better render thanks for his favours and that such sorrow may be the (evil-averting) rue for his world-adorning beauty. An instance of this occurred when the cortege of H.M. Sh̲āhin̲s̲h̲āh after arriving in Delhi had proceeded on the day of Bahman, Divine month, corresponding to Wednesday 28 Jamāda-al-awal, to visit the shrine of S̲h̲aik̲h̲ Niẓamu-d-dīn auliya. May his grave be holy! He was returning[3] from there to his dwelling, and when he reached the crossways (cahārsū) one of the death-destined ingrates was standing near Māham[2] Anaga's Madrasa. When H.M. had gone on beyond him, the latter discharged an arrow against that qibla of the world. It struck H.M.'s right shoulder and penetrated about the length of a span. A cry rose from heaven and earth, and devoted followers fell upon that wretch. They wished to examine him and not to kill him at once, but H.M. indicated that he should be speedily put to death lest a number of loyalists should fall under suspicion. In an instant they cut him to pieces. Though the hearts of the loyal and the minds of the superficial men of the world were perplexed as to the remedy, that spiritual and temporal king preserved his composure and comforted the faithful. He bade his followers extract the arrow. I have heard from the glorious tongue (Akbar's) that at first he thought someone had unwittingly thrown a fragment of a stone from a roof. In spite of such a wound he remained as before on his horse and proceeded to his palace. As the Divine protection and the prayers of the saints were guarding him, the wound was not serious, nor was lesion great. Skillful leeches who possessed *Jesus'* breath attended to the plastering and curing of it. Especially K̲h̲iz[5] K̲h̲wājah K̲h̲an and Hakim 'Ain-al-malk joined together in treating

64

the fresh wound and healing it by dry bandaging *(khushk-band).* Every
day they administered a fresh *fatila.*[6] In the course of a week a cicatrice
formed, and there was perfect restoration to health.

. . .

When H.M. was perfectly recovered he proceeded on 11 Bahman
Divine month, corresponding to Friday 6 Jamāda-al-a<u>kh</u>ira, 21 January,
1561, to Agra the capital. He made the journey by slow searches. Although
the wound had been cicatrised, and quite cured, yet out of consideration
for the fact that the wound was yet recent, and that he could not endure the
motion of a horse, he made most of the journey in a litter *(sūkāsan),* which
is the boat of dry land. When the shadow of his light-nourishing umbrella
cast its rays on the territory of Agra, mankind received fresh life and hastened to the acme of devotion, and had the bliss of going forth to welcome
him. They scattered gifts among his followers, and offered thanksgivings
for the Divine boon of his safety. H.M. on the 20th Bahman, Divine
month, corresponding to Sunday 15 Jamāda-al-a<u>kh</u>ira, alighted at the
palace. He busied himself in the administration of justice, and made fitting
regulations for the founding of empire and the cherishing of subjects. The
talented of the seven climes at the auspicious glance of the <u>Sh</u>āhin<u>sh</u>āh
emerged from their retirements and took part in active life, and became
constituents of increasing dominion. The evil received their punishment
and hastened to the hiding of annihilation. The world was cleansed of the
rubbish of the innmoderate and enjoyed the equability of spring.

. . .

Among the principal events of the year was the founding of the fort of
Agra. It is not concealed from the minds of the mathematical and the
acquainted with the mechanism of the spheres that since the world-adorning creator hath decked Time and the Terrene with the existence of the
<u>Sh</u>āhin<u>sh</u>āh in order that the series of creations might be perfected, that
wise-hearted one has exercised himself in bringing each individual life
from the secrecy of potentiality to the theatre of performance. At one time
he has prepared the constituents of rule by perfecting the earth for animated nature by improving agriculture by irrigation and the sowing of
seeds. At another time he establishes spiritual and temporal dominion by
building fortresses for the protection of products and the guarding of honour and prestige. Accordingly, he at this time gave directions for the build-

65

ing in Agra—which by position is the centre of Hindustan—of a grand fortress such as might be worthy thereof, and correspond to the dignity of his dominions. An order was then issued that the old fort which was built on the east bank of the Jamna, and whose pillars had been shaken by the revolutions of time and the shocks of fortune, should be removed, and that an impregnable fort should be built of hewn stone. It was to be stable like the foundation of the dominion of the sublime family and permanent like the pillars of its fortunes. Accordingly, lofty-minded mathematicians and able architects laid the foundations of this great building in an hour which was supreme for establishing a fortress. The excavations were made through seven strata of earth. The breadth of the wall was three *bādshāhī*[7] yards and its height sixty yards. It was provided with four gates whereby the doors of the dominion were opened towards the four quarters of the world. Every day 3 to 4,000 active builders and strong-armed labourers carried on the work. From the foundations to the battlements, the fortress was composed of hewn stone, each of which was polished like the world-revealing mirror, and was ruddy as the cheek of fortune. And they were so joined together that the end of a hair could not find place between them. This sublime fortress, the like of which had never been seen by a fabulous geometrician, was completed with its battlements, breastwork, and its loop-holes *(sang-andāz)* in the space of eight years under the faithful superintendence of Qāsim Khān Mīr Barr u Bahr.

. . .

MARCH OF THE SHĀHINSHĀH TO PUT DOWN THE SEDITION OF KHĀN ZAMĀN 'ALĪ QULĪ, ETC.

To those who have drunk[8] down to the lees of understanding it is no secret that[9] the "world is like wine in that it intensifies whatever exists already." If a man is of happy fortune, the acquisition of worldly things increases his auspiciousness and improves his personality so as to produce a thousand advantages to him. If, however, a man's destiny be evil, and his disposition bad, worldly success is productive in him of a thousand mischiefs. His outward prosperity is a cause of affliction to mankind, and his darkened heart becomes day by day more and more dark. His erring feet stray more and more, and he neither recognises the favours he has received nor does his duty to his benefactor. According as he is situated, he sometimes practises deceit and hypocrisy, and sometimes he withdraws the veil from before his actions and becomes openly as well as secretly a sedition-monger. The evil-ending career of 'Alī Qulī Khān Zamān is an instance of this. From the commencement of the coming into India, and the polishing of that great country which resulted from the Light of the Shāhinshāh fortune, he was always committing improprieties. The vessel of his nature was of small capacity, and so intoxication became apparent, and already some instances of this have been given.

H.M. the Shāhinshāh, from the breadth of his views, was continually washing the record of his faults and crimes from his own pure soul with the water of forgiveness. That black-fated one did not appreciate this clemency, but went on to accumulate wickednesses.

END NOTES

1. The spelling is given in the Āīn p. I. 207, top line. Apparently it is a corruption of the Sanskrit ūdar.
2. gilada lit. necklace, or collar, but used, like zinjār, to express number of elephants or leopards. See Vullers s.v.
3. The T. Alfī says he was returning from hunting.
4. In Syed Ahmad's Aṣṣār-i-ṣana did mention is made, p. 47, of a mosque and madrasra known as Mahām Begam's. The building had been destroyed, but Syed Ahmad gives the inscription. It ends in the chronogram Khair-al-munāzīl which yields the date 969=1561–62. Mahām Begam is doubtless Mahām Anaga for the inscription speaks of the exertions made in building the structure by Shihābu-d-dīn Ahmad, i.e. M. Anaga's friend and relative.
5. The T. Alfī says Khizr Khwajah was able to render assistance on account of his great experience in war and wounds. This is the last mention of Gutbadan's husband.
6. Fatila means a wick, and also a suppository or clyster, but I do not think it can mean the latter here. Perhaps it signifies a twisted or rolled bandage. There is a plant used in medicine called the fatīla-r-rah-bān (monks' match), and perhaps this may be what it meant here. See Not. et Ex., XXVI, p. 21.
7. It is not quite clear what is meant by the bādshāhī gaz, but most probably it is the Iskandari gaz which was introduced by Sikandar Lūdī and consisted of the width of 41 1/2 copper coins till Humayun increased it by half a coin, making the length 42 Iskandari coins. See Jang ret II. 11, where it is stated that the Hāi gaz was apparently made of universal application, 1. c. p. 68. The account in the Tab Akbari differes from Abul Fazl's. According to it the breadth of the wall was ten yards, and the height more than forty yards. The most was twenty yards wide and its depth ten yards. It also states that the work was finished in four years. Cf. also Blochmann, I do not fully understand A.F.'s statement that the excavations extended through seven strata or layers of earth. Apparently he is referring to the foundations generally and not to the moat. I suppose "seven layers" is merely a rhetorical expression for a great depth.

8. Text, *durd-kashan,* but many MSS. have *darya-kashan.*
9. This is a line or part of a line of verse.

QUESTIONS

1. What does a traveling Mughal court tell you about the ways that the Mughal government operated? Why might moving around have been effective for Akbar?

2. What is Akbar's relationship with his nobles? How do they receive him when he arrives?

3. How important is a leisure activity, such as hunting, to creating an imperial persona?

4. Why might Akbar have sponsored the building of a new fort in Agra? What role do you think architectural patronage plays in consolidating political power?

DOCUMENT

TRYING TO CHANGE CHINA

Matteo Ricci

For European missionaries and merchants in the sixteenth and seventeenth centuries, China presented almost irresistible opportunities. For merchants, the sheer size of the potential market and the possibility of purchasing exotic goods created visions of enormous wealth. For missionaries, the opportunity was in the possibility of offering salvation to China's huge population through conversion to Christianity. The first to arrive were the Jesuits, who quickly discovered that the hierarchical structure of Chinese society meant that successful conversion had to begin with the elite class. However, the missionaries were also confronted with the realization that the Chinese saw no need to embrace a doctrine preached by men they considered barbarians.

This selection is taken from the journals of pioneering Jesuit missionary Matteo (Matthew) Ricci (1552–1610), which were translated into Latin in 1615 by another missionary named Trigault and augmented by Trigault's own experiences. Ricci was by any account a phenomenally intelligent and learned man, and a keen observer of Chinese society. Born in Italy, he ultimately spent almost thirty years working in China during the reign of the Ming Dynasty (1368–1644), and although the number of Chinese he succeeded in converting to Christianity was small, he laid the foundation for those who followed.

Hanging on the wall of the reception room in the Mission House there was a cosmographical chart of the universe, done with European lettering. The

Reprinted by permission from *China in the Sixteenth Century: The Journals of Matthew Ricci: 1583–1610,* translated by Louis J. Gallagher. Copyright © 1953 by Random House, Inc.

more learned among the Chinese admired it very much and, when they were told that it was both a view and a description of the entire world, they became greatly interested in seeing the same thing done in Chinese. Of all the great nations, the Chinese have had the least commerce, indeed, one might say that they have had practically no contact whatever, with outside nations, and consequently they are grossly ignorant of what the world in general is like. True, they had charts somewhat similar to this one, that were supposed to represent the whole world, but their universe was limited to their own fifteen provinces, and in the sea painted around it they had placed a few little islands to which they gave the names of different kingdoms they had heard of. All of these islands put together would not be as large as the smallest of the Chinese provinces. With such a limited knowledge, it is evident why they boasted of their kingdom as being, the whole world, and why they called it Thienhia, meaning, everything under the heavens. When they learned that China was only a part of the great east, they considered such an idea, so unlike their own, to be something utterly impossible, and they wanted to be able to read about it, in order to form a better judgment. So the Governor consulted with Father Matthew Ricci and asked him, as he expressed it, if he, with the help of his interpreter, would make his map speak Chinese, assuring him that such a work would bring him great credit and favor with everyone.

Ricci had had considerable training in mathematics, which he studied for several years at Rome under Father Christophoro Clavius, Doctor of Science and Prince of Mathematicians of his day. In answer to the Governor's request, he went to work immediately at this task, which was not at all out of keeping with his ideas of preaching the Gospel. According to the disposition of Divine Providence, various ways have been employed at different times, and with different races, to interest people in Christianity. In fact this very attraction was to draw many of the Chinese into the net of Peter. The new chart was made on a larger scale than the original, so as to give more room for the Chinese written characters which are somewhat larger than our own. New annotations were also added, more in keeping with the Chinese genius, and more appropriate also to the author's intentions. When there was question of describing the various religious rites of the different nations, he took occasion to insert a mention of the sacred mysteries of the Christian faith, hitherto unknown to Chinese. In this way he hoped to spread the name and the fame of Christianity through the whole of China in a brief space of time. We must mention here another discovery which helped to win the good will of the Chinese. To them the heavens are round but the earth is flat and square, and they firmly believe that their empire is right in the middle of it. They do not like the idea of our geographies pushing their China into one corner of the Orient. They could not comprehend the demonstrations proving that the earth is a globe, made up of land and water, and that a globe of its very nature has neither beginning nor end. The geographer was therefore obliged to change his design and, by omitting the first meridian of the Fortunate Islands, he left a margin on either side of the map, making the Kingdom of China to appear right in the center. This was more in keeping with their ideas and it gave them a great deal of pleasure and satisfaction. Really, at that time and in the particular circumstances, one could not have hit upon a discovery more appropriate for disposing this people for the reception of the faith. This statement might appear to many to be somewhat of a paradox, so I shall briefly state the reason for making it, something which afterwards was confirmed by experience.

Because of their ignorance of the size of the earth and the exaggerated opinion they have of themselves, the Chinese are of the opinion that only China among the nations is deserving of admiration. Relative to grandeur of empire, of public administration and of reputation for learning, they look upon all other people not only as barbarous but as unreasoning animals. To them there is no other place on earth that can boast of a king, of a dynasty, or of culture. The more their pride is inflated by this ignorance, the more humiliated they become when the truth is revealed. When they first saw our delineation of the universe, some of the uneducated laughed at it and made fun of it, but it was different with the better instructed, especially when they studied the placement of the parallels and meridians and of the equator, relative to the tropics of Cancer and of Capricorn. Again, when they learned of the symmetry of the five zones, and after reading of the customs of so many different people, and seeing the names of many places in perfect accord with those given by their own ancient writers, they admitted that the chart really did represent the size and figure of the world. From that time on, they had a much higher opinion of the European system of education.

71

This, however, was not the only result. There was another, and of no less importance. When they saw on the map what an almost unlimited stretch of land and sea lay between Europe and the Kingdom of China, that realization seemed to diminish the fear our presence had occasioned. Why fear a people whom nature had placed so far away from them, and if this geographic fact of distance were generally known by all the Chinese, the knowledge would serve to remove a great obstruction to the spread of the Gospel throughout the kingdom. Nothing has impeded our work more than clouds of suspicion. This geographic study, frequently revised and refined and often reprinted, found its way into the courts of the Governor and of the Viceroy, where it was greatly admired, and finally into the palace of the King, on his own request. We shall say more later, relative to the way in which that was brought about. . . .

The geographic charts were such a huge success that Ricci took to making astronomical spheres and globes, out of copper and iron, illustrating the heavens and demonstrating the proper shape of the earth. At home he also painted sundials or engraved them on copper sheets, which he presented to friendly Magistrates, including the Viceroy. When these various devices were exhibited and their purpose explained showing the position of the sun, the courses of the stars and the central position of the earth, their designer and artisan was looked upon as the world's great astronomer. This nation measures all others according to its own standards, and they are thoroughly convinced that what is unknown to them is unknown to the rest of the world.

. . .

The European pictures and statues, the mathematical computations and the geographic relief maps also drew much attention. Our books, although printed in a language unknown to the Chinese, were greatly admired because of their unusual bindings and the splendor of the gilt work which was something altogether new in China. These people are delighted and amazed when you show them books containing descriptive maps, or specimens of building architecture illustrated in diagrams or designs. They simply marvel at the idea that whole countries can be viewed in one book, with cities, towns, palaces, lofty towers, arches and bridges and majestic temples. They are curiously interested in the thought of witnessing the grandeur of these things so widespread and distant from each other, and of seeing it all right at home in their own houses. The same may be said about their admiration of our musical instruments which they like for their soft tones and for their novelty of design. The effect of all this and of the conversation and discourses of the Fathers, which are always well adapted, seems to be that they have gradually formed a better opinion of Europe in general. They realize that fundamentally our sciences are more solid than their own and that the Chinese in general, and especially the educated classes, have had a wrong idea of foreigners up to the present, placing them all in the same category and calling them all barbarians. And so they have finally begun to make clear the real differences which exist between nations.

The Fathers have made an effort to merit a reputation for learning, not as a matter of vain-glory but with a view to the end for which they came here, namely, to further the cause of Christianity, which on all occasions they purposely weave into their conversations. The leaders among the Chinese do not easily pass over to a new religion, but most of them admire the truth, and do not hesitate to publish it, once it is known. . . .

. . . So Father Matthew told the Father Visitor that he thought it would be to the advantage of the Christian faith if they would let their beards grow and wear their hair longer, so they would not be taken for idol worshippers, or worse still for such as offer sacrifice to the idols. With these, as he explained, it was a set rule to be clean shaven and to wear the hair close cropped. He also asserted that experience had taught him that the Fathers should wear the same costume and ornaments as the highly educated Chinese, and that each of them should have a silk habit which he should wear when visiting a Magistrate, and without which, in the eyes of the Chinese, one was never considered to be the equal of a Magistrate or even of one of the educated class. . . .

The Fathers at Xaucea gradually accustomed themselves to this new mode of appearance, which proved to be quite pleasing to their friends, because according to their ritual they could now confer with the Fathers as equals and more at ease, which they could not do with their own priests who offered sacrifice to idols. The Magistrates and the upper class Chinese had always been very respectful to the Fathers because of the opinions they entertained of their learning and their virtue, both of which were noticeably lacking in the native clergy. The common people, on the other hand, who were too stupid to notice such things, thought that all priests were the same. So it was partly the fault of the Fathers that the upper classes could not treat them as their equals, for fear of overstepping the bounds of civility and of good taste by associating with those who dressed in a manner which was contrary to the custom of the country. When the missionaries went to the palace of the Magistrates, they observed the ceremonies of visiting intellectuals, which differed from those of the common people, and this in itself was an invitation to the Magistrates to do the same when visiting the Mission.

It might be opportune here to digress for a moment, to disabuse certain people in Europe of the idea that the Jesuit Fathers in China endeavor to acquire the academic degrees which are offered here. They are known here as Europeans, not as educated Chinese. The Chinese favor the universal idea that the class of the Literati, or the intellectuals, wherever they may live, should comport themselves as such, following the customs and wearing the clothes demanded by the customs of the country in which they reside. Unfortunately, in the Province of Canton, the Fathers had not been able to shake off the obnoxious title of sacrificers. Happily, and much to their benefit, from the time of their arrival in the other provinces, they were identified with the class of the learned.

. . .

Here in China, as was mentioned in the first book of the Diary, literary studies are cultivated to such an extent that there are very few people who are not interested in them to some degree. It is also distinctive of the Chinese, that all their religious sects are spread, and their religious doctrine promulgated, by written books, rather than by the spoken word. They have a great dislike to people gathering together in crowds, and so news is spread chiefly by writing. But this did not hamper the work of the Missionaries, because a book-reading people were probably more readily persuaded by something they would read at leisure, than by something said from a pulpit by a preacher who was not thoroughly acquainted with their language. This does not mean that the Fathers did no preaching to their converts on Sundays and on feast days. The reference is rather to the pagans, who are attracted by books, and who spread about the ideas they find in them, in their private conversations. From this common custom it happened at times that someone, while reading a pious book at home, would come across a passage relative to Christianity, which be committed to memory, and then repeated to his relatives and friends. This proved to be of interest to the Fathers and it served as an incentive to their learning to write in Chinese. This is always a long and a tedious task but, with the grace of God, the time and the attention they gave to overcoming the difficulties and the drudgery of it, proved to be very well spent. . . .

Father Ricci was the first one to begin the study of Chinese literature and he was so well versed in what he learned that he became the admiration of the Chinese lettered class who, in their reading, had never before encountered a foreigner from whom they could learn anything. We are purposely treating of this subject here, so that posterity may know what a great advantage was derived from the knowledge of Chinese, and so that Europeans who read this may realize that the interest the Fathers took in the genius of the people was well placed.

QUESTIONS

1. What strategies did the Jesuit missionaries adopt to generate the respect and attention of Chinese elites?
2. What types of Jesuit knowledge, abilities, and behavior most impressed the Chinese? Why?
3. Why did the missionaries have to take a roundabout approach before they could proselytize among the Chinese, especially the literati elite? What did this situation reveal about the mindset of the Chinese elite at this time?
4. Why might Ricci's strategy have attracted criticism from other missionaries? How was he deviating from the course missionaries ordinarily follow?

A FRENCH PHYSICIAN DESCRIBES THE MUGHAL EMPIRE

François Bernier

François Bernier was an indefatigable traveler, writer, and physician who traversed the extensive domains of the Mughal Empire between 1656 and 1667. The empire, founded in the sixteenth century by Muslim warrior kings from central Asia, had grown to dominate most of north and central India by the mid-seventeenth century. Bernier observed the internecine conflicts that ended the reign of the emperor Shah Jahan (d. 1658), as his warring sons fought over the imperial succession. He also witnessed the early years of the emperor Aurangzeb (1658–1707), who presided over a further period of military and territorial expansion.

Bernier dedicated his book, "Travels in the Mogul Empire," first published in 1670, to the French king, Louis XIV, and he included a long letter (from which the following passage is taken) to Colbert, the French finance minister, concerning the economy of India and "the principal Cause of the Decline of the States of Asia." Bernier argued that India enjoyed abundant riches from all over the world in exchange for Indian textiles and spices. But he thought that the great potential wealth of India was undermined by the despotic system of Mughal government, in which the ruler kept his subjects as slaves, and kept all property for himself. One of the main claims of Bernier's

Reprinted from *Travels in the Mogul Empire,* translated by Archibald Constable, 1916.

treatise was that the Mughal emperor owned all the land in his empire, and that there was no private property in land.

Historians now think that Bernier's view was a massive distortion of the nature of Mughal government and early modern India. It now appears that Mughal rule ushered in a period of economic growth in India, marked by the expansion of commerce and agriculture, and the consolidation of new forms of property and exchange. But Bernier's views were very influential in shaping European views of Mughal India in the eighteenth and nineteenth centuries.

Before I conclude, I wish to explain how it happens that, although this Empire of the *Mogol* is such an abyss for gold and silver, as I said before, these precious metals are not in greater plenty here than elsewhere; on the contrary, the inhabitants have less the appearance of a moneyed people than those of many other parts of the globe.

In the first place, a large quantity is melted, re-melted, and wasted, in fabricating women's bracelets, both for the hands and feet, chains, earrings, nose and finger rings, and a still larger quantity is consumed in manufacturing embroideries; *alachas,* or striped silken stuffs; *touras,*[1] or fringes of gold lace, worn on turbans; gold and silver cloths; scarfs, turbans, and brocades.[2] The quantity of these articles made in *India* is incredible. All the troops, from the *Omrah* to the man in the ranks, will wear gilt ornaments; nor will a private soldier refuse them to his wife and children, though the whole family should die of hunger; which indeed is a common occurrence.

In the second place, the *King,* as proprietor of the land, makes over a certain quantity to military men, as an equivalent for their pay; and this grant is called *jah-ghir,* or, as in Turkey, *timar;* the word *jah-ghir* signifying the spot from which to draw, or the place of salary. Similar grants are made to governors, in lieu of their salary, and also for the support of their troops, on condition that they pay a certain sum annually to the King out of any surplus revenue that the land may yield. The lands not so granted are retained by the King as the peculiar domains of his house, and are seldom, if ever, given in the way of *jah-ghir;* and upon these domains he keeps contractors,[3] who are also bound to pay him an annual rent.

The persons thus put in possession of the land, whether as *timariots,*

governors, or contractors, have an authority almost absolute over the peasantry, and nearly as much over the artisans and merchants of the towns and
villages within their district; and nothing can be imagined more cruel and
oppressive than the manner in which it is exercised. There is no one before
whom the injured peasant, artisan, or tradesman can pour out his just com-
plaints; no great lords, parliaments, or judges of local courts, exist, as in
France, to restrain the wickedness of those merciless oppressors, and the
Kadis, or judges, are not invested with sufficient power to redress the
wrongs of these unhappy people. This sad abuse of the royal authority
may not be felt in the same degree near capital cities such as *Dehly* and
Agra, or in the vicinity of large towns and seaports, because in those
places acts of gross injustice cannot easily be concealed from the court.

This debasing state of slavery obstructs the progress of trade and influences the manners and mode of life of every individual. There can be little
encouragement to engage in commercial pursuits, when the success with
which they may be attended, instead of adding to the enjoyments of life,
provokes the cupidity of a neighbouring tyrant possessing both power and
inclination to deprive any man of the fruits of his industry. When wealth is
acquired, as must sometimes be the case, the possessor, so far from living
with increased comfort and assuming an air of independence, studies the
means by which he may appear indigent: his dress, lodging, and furniture,
continue to be mean, and he is careful, above all things, never to indulge in
the pleasures of the table. In the meantime, his gold and silver remain
buried at a great depth in the ground; agreeable to the general practice
among the peasantry, artisans and merchants, whether *Mahomelans* or
Gentiles, but especially among the latter, who possess almost exclusively
the trade and wealth of the country, and who believe that the money concealed during life will prove beneficial to them after death. A few individuals alone who derive their income from the King or from the *Omrahs,* or
who are protected by a powerful patron, are at no pains to counterfeit
poverty, but partake of the comforts and luxuries of life.

I have no doubt that this habit of secretly burying the precious metals,
and thus withdrawing them from circulation, is the principal cause of their
apparent scarcity in *Hindoustan.*

From what I have said, a question will naturally arise, whether it
would not be more advantageous for the King as well as for the people, if

the former ceased to be sole possessor of the land, and the right of private property[4] were recognised in the *Indies* as it is with us? I have carefully compared the condition of *European* states, where that right is acknowledged, with the condition of those countries where it is not known, and am persuaded that the absence of it among the people is injurious to the best interests of the Sovereign himself. We have seen how in the *Indies* the gold and silver disappear in consequence of the tyranny of Timariots, Governors, and Revenue contractors—a tyranny which even the monarch, if so disposed, has no means of controlling in provinces not contiguous to his capital—a tyranny often so excessive as to deprive the peasant and artisan of the necessaries of life, and leave them to die of misery and exhaustion—a tyranny owing to which those wretched people, either have no children at all, or have them only to endure the agonies of starvation, and to die at a tender age—a tyranny, in fine, that drives the cultivator of the soil from his wretched home to some neighbouring state, in hopes of finding milder treatment, or to the army, where he becomes the servant of some trooper. As the ground is seldom tilled otherwise than by compulsion, and as no person is found willing and able to repair the ditches and canals for the conveyance of water, it happens that the whole country is badly cultivated, and a great part rendered unproductive from the want of irrigation. The houses, too, are left in a dilapidated condition, there being few people who will either build new ones, or repair those which are tumbling down. The peasant cannot avoid asking himself this question: 'Why should I toil for a tyrant who may come to-morrow and lay his rapacious hands upon all I possess and value, without leaving me, if such should be his humour, the means to drag on my miserable existence?'—The Timariots, Governors, and Revenue contractors, on their part reason in this manner: 'Why should the neglected state of this land create uneasiness in our minds? and why should we expend our own money and time to render it fruitful? We may be deprived of it in a single moment, and our exertions would benefit neither ourselves nor our children. Let us draw from the soil all the money we can, though the peasant should starve or abscond, and we should leave it, when commanded to quit, a dreary wilderness.'

The facts I have mentioned are sufficient to account for the rapid decline of the *Asiatic* states. It is owing to this miserable system of government that most towns in *Hindoustan* are made up of earth, mud, and other wretched materials; that there is no city or town which, if it be not already ruined and deserted, does not bear evident marks of approaching decay. Without confining our remarks to so distant a kingdom, we may judge of the effects of despotic power unrelentingly exercised, by the present condition of *Mesopotamia, Anatolia, Palestine,* the once wonderful plains of *Antioch,* and so many other regions anciently well cultivated, fertile, and populous, but now desolate, and in many parts marshy, pestiferous, and unfit for human habitation. *Egypt* also exhibits a sad picture of an enslaved country. More than one-tenth part of that incomparable territory has been lost within the last eighty years, because no one will be at the expense of repairing the irrigation channels, and confining the *Nile* within its banks. The low lands are thus violently inundated, and covered with sand, which cannot be removed without much labour and expense. Can it excite wonder, that under these circumstances, the arts do not flourish here as they would do under a better government, or as they flourish in our happier *France*? No artist can be expected to give his mind to his calling in the midst of a people who are either wretchedly poor, or who, if rich, assume an appearance of poverty, and who regard not the beauty and excellence, but the cheapness of an article: a people whose grandees pay for a work of art considerably under its value, and according to their own caprice, and who do not hesitate to punish an importunate artist, or tradesman, with the *korrah,* that long and terrible whip hanging at every *Omrah's* gate. Is it not enough also to damp the ardour of any artist, when he feels that he can never hope to attain to any distinction; that he shall not be permitted to purchase either office or land for the benefit of himself and family; that he must at no time make it appear he is the owner of the most trifling sum; and that he may never venture to indulge in good fare, or to dress in fine apparel, lest he should create a suspicion of his possessing money?[5] The arts in the *Indies* would long ago have lost their beauty and delicacy, if the Monarch and principal *Omrahs* did not keep in their pay a number of artists who work in their houses,[6] teach the children, and are stimulated to exertion by the hope of reward and the fear of the *korrah*. The protection afforded by powerful patrons to rich merchants and tradesmen who pay the workmen rather higher wages, tends also to preserve the arts. I say rather higher wages, for it should not be inferred from the goodness of the manufactures, that the workman is held in esteem, or arrives at a state of independence. Nothing but sheer necessity or blows from a cudgel keeps him employed; he never can become rich, and he feels it no trifling matter if he have the means of satisfying the cravings of hunger, and of covering his body with the coarsest raiment. If money be gained, it does not in any measure go into his pocket, but only serves to increase the wealth of the merchant who, in his turn, is not a little perplexed how to guard against some act of outrage and extortion on the part of his superiors.

A profound and universal ignorance is the natural consequence of such a state of society as I have endeavoured to describe. Is it possible to establish in *Hindoustan* academies and colleges properly endowed? Where shall we seek for founders? or, should they be found, where are the scholars? Where the individuals whose property is sufficient to support their children at college? or, if such individuals exist, who would venture to display so clear a proof of wealth? Lastly, if any persons should be tempted to commit this great imprudence, yet where are the benefices, the employments, the offices of trust and dignity, that require ability and science and are calculated to excite the emulation and the hopes of the young student?

Nor can the commerce of a country so governed be conducted with the activity and success that we witness in *Europe;* few are the men who will voluntarily endure labour and anxiety, and incur danger, for another person's benefit,—for a governor who may appropriate to his own use the profit of any speculation. Let that profit be ever so great, the man by whom it has been made must still wear the garb of indigence, and fare no better, in regard to eating and drinking, than his poorer neighbours, In cases, indeed, where the merchant is protected by a military man of rank, he may be induced to embark in commercial enterprises; but still he must be the slave of his patron, who will exact whatever terms he pleases as the price of his protection.

The *Great Mogol* cannot select for his service, princes, noblemen and gentlemen of opulent and ancient families; nor the sons of his citizens, merchants and manufacturers; men of education, possessing a high sense of propriety, affectionately attached to their Sovereign, ready to support, by acts of valour, the reputation of their family, and, as the occasion may arise, able and willing to maintain themselves, either at court or in the army, by means of their own patrimony; animated by the hope of better times, and satisfied with the approbation and smile of their Sovereign. Instead of men of this description, he is surrounded by slaves, ignorant and brutal; by parasites raised from the dregs of society; strangers to loyalty and patriotism; full of insufferable pride, and destitute of courage, of honour, and of decency.

The country is ruined by the necessity of defraying the enormous charges required to maintain the splendour of a numerous court, and to pay a large army maintained for the purpose of keeping the people in subjection. No adequate idea can be conveyed of the sufferings of that people. The cudgel and the whip compel them to incessant labour for the benefit of others; and driven to despair by every kind of cruel treatment, their revolt or their flight is only prevented by the presence of a military force.

The misery of this ill-fated country is increased by the practice which prevails too much at all times, but especially on the breaking out of an important war, of selling the different governments for immense sums in hard cash. Hence it naturally becomes the principal object of the individual thus appointed Governor, to obtain repayment of the purchase-money, which he borrowed as he could at a ruinous rate of interest. Indeed whether the government of a province has or has not been bought, the Governor, as well as the *timariot* and the farmer of the revenue, must find the means of making valuable presents, every year, to a *Visir,* a *Eunuch,* a lady of the *Seraglio,* and to any other person whose influence at court he considers indispensable. The Governor must also enforce the payment of the regular tribute to the King; and although he was originally a wretched slave, involved in debt, and without the smallest patrimony, he yet becomes a great and opulent lord.

Thus do ruin and desolation overspread the land. The provincial governors, as before observed, are so many petty tyrants, possessing a boundless authority; and as there is no one to whom the oppressed subject may appeal, he cannot hope for redress, let his injuries be ever so grievous or ever so frequently repeated.

END NOTES

1. From the Persian word *turreh,* a lock of hair. Fringes, with which the ends of turban cloths are finished off.

2. Recent travellers have remarked upon this 'abyss for gold and silver,' to use Bernier's forcible language, in the East generally, and in an interesting special article in *The Times* of March 13th, 1891, describing the cutting of the top-knot (a 'coming of age' ceremony) of the heir-apparent to the Crown of Siam which took place on the 19th of January, we read, *à propos* of the grand procession:—

   'But a Siamese procession is in itself a marvel, compared with which the most ambitious Lord Mayor's Show is a very one-horse affair. The Royal crown alone worn by the King in his palanquin, would, if converted into pounds sterling, pay for a great many such shows. So would his jewelled uniform, and so would the crown of the small Prince. Many thousands of pounds' worth of pure gold is carried along on the belts and Court uniforms of the grandees; and an inventory of the other "properties" displayed would rather astonish a manager of stage processions in Europe.'

3. In the original, *Fermiers.*

4. In the original, *ce Mien et ce Tien.*

5. In 1882 on the occasion of the formation of a Loan Collection of arts and manufactures in connection with an Agricultural Exhibition at Lucknow, many of the possessors of various ancient family jewels, amulets, and other works of art, were at first unwilling to lend them, lest by their doing so they should acquire the reputation of being wealthy and be assessed at a high rate for Income-tax.

6. See p. 258 text, and footnote 2.

QUESTIONS

1. What primary reasons does Bernier give why Indian people do not appear to be more wealthy?

2. What effects follow, in Bernier's view, from the fact that the Mughal emperor or "king" is the "proprietor of the land"?

3. Which other regions, in Bernier's view, suffer from the same kind of despotic rule?

4. Why do you think Bernier addressed this letter on the Indian economy to the French finance minister, Colbert?

DOCUMENT

SLAVE TRADE IN THE KINGDOM OF LOANGO IN THE EIGHTEENTH CENTURY

Abbé Proyart

Abbé Proyart's Histoire de Loango, Kakongo et autres royaumes d'Afrique *was published in 1776 and quickly became a seminal text on the geography and economy of Central Africa. The regions of Loango and Kakongo are in the region of present-day Congo and Angola. The precision and detail of the account indicate that it relies on firsthand observation, but it is unclear whether it is based on Proyart's own experiences or on those of other travelers.*

The main trade of these people is in slaves whom they sell to the Europeans, that is to say, to the French, English and Dutch who then ship them to their colonies in America. Slaves originating from Loango and the neighbouring kingdoms are considered as the darkest and the strongest in Africa. They have been captured in battle by those who sell them.

Those who captured them either sell them to native merchants or take them to the coast, but they are absolutely forbidden to sell them directly to the Europeans. They must go through brokers, appointed by the Minister of Commerce, who deal with ship captains. These slaves are valued according to their age, sex and physical strength. Goods from Europe are used in payment.

Although the different Kingdoms about which we are talking are quite close to one another, the manner of evaluating goods as against slaves is not the same. On the coasts of Malimbe and Cabinde, that is to say the Kingdoms of Kakongo and n'Goio, the calculation is done in *wares,* and in Loango it is in *pieces.* A *ware* is a piece of calico or Indian linen measuring 12 to 16 metres. Before selling, the blacks go to the warehouse of the captain, which is on the sea shore, to indicate the pieces of material that they will accept. A man who sold four slaves at fifteen *wares* per head, will receive sixty pieces of a designated material. In Kingdoms where buying is done in *wares,* it is usual to give, for each slave, what is known as *bonus,* which normally consists of three or four bottles of brandy, fifteen pounds of gun powder and some dozens of Knives. Other goods can be given in place of those mentioned.

In Loango the calculation is done in *pieces.* Here all sorts of goods are put together with linen materials to form a *piece.* Thus, when a slave is said to cost thirty pieces, it does not mean that he is worth thirty pieces of linen fabric, but rather thirty times an ideal value considered adequate to be called *piece,* such that a single piece of linen fabric is sometimes estimated at two or three *pieces,* just as several objects are sometimes required to make one piece. This difference in ways of counting is of little import in the final analysis as the price of slaves is roughly the same in all neighbouring Kingdoms of

A scrutiny of the account that follows will help us to estimate the real value of the *piece* and to see what goods are commonly passed on to blacks in exchange for their slaves.

I paid to Ma-nboukou, for the slave Makouta, aged twenty-two years, whom he sold to me for thirty pieces:

One Indian linen material 16 metres long,
valued at two ad half pieces.. .. ..   2 1/2p
Two guineas (dark blue calico) valued at
two and a half pieces each   5
One chasselat and one bajuta skin measuring
16 metres each (calico materials) valued at four pieces   4
One neganoskin 16 metres long and one 12 metres
long, "nicané" (other calico materials) valued at
three and a half pieces .. ..gg.. .. ..   3 1/2

One piece of cambric of 11 metres, valued at 1 1/2 pieces	1 1/2
One belt made of red cloth (1.2 metres long and one foot wide) valued at one piece	1
One rod (approximately two metres thick linen fabric) valued at one piece	1
Two standard guns, valued at two pieces	2
Two barrels of gun powder (approximately	5
pounds each), valued at two pieces	2
Two bags of bullets (weighing three pounds each) valued at half piece	1/2
Two sabres at a quarter piece each	1/2
Two dozens of standard knives with sheaths valued at half piece	1/2
Two iron bars weighing both 20 lbs valued at one piece	1
Five earthenware pots valued at half piece	1/2
Four barrels of brandy (each containing five bottles) valued at four pieces	4
Ten lines of glass stones (for making chaplets) valued at half piece	1/2
Total	30 pieces
In addition, I paid to the broker for his services, the value of six pieces in guns, gun powder, sabres and brandy	6
Grand Total	36 pieces

Apart from the agreed price for each slave, it is still necessary for the captain, at the conclusion of his business, to present gifts to the Minister of Commerce and to those brokers who have been of service to him and to whom he may have become attached. Such presents are in corals, silverware, rugs and other more or less precious commodities.

At the moment slaves are much more expensive that they were in the past, at least for French people; for it is possible for them to be relatively more expensive for one nation than for another. The French, the English and the Dutch all do their exchange with goods but these goods are different. Thus the expensiveness of slaves for a nation depends on the price that this nation puts on the goods she sends to the blacks; and again this price, as one would imagine, varies more or less with the level of understanding existing between the individuals engaged in the same trade.

The function of brokers is not limited to enhancing the trade in slaves; they are also responsible for ensuring that regulations made by the king or the Minister of commerce are implemented. The most slaves bought from outside the country can be sold as slaves to Europeans. Every slave born in the Kingdom is under the protection of the Commerce Minister and can invoke this protection against his master who may wish to sell him to the Europeans, unless he has given his master cause, through misconduct, to so sell him. For the law permits the master to dispose of a slave, no matter who he is, who is found guilty of infidelity, of rebellion or of any other criminal act. In order to prevent the violent and fraudulent practices that could characterize such a trade, the Commerce Minister of Kakongo forbade all brokers to carry out slave deals during the night. In addition, they are not allowed to send slaves to the European warehouses under the pretext of letting the captain have a preview. They are also forbidden to receive advance payments on slaves that they have not delivered without obtaining permission.

The slave trade is the only business that the French are doing on these coasts: trading in ivory, monkeys, parrots and some other such commodities is so negligible that it can be considered as non-existent. The English carry away, every year, from the forest of lomba, several shiploads of a particular red wood which is very good for dyeing, although inferior to that obtained from Brazil.

As has already been mentioned, the commerce that takes place on the coasts with foreigners involves only a small number of individuals, whom one can consider as the rich and powerful in the country. As for the masses, having no other needs but to feed and clothe themselves, in the most vulgar and simple manner, trading for them is limited to a few commodities. There is daily market in the towns and large villages; it takes place at the public square, under some big trees. Smoked fish, cassava and other tubers, salt, coconuts, sugar cane, bananas, plantains and some other fruits are sold there. It is on feast days that one notices greater crowds of sellers and buyers in these markets. There is no cheating in these markets.

A mother can send a child of six years to the markets, assured that no one will cheat the child. One does not have to understand the native language to buy from these markets: prices are never haggled. All commodities are divided into small equal portions, of the prescribed weight, and each portion is worth one macoute. There is no risk of a buyer being cheated in quality or quantity of what he is buying: the salt and cassava being displayed by one seller are just like the salt and cassava displayed by the other seller. Thus, without taking the trouble of comparing the commodities of one merchant with another's, you take, from the first person you meet, as many little packets as the macoutes you have can buy, and you give way to others.

QUESTIONS

1. How are the calculations of prices undertaken in Kakongo and Loango?
2. What is the role of brokers in the slave trade?
3. According to Proyart's account, how do Africans and Europeans each seek to direct the trade in slaves? Which side seems to be most successful in exerting control?
4. What does Proyart's list of goods traded for a slave suggest about life in eighteenth-century Central Africa?

THE CONCLUSIVE ARGUMENT FROM GOD

Shah Wali Ullah

Shah Wali Ullah (1703–1762) lived during the period of the Mughal Empire's decline. The son of a Sufi shaikh, and himself an initiate of the Naqshbandi and Qadiri Sufi orders, Wali Ullah sought to curb the excesses of Sufism and inject new life into political Islam through a series of works on the necessity of reforming the Muslims of India.

Wali Ullah sought to revitalize the Muslim community at the level of the spiritual, the political, and the personal. He did so by stressing the need for a return to the example of Qur'an and the Prophet Muhammad's practice (sunna), the twin foundations of Islamic Shari'ah law. He criticized what he saw as "un-Islamic" customs that had crept into Muslim practice, such as the veneration of living and deceased saints; the bias against the remarriage of widows; the unbridled pursuit of hedonistic pleasure; and the use of intoxicants, amulets, and charms. To the ruling and scholarly classes he addressed a series of treatises advising them to abandon their exploitative practices and to cultivate exemplary moral qualities, a sense of duty to the state and to the people it ruled, and loyalty to their fellow Muslims. He chastised ordinary Muslims for paying more attention to saints' shrines than to knowledge of God and his laws. He condemned contemporary Sufis for their deviation from the path of righteousness that had been laid by their spiritual ancestors, and warned ordinary people to avoid the company of corrupt shaikhs. Rather than dismissing the popular ideas of Ibn Arabi about the unity of being (wahdat al-wujud), which held that God and his creation were fundamentally one, Wali Ullah sought to achieve a synthesis between this and the idea proposed by Shaikh Ahmad Sirhindi on the unity of experience (wahdat ash-shuhud), which argued that this apparent unity was only in the mystic's perception.

The teachings of Shah Wali Ullah had a limited impact in his own time, but they influenced successive reform movements, such as that represented by the Deobandi school, founded in the mid-nineteenth century in Northern India. The Deobandis, and thus the ideas of Shah Wali Ullah, remain highly influential in South Asia and elsewhere in the Muslim world even today.

THE EXPLANATION OF THE CATEGORIES OF THE PROPHET S KNOWLEDGE, MAY THE PEACE AND BLESSINGS OF GOD BE UPON HIM

Be informed that what was reported from the Prophet, may the peace and blessings of God be upon him, and recorded in the books of hadith falls under two categories.

1) The first category (of the Prophetic sciences) comprises those things which are a means for the propagation of the message, and God's, may He be exalted, saying applies to it: "What the Prophet gives you, take, and what he forbids, abstain from."[1] These are:

a) Knowledge about the next life and the wonders of Malakūt, and all of this is based on revelation.

b) The divine laws, and the determining of the acts of worship and the supports of civilization according to the ways of determination mentioned previously. Some of these depend on revelation, while others depend on independent reasoning *(ijtihād)*. The independent reasoning of the Prophet, may the peace and blessings of God be upon him, is at the level of revelation, because God made him safeguarded from having his opinion settle on error. It is not required that his independent reasoning be inferred from revealed statements as has been thought, but rather in most cases God, may He be exalted, used to teach him the intentions behind the divine law and the principle of legislation, facilitation, and the rulings, then he explained the intentions that he learned through revelation according to this principle.

90

c) Practical wisdom and general beneficial purposes which he did not appoint for a specific time, nor did he set their limits; as when he explained good character and its opposite. These generally depended on individual reasoning *(ijtihād)* in the sense that God, may He be exalted, had informed him of the principles of the supports of civilization from which he then inferred an underlying reason *(ḥikma)* and made this a general principle.

d) The virtues of deeds and the outstanding traits of those who do good deeds and I think that some of these depend on revelation and some on independent reasoning.

The explanation of these principles has already been given. We intend to comment on and explain the meanings (of the issues stemming from the principles involved in this category of the Prophet's sayings).

2) The second category (of the Prophet's sayings) comprises whatever does not come under the topic of propagating the message. Concerning this we have the Prophet's saying, "I am only a man, and when I order you to do something regarding your religion, accept it, and if I order you with something according to my own opinion, then I am only a human being,"[2] and his saying in the story of pollinating the palms, "I only made a conjecture, so don't blame me for that opinion, but if I tell you something about Allah, then accept (it) for I will never lie about God."[3]

Included in this section is medicine, and also topics like the Prophet's saying, may the peace and blessings of God be upon him, "Be keen to acquire (as best for Jihād) a black horse; with a whitish blaze on its forehead,"[4] and this was based on experience. Included (in this) are what the Prophet, may the peace and blessings of God be upon him, did as part of his daily routine, not as religious practice; and incidentally, not intentionally. Under this category also fall things he used to speak about just like other people, such as the hadith of Umm Zara' and the hadith of Khurāfa,[5] and this is the saying of Zaid ibn Thābit when a group of people came to him and said, "Tell us some sayings of the Prophet of God, may peace and blessings be upon him." He said, "I was his neighbor, and it happened that whenever revelation came to him, he used to send for me, and I wrote it down for him. If we were talking about the life of this world he would talk about it with us, and if we spoke of the next life he would speak about it with us, and if we spoke about food he would speak about it with us, so I would have to report to you all of these things as hadiths from the Prophet of God." Included here are things from which he intended a specific beneficial effect at that time, and not as things incumbent upon the whole community, for example when a Caliph gives a command regarding mobilizing the armies and specifying the banner. This is the saying of 'Umar, may God be pleased with him, "There was no reason for us to do *ramal*[6] except that we wanted to make a show of force to a people (the pagans) and now Allah has destroyed them."[7] Then he feared that for the ramal there might be some other cause.[8] Many of the rules can be traced back to a specific beneficial purpose such as the saying of the Prophet, may the peace and blessings of God be upon him, "Who ever kills someone (in the *Jihād*) can keep his arms and clothing."[9] Included under this are specialized rulings and decrees, and in these he, may the peace and blessings of God be upon him, used to accept evidence and oaths and this is his, may the peace and blessings of God be upon him, saying to 'Alī, may God be pleased with him, "The one who is present sees something that the absent one does not."[10]

THE DIFFERENCE BETWEEN THE BENEFICIAL PURPOSES (MASĀLIH) AND THE RELIGIOUS LAWS

Be informed that the law-giver benefited us with two types of knowledge which are distinct in their rulings and dissimilar in their ranking.

1) One of the two types is the knowledge of the beneficial purposes and the causes of sin, by which I mean whatever he explained about refining the soul through the acquisition of virtues which aid in this world and in the next life, and by the elimination of their opposites. Therefore how to manage a household, the manner of livelihood, and the governing of the city were not quantified by specific amounts, nor did he render the ambiguous precise by fixed limits, nor did he distinguish the obscure issues through determined signs. Rather the Prophet, may the peace and blessings of God be upon him, encouraged praiseworthy things and urged abstention from vices, leaving his speech as it would be normally be understood by people in basing demanding or forbidding on the beneficial purposes themselves, not on anticipated sources *(mazānn)* attached to them, or signs which would made them recognizable. For example, he

praised cleverness and courage, and commanded friendship, showing affection, and adopting a middle course as a way of life; but he did not explain the definition of cleverness on which the call for it was based, nor did he explain any anticipated source for it on the basis of which the people could be taken to task (for disregarding it).

Every beneficial purpose to which the divine law incites us and every cause of evil from which it keeps us, unavoidably goes back to one of three principles.

1) The first is the refinement of the soul through the acquisition of the four virtues[11] beneficial for the next life and the rest of the virtues which are of benefit in this life. The second of them is the propagation of the word of God and the consolidation of the divine laws and making efforts to spread them. The third is the organization of the order of mankind and the improvement of their supports of civilization, and the refinement of their conventions.

The meaning of their (the beneficial purposes and the causes of evil) going back to these principles is that a thing has some role in these matters either by affirming or negating them, in that it is a ramification of one of their properties or opposes this ramification, or it is an anticipated source of their presence or absence, or it is bound up with them or with their opposite, or it is a path to them or diverts from them. God's pleasure is originally connected with these beneficial purposes, and His anger is also attached to these evil deeds, before His sending the prophets and after it equally. If it were not for the connection of His satisfaction and anger with these two types of behavior (good and evil), the prophets would not have been sent. This is because the divine laws and the punishments only came after the mission of the prophets, so that initially there was no grace from God in having these laws imposed and being held to them, but rather the beneficial purposes and the causes of evil were effective in requiring the refinement of the soul or its being corrupted, or in putting their affairs in order or ruining them, already, before the sending of the prophets. Thus the grace of God decreed that people should have (at the same time) an understanding of what was important for them, and that they should have imposed on them whatever was incumbent on them, and this could not be effected except through setting stipulations and laws, so the grace of God decreed this sort of thing as the occasion arose. This type of thing is rationally comprehensible, but among it is a portion which the intelligence of the common man can understand on its own and a portion which can only be understood by the minds of the most intelligent on whom emanates the light from the hearts of the prophets. The law alerted them, so that they were alerted, and pointed out to them, so that they understood. The person who masters the principles which we have mentioned will not waver on any aspect of them.

2) The second type of knowledge is knowledge of the divine laws, the punishments *(ḥudūd),* and the obligatory religious duties. I mean whatever the divine law explained by way of the appointed quantities, so that it fixed anticipated sources and precise, well-known signs for the beneficial purposes, and based the ruling on them, and imposed them on the people. The types of pious actions were set by determining the pillars, conditions, and proper behaviors, and for every type a limit was set to be sought from the group which was compulsory, and a limit which was recommended without compulsion. In every pious act a number which was compulsory was chosen and another which was recommended, thus the obligation was directed to these very anticipated sources, and the rulings were based on these very signs, and this type of knowledge is a basis for the rules of religious regulation. Not every anticipated source of a beneficial purpose is made compulsory for people, but only those which are precise and tangible or possess an obvious description which both the elite and the masses can recognize. Sometimes there are incidental reasons for the compulsory and the forbidden which result in their being recorded among the Highest Council, and There above is confirmed the form of the compulsory and the forbidden; such as a certain question of an inquirer, and a particular desire of a group for something or their rejecting it. All of this is not rationally comprehensible in the sense that even if we knew the rules of determining amounts and (divine) legislation, we would not know that they had actually been recorded among the Highest Council and that the form of the compulsory had been established with the Holy Enclave, except through the explicit statement of the divine law.[12] This is one of the things that there is no way to understand except through the reports of God's sayings, and this is comparable to ice—we know that the cause for its coming into being is a coldness which affects the water, but we don't know whether the water in a large cup at this time has frozen or not except through seeing it ourselves

or through being told by one who saw it. On this analogy we know that the minimum taxable holding for the alms tax must be set, and we know that two hundred dirhems and five *ausāq* is the proper amount for the minimum taxable holding, because the one who has this much is reckoned as being able to spare (the tax), and these two are things in confirmed usage among the people; but we do not know that God, may He be exalted, decided this share for us, and based on it His being satisfied and angry, except through the text of the divine law. Indeed how could we, and how many causes are there which we have no way of knowing except through a report, and this is the Prophet's saying: "The Muslim who harms Muslims most"[13] and his saying, "I feared that it would become prescribed for you."[14]

The learned scholars of repute have agreed that analogical reasoning *(qiyās)* does not apply in the topic of set amounts, and that the proper methodology of analogical reasoning is extending the ruling on the original case *(aṣl)* to the assimilated case *(far')* through a shared reason for legislation *('illa),*[15] not that the symbol or anticipated source of a beneficial purpose should be made a reason for legislation, nor that some thing related to it should be made a pillar or a condition.[16] They also agreed that analogical reasoning does not apply due to the existence of the beneficial purpose but because of a precise reason for legislation on which the rule may be based. Therefore an analogy is not drawn from what determines "hardship" for the traveler in his being allowed a dispensation in prayer and fasting, since the prevention of "hardship" is the beneficial purpose behind receiving a dispensation, and not the reason for the legislation to shorten the prayers and break the fast. Rather, the reason for the legislation *('illa)* is being on a journey. Therefore, on the whole, the religious scholars do not differ about such cases, but most of them support bringing them out in more detail. This is because sometimes the beneficial purpose becomes confused with the reason for legislation and the act of legislation. Some of the legal scholars, when they went deeply into analogical reasoning became confused, and insisted on some of the determined amounts, and forbade exchanging them for things similar to them, while they were tolerant about others and allowed substitutions for them. An example of their fixing amounts is their setting the minimum share of cotton liable for the *zakāt* tax as five loads, and their making riding on a ship the anticipated source of seasickness so that they based the dispensation to remain seated during prayer (while at sea) on this, while they set the amount of water at ten by ten.[17]

Whenever the law made the beneficial purpose understood in a case and we find this (same) beneficial purpose in another case; then we should recognize that the pleasure of God is connected with it in its own right, not by the particularities of that case, in contrast to the determined amounts, for there God's pleasure attaches to these determined amounts themselves. To elaborate this; when someone does not perform the prayer on time it is a sin, even if at that time he is occupied in the remembrance of God and other acts of worship. The person who does not pay the tax incumbent on him but spends more than that amount in good works, still commits a sin. Likewise to dress in silk and gold in privacy where it won't wound the hearts of the poor, nor lead people to be more worldly, and when luxury is not intended by it, still is a sin; likewise to drink wine with the intention of medicinal use, when there is neither immoral purpose nor abandonment of the prayers—is still a sin because the pleasure and anger of God are connected to those acts themselves, even if the essential goal was to avert people from sin and to bring them to the beneficial purpose. God knew, however, that the regulation of the community would not be possible at that time except through compelling these very acts and forbidding them, and thus he directed His pleasure and anger to them in themselves, and this was recorded among the Highest Council.

This is in contrast to someone who wears the finest wool which is better and more costly than silk, and who uses vessels of ruby, for he does not sin by those actions in themselves. However, if breaking the hearts of the poor, leading other people to do these things, or seeking luxurious living are the result, then he is far from the mercy of God because of these sins, and if not, then he is not.

Wherever you find the Companions and the Successors doing something which resembles setting specific quantities,[18] their intent was only to clarify the beneficial purpose and to incite to it, and to clarify the evil and to deter against it. They only brought out this case by way of exemplification, and they did not mean to specify by it,[19] for they only had in mind conveying the meanings, although on the surface the matter is confusing.

Whenever the divine law allows exchanging a set thing for its price, such as the two year old camel for a price according to one report; then even if we accept this report, this is also a type of setting a quantity, and this is because it is not possible to do a minute investigation into quantification in so far as this would lead to hardship. Rather, sometimes an amount is set for something common to many things, such as the two year old camel itself, for sometimes one such camel will be superior to another. Sometimes setting an amount by value sets a limit which is universal, such as setting the threshold for which a person's hand would cut off for theft at something that has the value of a quarter of a dinar or three dirhems.

Be informed that making things obligatory and forbidden (as such) are two types of assessment and this is because often what appears to be a beneficial purpose or a cause of evil has many forms. One form is settled upon to be commanded or forbidden because it is exact or because it is something whose status was recognized among the preceding religions, or because people strongly desired it. Therefore the Prophet, may the peace and blessings of God be upon him, excused himself saying, "I feared that it would become prescribed for you."[20] And he said, "Were it not that I would be hard on my community I would have ordered them to clean their teeth (before every prayer)."[21] Since this is the situation, it is not legitimate to construe something whose ruling was not stipulated by the textual pronouncement on the basis of something that was.

As for being something being recommended or reprehensible,[22] in these there are further detailed aspects. Whichever recommended thing the law-giver commanded per se, praised, and laid down as a customary practice for the people—has the same force as the obligatory. Any recommended thing in which the Prophet confined himself to explaining its beneficial purpose, or which he himself chose to do without etablishing it as a practice (sunna), and without emphasizing its significance; remains in the state which it had before the legislation, and reward for it will be through the beneficial purpose found within it, not the performance of the action itself.[23] Likewise is the situation of the reprehensible according to this more detailed explanation.

When you have really grasped this introduction it will become apparent to you that most of the analogies of which this group[24] are proud and on account of which they have become arrogant towards the group of the People of the Hadith lead to and evil cosequence for them without their realizing it.[25]

END NOTES

1. Qur'ān 59:7.
2. Bukhārī Ṣalāt 31, Mazālim 16, Haid 10, Aḥkām 20, 29, 31, Muslim, Abū Dāwūd, Tirmidhī, Nasā'ī, Ibn Mājah, Muwaṭṭa', Ibn Ḥanbal. *Mishkāt,* p. 40.
3. The Prophet at one point ordered the Medinans not to fecundate their palm trees but when they found that the crop was less abundant this order was rescinded. Muslim Fadā'il 139, Ibn Ḥanbal. *Mishkāt,* p. 40.
4. Tirmidhī III:120 #1747 Jihād 20, Ibn Mājah, Ibn Ḥanbal. *Mishkāt,* p. 823.
5. The hadith of Umm Zara' was related by 'Ā'isha and involves a story of eleven women telling about their husbands, Siddiqi trans. *Ṣaḥīḥ* Muslim IV:1302. In the hadith of Khurāfa, the Prophet explains that Khurāfa was a marvelous story teller who was kidnapped by the jinn and then returned to tell about them, such tales are known by the people as "hadith Khurāfa". Ibn Ḥanbal VI:157.
6. *Ramal* is fast walking accompanied by movements of the arms and legs to show one's physical strength. When Muḥammad and his Companions came to Mecca for pilgrimage and the Quraish were still in control, the pagans said that they had been weakened by the fever of Yathrib so the Prophet ordered them to do "*ramal*" in the first three circumambulations of the Ka'ba.
7. Bukhārī Hajj 57. Khan trans. II:393.
8. So 'Umar added, "Nevertheless, the Prophet did that (ramal), and we do not want to abandon it."
9. That is, these articles would not be subject to having the one-fifth share of the Prophet assessed on them. Bukhārī Khums 18, Maghāzī 54, Muslim, Abū Dāwūd, Tirmidhī, Ibn Mājah, Muwaṭṭa', Ibn Ḥanbal.
10. Cited in Chapter 40. Ibn Ḥanbal I:83.
11. Purity, humility, magnanimity, and justice. Previously discussed in Ch. 32.
12. "*naṣṣ al-shar'*".
13. The Muslim who harms Muslims most is the one who asked about a thing so that it was forbidden because of his questioning, Bukhārī I'tiṣām 3, Muslim, Abū Dāwūd, *Mishkāt.* p. 42. This hadith was previously mentioned in the introduction and Chapter 57.
14. *Mishkāt,* p. 270. Transmitted by Bukhārī Tahajjud 4. Khan trans. II:128. This hadith refers to the Prophet's allowing people to pray the special night prayers at home during Ramaḍān, and was cited in the introduction and Chapter 60.
15. This is a reference to the technical syllogistic method of juridical *qiyās*.
16. The idea of "condition" (*sharṭ*) is a fairly technical one discussed in works of *uṣūl al-fiqh* and varying somewhat from one legal school to another. A discussion of the term may be found in al-Thanavī, Muḥammad, *al-Kashshāf fī Istilāḥāt al-Funūn,* (Calcutta, 1862), 754.
17. The size of a pond whose water may be considered pure for the ritual bath according to some Ḥanafī jurists. See *Ḥujjat Allah al-Bāligha* II:183–183 "Rules About Water."
18. Such as in defining the length of a "journey" as being a specific distance.
19. For example, when they set the distance traveled on "a journey" as being four *burūd*.
20. Hadith cited above in this Chapter.
21. *Mishkāt,* p. 79. Bukhārī Juma' 8, Tamannā 9, Ṣaum 27, Muslim, Abū Dāwūd, Tirmidhī, Nasā'ī, Ibn Mājah, Muwṭṭa', Ibn Ḥanbal. Hadith cited previously in Chapter 60.
22. According to most schools of Islamic law there are five degrees of actions—compulsory, recommended (*mandūb* or *mustahabb*), neutral (*mubāh*), reprehensible (*makrūh*), and forbidden (*ḥarām*). This therefore refers to two of the categories between compulsory and forbidden.

23. This distiction in Islamic Law is recognized as that between a confirmed practice *(suna mu' akkada)* and a non-confirmed practice *(sunna ghair mu' akkada)* of the Prophet.
24. Meaning those jurists who rely more on reason rather than on literal readings of revealed texts.
25. Thus Shāh Walī Allāh is critisizing the exessive use of *qiyās,* particularly if it is not strictly based on the Qur'ān and the hadith.

QUESTIONS

1. In Wali Ullah's thinking, why is Islamic Law (Shari'ah) important for the cultivation of mystical awareness?
2. What were the major moral failings of Muslims, according to Shah Wali Ullah?
3. Who is the main audience for this treatise and of whom is Shah Wali Ullah being critical?
4. What does virtuous behavior consist of, according to Shah Wali Ullah?

from CHAPTER 3, "THE SLAVESHIP" *in* EQUIANO'S TRAVELS

Olaudah Equiano

Olaudah Equiano was born around 1745 in what is now Nigeria. Equiano was kidnapped and enslaved at about the age of ten. After a period of bondage in Africa, Equiano was transported to the West Indies, and from there to Virginia, where he was sold to a planter. Resold to an officer in the British navy, Equiano—renamed Gustavo Vassa by his new master—witnessed the hostilities of the Seven Years War aboard a Royal Navy ship. In 1762, the naval officer reneged on an earlier promise to free Equiano, and instead sold him in the West Indies. Equiano was able to purchase his own freedom in 1766, using funds he had earned through personal enterprise. As a freedman, Equiano was involved in several commercial voyages, sailing as far as the North Pole before he settled in London. There, Equiano converted to Methodism and emerged as an outspoken opponent of the slave trade. He married Susanna Cullen, an Englishwoman, in 1792, and left a sizable estate to their daughter when he died in 1797.

The Interesting Narrative was published in 1789. It was one of a series of works by authors of African birth or descent to appear before the public during this period. Writings by James Albert Ukawsaw Gronniosaw, Phillis Wheatley, and Ignatius Sancho were also published in Britain in the 1770s and 1780s. Like these publications, Equiano's work offered convincing evidence of the intellectual capability of Africans. But as the first Afro-Briton account to offer an indictment

---

Reprinted from *The Interesting Narrative and Other Writings*, 1789.

of the slave trade, the Interesting Narrative *was unique. It was praised by Mary Wollstonecraft and John Wesley, and ran through nine English language editions during Equiano's lifetime. Equiano's* Interesting Narrative *also reminds us of the mobility and mixing of cultures that characterized the Atlantic world in the eighteenth century. In this passage, Equiano described how he was transported aboard a slave ship to the Americas.*

The first object which saluted my eyes when I arrived on the coast was the sea, and a slave-ship, which was then riding at anchor, and waiting for its cargo. These filled me with astonishment, which was soon converted into terror, which I am yet at a loss to describe, nor the then feelings of my mind. When I was carried on board I was immediately handled, and tossed up, to see if I were sound,[1] by some of the crew; and I was now persuaded that I had gotten into a world of bad spirits, and that they were going to kill me.[2] Their complexions too differing so much from ours, their long hair, and the language they spoke, which was very different from any I had ever heard, united to confirm me in this belief. Indeed, such were the horrors of my views and fears at the moment, that, if ten thousand worlds had been my own, I would have freely parted with them all to have exchanged my condition with that of the meanest slave in my own country. When I looked round the ship too, and saw a large furnace of copper boiling, and a multitude of black people of every description chained together, every one of their countenances expressing dejection and sorrow, I no longer doubted of my fate, and, quite overpowered with horror and anguish, I fell motionless on the deck and fainted. When I recovered a little, I found some black people about me who I believed were some of those who brought me on board and had been receiving their pay; they talked to me in order to cheer me, but all in vain. I asked them if we were not to be eaten by those white men with horrible looks, red faces, and long hair.[3] They told me I was not; and one of the crew brought me a small portion of spirituous liquor in a wine glass; but, being afraid of him, I would not take it out of his hand. One of the blacks therefore took it from him and gave it to me, and I took a little down my palate, which, instead of reviving me, as they thought it would, threw me into the greatest consternation at the strange feeling it produced, having never tasted any such liquor before. Soon after this, the blacks who brought me on board went off, and left me abandoned to despair. I now saw myself deprived of all chance of returning to my native country, or even the least glimpse of hope of gaining the shore, which I now considered as friendly: and I even wished for my former slavery in preference to my present situation, which was filled with horrors of every kind, still heightened by my ignorance of what I was to undergo. I was not long suffered to indulge my grief; I was soon put down under the decks, and there I received such a salutation in my nostrils as I had never experienced in my life; so that with the loathsomeness of the stench, and crying together, I became so sick and low that I was not able to eat, nor had I the least desire to taste any thing. I now wished for the last friend, Death, to relieve me; but soon, to my grief, two of the white men offered me eatables; and, on my refusing to eat, one of them held me fast by the hands, and laid me across, I think, the windlass[4] and tied my feet, while the other flogged me severely. I had never experienced any thing of this kind before; and although, not being used to the water, I naturally feared that element the first time I saw it; yet, nevertheless, could I have got over the nettings,[5] I would have jumped over the side, but I could not; and, besides, the crew used to watch us very closely who were not chained down to the decks, lest we should leap into the water; and I have seen some of these poor African prisoners most severely cut for attempting to do so, and hourly whipped for not eating. This indeed was often the case with myself. In a little time after, amongst the poor chained men, I found some of my own nation, which in a small degree gave ease to my mind. I inquired of these what was to be done with us? they gave me to understand we were to be carried to these white people's country to work for them. I then was a little revived, and thought, if it were no worse than working, my situation was not so desperate: but still I feared I should be put to death, the white people looked and acted, as I thought, in so savage a manner; for I had never seen among any people such instances of brutal cruelty; and this not only shewn towards us blacks, but also to some of the whites themselves.[6] One white man in particular I saw, when we were permitted to be on deck, flogged so unmercifully with a large rope near the foremast,[7] that he died in consequence of it; and they tossed him over the side as they would have done a brute. This made me fear these people the more; and I expected nothing less than to be treated in the same manner. I could not help expressing my fears and apprehensions to some of my countrymen: I asked them if these people had no country, but lived in this

102

hollow place the ship? they told me they did not, but came from a distant one. "Then," said I, "how comes it in all our country we never heard of them?" They told me, because they lived so very far off. I then asked where were their women? had they any like themselves! I was told they had: "And why," said I, "do we not see them?" they answered, because they were left behind. I asked how the vessel could go? they told me they could not tell; but that there were cloths put upon the masts by the help of the ropes I saw, and then the vessel went on; and the white men had some spell or magic they put in the water when they liked in order to stop the vessel.[8] I was exceedingly amazed at this account, and really thought they were spirits. I therefore wished much to be from amongst them, for I expected they would sacrifice me: but my wishes were vain; for we were so quartered that it was impossible for any of us to make our escape. While we staid on the coast I was mostly on deck; and one day, to my great astonishment, I saw one of these vessels coming in with the sails up. As soon as the whites saw it, they gave a great shout, at which we were amazed; and the more so as the vessel appeared larger by approaching nearer. At last she came to an anchor in my sight, and when the anchor was let go, I and my countrymen who saw it were lost in astonishment to observe the vessel stop; and were now convinced it was done by magic. Soon after this the other ship got her boats[9] out, and they came on board of us, and the people of both ships seemed very glad to see each other. Several of the strangers also shook hands with us black people, and made motions with their hands, signifying, I suppose, we were to go to their country; but we did not understand them. At last, when the ship we were in had got in all her cargo, they made ready with many fearful noises, and we were all put under deck, so that we could not see how they managed the vessel. But this disappointment was the least of my sorrow. The stench of the hold while we were on the coast was so intolerably loathsome, that it was dangerous to remain there for any time, and some of us had been permitted to stay on the deck for the fresh air; but now that the whole ship's cargo were confined together, it became absolutely pestilential. The closeness of the place, and the heat of the climate, added to the number in the ship, which was so crowded that each had scarcely room to turn himself, almost suffocated us. This produced copious perspirations, so that the air soon became unfit for respiration, from a variety of loathsome smells, and brought on a sickness among the slaves, of which many died, thus falling victims to the improvident avarice, as I may call it, of their purchasers. This wretched situation was again aggravated by the galling of the chains, now become insupportable; and the filth of the necessary tubs, into which the children often fell, and were almost suffocated.[10] The shrieks of the women, and the groans of the dying, rendered the whole a scene of horror almost inconceiveable. Happily perhaps for myself I was soon reduced so low here that it was thought necessary to keep me almost always on deck; and from my extreme youth I was not put in fetters. In this situation I expected every hour to share the fate of my companions, some of whom were almost daily brought upon deck at the point of death, which I began to hope would soon put an end to my miseries. Often did I think many of the inhabitants of the deep much more happy than myself; I envied them the freedom they enjoyed, and as often wished I could change my condition for theirs. Every circumstance I met with served only to render my state more painful, and heighten my apprehensions, and my opinion of the cruelty of the whites. One day they had taken a number of fishes; and when they had killed and satisfied themselves with as many as they thought fit, to our astonishment who were on the deck, rather than give any of them to us to eat, as we expected, they tossed the remaining fish into the sea again, although we begged and prayed for some as well as we could, but in vain; and some of my countrymen, being pressed by hunger, took an opportunity, when they thought no one saw them, of trying to get a little privately; but they were discovered, and the attempt procured them some very severe floggings.

One day, when we had a smooth sea, and moderate wind, two of my wearied countrymen, who were chained together (I was near them at the time), preferring death to such a life of misery, somehow made through the nettings, and jumped into the sea: immediately another quite dejected fellow, who, on account of his illness, was suffered to be out of irons, also followed their example; and I believe many more would very soon have done the same, if they had not been prevented by the ship's crew, who were instantly alarmed. Those of us that were the most active were, in a moment, put down under the deck; and there was such a noise and confusion amongst the people of the ship as I never heard before, to stop her, and get the boat out to go after the slaves. However, two of the wretches were drowned, but they got the other, and afterwards flogged him unmercifully, for thus attempting to prefer death to slavery. In this manner we continued to undergo more hardships than I can now relate; hardships which are inseparable from this accursed trade.—Many a time we were near suffocation, from the want of fresh air, which we were often without for whole days together. This, and the stench of the necessary tubs, carried off many. During our passage I first saw flying fishes, which surprised me very much: they used frequently to fly across the ship, and many of them fell on the deck. I also now first saw the use of the quadrant.[11] I had often with astonishment seen the mariners make observations with it, and I could not think what it meant. They at last took notice of my surprise; and one of them, willing to increase it, as well as to gratify my curiosity, made me one day look through it. The clouds appeared to me to be land, which disappeared as they passed along. This heightened my wonder: and I was now more persuaded than ever that I was in another world, and that every thing about me was magic. At last we came in sight of the island of Barbadoes, at which the whites on board gave a great shout, and made many signs of joy to us. We did not know what to think of this; but as the vessel drew nearer we plainly saw the harbour, and other ships of different kinds and sizes: and we soon anchored amongst them off Bridge Town. Many merchants and planters now came on board, though it was in the evening. They put us in separate parcels,[12] and examined us attentively. They also made us jump,[13] and pointed to the land, signifying we were to go there. We thought by this we should be eaten by these ugly men, as they appeared to us; and, when soon after we were all put down under the deck again, there was much dread and trembling among us, and nothing but bitter cries to be heard all the night from these apprehensions, insomuch that at last the white people got some old slaves from the land to pacify us. They told us we were not to be eaten, but to work, and were soon to go on land, where we should see many of our country people. This report eased us much; and sure enough, soon after we were landed, there came to us Africans of all languages. We were conducted immediately to the merchant's yard, where we were all pent up together like so many sheep in a fold, without regard to sex or age. As every object was new to me, every thing I saw filled me with surprise. What struck me first was, that the houses were built with bricks, in stories,[14] and in every other respect different from those in I have seen in Africa:[15] but I was still more astonished on seeing people on horseback. I did not know what this could mean; and indeed I thought these people were full of nothing but magical arts. While I was in this astonishment, one of my fellow prisoners spoke to a countryman of his about the horses, who said they were the same kind they had in their country. I understood them, though they were from a distant part of Africa, and I thought it odd I had not seen any horses there; but afterwards, when I came to converse with different Africans, I found they had many horses amongst them, and much larger than those I then saw. We were not many days in the merchant's custody before we were sold after their usual manner, which is this:—On a signal given, (as the beat of a drum), the buyers rush at once into the yard where the slaves are confined, and make choice of that parcel they like best.[16] The noise and clamour with which this is attended, and the eagerness visible in the countenances of the buyers, serve not a little to increase the apprehensions of the terrified Africans, who may well be supposed to consider them as the ministers of that destruction to which they think themselves devoted.[17] In this manner, without scruple, are relations and friends separated, most of them never to see each other again. I remember in the vessel in which I was brought over, in the men's apartment, there were several brothers, who, in the sale, were sold in different lots; and it was very moving on this occasion to see and hear their cries at parting. O, ye nominal Christians! might not an African ask you, learned you this from your God? who says unto you, Do unto all men as you would men should do unto you? Is it not enough that we are torn from our country and friends to toil for your luxury and lust of gain? Must every tender feeling be likewise sacrificed to your avarice? Are the dearest friends and relations, now rendered more dear by their separation from their kindred, still to be parted from each other, and thus prevented from cheering the gloom of slavery with the small comfort of being together and mingling their sufferings and sorrows? Why are parents to lose their children, brothers their sisters, or husbands their wives? Surely this is a new refinement in cruelty, which, while it has no advantage to atone for it, thus aggravates distress, and adds fresh horrors even to the wretchedness of slavery.

END NOTES

1. Sound: healthy.
2. These two sentences were revised twice: the 1st ed. reads ". . . into terror when I was carried on board. I was immediately . . ."; the 3rd ed. reads ". . . into terror, which I am yet at a loss to describe; and the then feelings of my mind when carried on board. I was immediately . . ."; the final revision first appears in the 5th ed.
3. Long hair: only ed. 1 reads "loose hair."
4. Windlass: a winch, or crank, used to wind a heavy rope or chain to lift a weight.
5. Nettings: "a sort of fence, formed of an assemblage of ropes, fastened across each other" (William Falconer (1732–1769), *An Universal Dictionary of the Marine* [London, 1784; first published in 1769], hereafter cited in the notes as Falconer). These nettings were placed along the sides of the ship to form a caged enclosure to prevent the slaves from jumping overboard to try to escape or commit suicide.
6. The abolitionists frequently argued that the slave trade brutalized the enslavers as well as the enslaved. The tyrannical captain became almost a stock figure in the literature. The apologists for slavery argued that the trade served as a nursery for seamen. Evidence supports the abolitionists' claims that the trade was even more lethal, on an average percentage basis, for the crews than for the slaves. The Privy Council in 1789 estimated that the average mortality rate for slaves during the middle passage was 12.5 percent. Modern estimates of the mortality rate of 15 percent for slaves mean that of the approximately 10 million Africans taken to the Americas between 1600 and 1900, about 1.5 million died at sea. More than twice that number of African slaves died during the same period either while still in Africa or on their way to the Orient. The mortality rate of the much smaller number of marine slavers is estimated at about 20 percent. For both slaves and enslavers, the death rate varied with length of voyage, time, and age.
7. Foremast: the term *ship* was "particularly applied to a vessel furnished with three masts, each of which is composed of a lower mast, top mast, and top-gallant mast, with the usual machinery thereto belonging. The mast . . . placed at the middle of the ship's length, is called the main-mast, . . . that which is placed in the fore-part, the fore-mast, . . . and that which is towards the stem [the rear] is termed the mizen-mast" (Falconer).
8. Spell or magic: the anchor.
9. Boat: "a small open vessel, conducted on the water by rowing or sailing" (Falconer).
10. Necessary tubs: latrines.
11. Quadrant: "an instrument used to take the altitude of the sun or stars at sea, in order to determine the latitude of the place; or the sun's azimuth, so as to ascertain the magnetical variation" (Falconer).
12. Parcels: groups.
13. Made us jump: as a sign of health and strength.
14. The 1st ed. reads ". . . the houses were built with stories . . ."; the 2nd ed. reads ". . . the houses were built with bricks and stories . . ."; the final revision first appears in the 5th ed.
15. From . . . Africa: only ed. 1 reads "from those in Africa."
16. Equiano refers to what was known as the *scramble*, described from the perspective of an observer by Alexander Falconbridge (d. 1792) in *An Account of the Slave Trade on the Coast of Africa* (London, 1788):

> On a day appointed, the negroes were landed, and placed altogether in a large yard, belonging to the merchants to whom the ship was consigned. As soon

as the hour agreed on arrived, the doors of the yard were suddenly thrown open, and in rushed a considerable number of purchasers, with all the ferocity of brutes. Some instantly seized such of the negroes as they could conveniently lay hold of with their hands. Others, being prepared with several handkerchiefs tied together, encircled with these as many as they were able. While others, by means of a rope, effected the same purpose. It is scarcely possible to describe the confusion of which this mode of selling is productive. It likewise causes much animosity among the purchasers, who, not unfrequently upon these occasions, fall out and quarrel with each other. The poor astonished negroes were so much terrified by these proceedings, that several of them, through fear, climbed over the walls of the court yard, and ran wild about the town; but were soon hunted down and retaken (34).

Falconbridge's *Account* was written at the behest of the Society for Effecting the Abolition of the Slave Trade, which printed and distributed six thousand copies of it.

17. Devoted: doomed.

QUESTIONS

1. Equiano had encountered slavery in Africa, and he contrasts it to the slavery he experienced at the hands of the English. What contrasts does he draw?

2. What kind of language does Equiano use to describe his captors? What does he think of their behavior, not only to himself and other Africans, but to one another as well?

3. What account does Equiano give of slave sales?

4. How does Equiano use ideas—religious, social, and moral—embraced by the English to chastise them for the practice of slavery?

LETTER TO LORD MANSFIELD, 21 MARCH 1774

Warren Hastings

Warren Hastings (1732–1818) was the first governor-general of India, appointed to the position in 1773 and serving until he left India in 1785. He was a great patron of orientalist scholarship, founding the Asiatic Society in 1784 to promote further learning about Sanskrit, Persian, and Arabic texts produced in India. He also authorized the translation of various codes and digests of laws so that the British would be better able to adjudicate law in India in line with local norms and practices. His judicial reform was a hallmark of his administration and of colonial rule in India because he argued that Hindus and Muslims ought to have their own laws protected by the East India Company government, rather than having English common law thrust upon them. This speech addresses his position in a letter he wrote early in his administration.

When Hastings returned to England, he was accused by Edmund Burke, political thinker and statesman, of illegally expanding the political reach of the British territories in India by trampling on the rights and sovereignty of Indians and their government. Hastings was impeached by the British Parliament in a trial that lasted from 1788 to 1795 and resulted in an acquittal.

TO LORD MANSFIELD.

FORT WILLIAM, 21ST MARCH, 1774, (PER RESOLUTION.)
DUPLICATE (PER SWALLOW) 25TH AUGUST, 1774.

My Lord,—I feel a very sensible regret that I have not endeavoured to improve the opportunities which I possessed by an early introduction to your Lordship's acquaintance of acquiring a better right to the freedom which I now assume in this address. The great veneration which I have ever entertained for your Lordship's character, and the unimportant sphere in which, till lately, it has been my lot to act, were sufficient checks to restrain me from such an attempt, however my wishes might have impelled me to it.

I know not whether you will admit the subject of this letter to merit your attention by its importance. My only motive for introducing it to your Lordship is, that I believe it to be of that importance, as it regards the rights of a great nation in the most essential point of civil liberty, the preservation of its own laws, a subject, of which I know no person equally able to judge, or from whom I could hope for a more ready or effectual support of any proposition concerning it.

Among the various plans which have been lately formed for the improvement of the British interests in the provinces of Bengal, the necessity of establishing a new form of judicature, and giving laws to a people who were supposed to be governed by no other principle of justice than the arbitrary wills, or uninstructed judgments, of their temporary rulers, has been frequently suggested; and this opinion I fear has obtained the greater strength from some publications of considerate merit in which it is too positively asserted that written laws are totally unknown to the Hindoo, or original inhabitants of Hindostan. From whatever cause this notion has proceeded, nothing can be more foreign from truth. They have been in possession of laws, which have continued unchanged, from the remotest antiquity. The professors of these laws, who are spread over the whole empire of Hindostan, speak the same language, which is unknown to the rest of the people, and receive public endowments and benefactions from every state and people, besides a degree of personal respect amounting almost to idolatry, in return for the benefits which are supposed to be derived from their studies. The consequence of these professors has suf-

110

fered little diminution from the introduction of the Mahomedan government which has generally left their privileges untouched, and suffered the people to remain in quiet possession of the institutes which time and religion had rendered familiar to their understandings and sacred to their affections. I presume, my Lord, if this assertion can be proved, you will not deem if necessary that I should urge any argument in defence of their right to possess those benefits under a British and Christian administration which the bigotry of the Mahomedan government has never denied them. It would be a grievance to deprive the people of the protection of their own laws, but it would be a wanton tyranny to require their obedience to others of which they are wholly ignorant, and of which they have no possible means of acquiring a knowledge.

I cannot offer a better proof of what I have before affirmed, than by presenting you with a specimen of the laws themselves, which it will be necessary to preface with the following brief history of the manner in which it came into my hands.

A short time after my appointment to the government of this presidency, the Company were pleased to direct the administration here to take possession of the Dewanny, or territorial government of these provinces, in their name, without using any longer the intervention of an officer of the ancient Mogul government under the title of their Naib, or deputy, and gave them full powers to constitute such regulations for the collection and management of the revenue as the should judge most beneficial to the Company and the inhabitants.

In the execution of this commission, it was discovered that the due administration of justice had so intimate a connexion with the revenue, that in the system which was adopted, this formed a very considerable part. Two courts were appointed for every district, one for the trial of crimes and offences, and the other to decide causes of property. The first consisted entirely of Mahomedans, and the latter of the principal officers of the revenue, assisted by the judges of the criminal courts, and by the most learned pundits (or professors of the Hindoo law), in cases which depended on the peculiar usages or institutions of either faith. These courts were made dependent on two supreme courts which were established in the city of Calcutta, one for ultimate reference in capital cases, the other for appeals.

111

In this establishment no essential change was made in the ancient constitution of the province. It was only brought back to its original principles, and the line prescribed for the jurisdiction of each Court, which the looseness of the Mogul government for some past had suffered to encroach upon each other.

It would swell this letter to too great a bulk were I to enter into a more minute description, although I feel the necessity of making it more comprehensive to convey an adequate idea of the subject.

As it has never been the practice of this country for the pundits or expounders of the Hindoo law, to sit as judges of it, but only to give their opinions in such cases is might be proposed to them, and is these perpetually occurring occasioned very great delays in our proceedings, or were decided at once by the officers of the Courts, without any reference, it was judged advisable for the sake of giving confidence to the people, and of enabling the Courts to decide with certainty and despatch, to form a compilation of the Hindoo laws with the best authority which could be obtained; and for that purpose ten of the most learned pundits were invited to Calcutta from different parts of the province, who cheerfully undertook this work, have incessantly laboured in the prosecution of it, and have already, as they assure me, completed it, all but the revisal and correction of it.

This code they have written in their own language, the Shanscrit. A translation of it is begun under the inspection of one of their body into the Persian language, and from that into English. The two first chapters I have now the honour to present to your Lordship with this, is a proof that the inhabitants of this land are not in the savage state in which they have been unfairly represented, and as a specimen of the principles which constitute the rights of property among them.

Although the second chapter has been translated with a despatch that has not allowed time for rendering it quite so correct as I could wish to offer it to your Lordship's view, yet I can venture to vouch for the fidelity with which it is generally executed, such parts of it as I have compared with the Persian copy having been found literally exact.

Your Lordship will find a great mixture of the superstitions of their religion in this composition. Many passages in the first chapter are not to be reconciled to any rule known to us, but may be supposed to be perfectly consonant to their own maxims, as your Lordship will perceive that they have been scrupulous exact in marking such cases is have received a different decision in the different originals from which this abstract is selected.

Upon the merit of the work itself I will not presume to offer an opinion. I think it necessary to obviate any misconception which you may entertain from the similitude in the arrangement and style to our own productions, by saying that I am assured they are close and genuine transcripts from the original.

With respect to the Mahometan law, which is the guide at least of one fourth of the natives of this province, your Lordship need not be told that this is as comprehensive, and as well defined, as that of most states in Europe, having been formed at a time in which the Arabians were in possession of all the real learning which existed in the western parts of this continent. The book which bears the greatest authority among them in India is a digest formed by the command of the Emperor Aurungzebe, and consists of four large folio volumes which are equal to near twelve of ours.

I have only to add that the design of this letter is to give your Lordship a fair representation of a fact of which the world has been misinformed, to the great injury of this country, and to prevent the ill effects which such an error may produce in a public attempt to deprive it of the most sacred and valuable of its rights. Even the most injudicious or most fanciful customs which ignorance or superstition may have introduced among them, are perhaps preferable to any which could be substituted in their room. They are interwoven with their religion, and are therefore recovered as of the highest authority. They are the conditions on which they hold their place in society, they think them equitable, and therefore it is no hardship to exact their obedience to them. I am persuaded they would consider the attempt to free them from the effects of such a power as a severe hardship. But I find myself exceeding the bounds which my deference for your Lordship's great wisdom had prescribed, and therefore quit the subject.

I know the value of your Lordship's time, and reluctantly lay claim to so great a share of it as may be required for the perusal of this letter. I assure myself that you will approve my intention. My only apprehension is, that it may arrive too late to produce the effect which I hope to obtain from it. I would flatter myself that the work which it introduces may be of use in your Lordship's hands towards the legal accomplishment of a new system which shall found the government in Bengal on its authority of the British ancient laws, and serve to point out the way to rule this people with case and moderation according to their own ideas, manners, and prejudices. But although I should be disappointed in this expectation, I still please myself with the persuasion that your Lordship will receive it with satisfaction as an object of literary curiosity, whatever claim it may have to your attention from it's Intrinsic merit; as it contains the genuine sentiment, of a remote and ancient people at a period of time In which it was impossible for them to have had the smallest connexion or communication with the inhabitants of Europe, on a subject in which all mankind have a common interest and is, I believe, the first production of the kind hitherto made known amongst us.—I have the, honour to be, my Lord, your Lordship's most obedient and most humble servant.

QUESTIONS

1. What kinds of legal practice does Hastings propose for the British administration and why? Is it something dramatically new or is it a continuation of old practices?
2. What does Hastings call the "ancient constitution" and why should the British administration defend it?
3. In this letter, Hastings is informing the recipient Lord Mansfield of various facts about India: What kinds of knowledge does Hastings feel he must pass on? What kinds of misinformation is he hoping to correct?
4. How do Hindus and Muslims compare in their legal practices, as Hastings understands it? How does this affect the ways that legal codes were constructed in colonial India?

CHINA REJECTS THE WEST

The Qianlong Emperor

Midway through China's last dynasty, the Qing (1644–1911), China was deeply convinced of its own superiority, not only in East Asia, but throughout the world. The Emperor of China saw himself as ruler of a vast kingdom that sat, not coincidentally, at the center of the world. Other peoples who wished to trade with China, and there were many, were incorporated into the tribute system. They bore tribute to China's imperial court, ritually acknowledged Chinese superiority (generally by performing the ketou *or kowtow, a prostration accompanied by the knocking of one's forehead on the ground as a sign of submission), and then were usually graciously permitted to conduct commerce and assured of Chinese protection for their countries. Many tributary regimes in East Asia, particularly Korea and Vietnam, were deeply influenced by China. By the eighteenth century, Chinese goods and the enormous Chinese market had also drawn eager merchants from a number of European nations. For Great Britain, the major attraction was tea, to which its people had become addicted.*

This selection features two edicts issued in 1793 by the Qianlong Emperor (Ch'ien-lung; 1711–1799) and addressed to King George III of England in response to the mission of Lord George Macartney. Macartney had been sent to China to convince the Chinese to allow a British diplomatic or trade envoy to live in the capital and to convince them to lift many Chinese constraints on foreign trade. Those constraints were often referred to as the "Canton system"

Reprinted by permission from *Changing China*, edited by J. Mason Gentzler. Copyright © 1977 by Greenwood Publishing Group, Inc.

because foreign trade was confined to an area just outside the port city of Canton (Guangzhou) and foreign traders had to adhere to a very strict set of conditions if they wished to conduct commerce with the Chinese. (Non-Chinese were also allowed to reside at the port of Macao.) A small number of Chinese firms (hongs) *were given the monopoly on foreign trade. The British, with their zeal for free trade, deeply resented these restrictions. Macartney was politely received in the imperial court in Peking (Beijing), and given a special reception that did not require the ketou—which he said he would refuse to perform—but as these documents indicate, his requests were turned down.*

Despite his Manchu origins, Qianlong (r. 1736–1795) is considered one of China's most competent and intelligent emperors, and these edicts provide a glimpse into the mindset of this revered ruler at the height of his power. By the 1840s, however, Great Britain had taken advantage of China's technological backwardness to win the famous Opium War (1839–1842) and dismantle the Canton system.

TWO EDICTS FROM THE CH'IEN-LUNG EMPEROR TO KING GEORGE III OF ENGLAND

[September 1793, on the Occasion of Lord Macartney's Mission to China]

(a)

You, O King, live beyond the confines of many seas, nevertheless, impelled by your humble desire to partake of the benefits of our civilization, you have dispatched a mission respectfully bearing your memorial. Your Envoy has crossed the seas and paid his respects at my Court on the anniversary of my birthday. To show your devotion, you have also sent offerings of your country's produce.

I have perused your memorial: the earnest terms in which it is couched reveal a respectful humility on your part, which is highly praiseworthy. In consideration of the fact that your Ambassador and his deputy have come a long way with your memorial and tribute, I have shown them high favour and have allowed them to be introduced into my presence. To manifest my indulgence, I have entertained them at a banquet and made them numerous gifts. I have also caused presents to be forwarded to the Naval Commander and six hundred of his officers and men, although they did not come to Peking, so that they too may share in my all-embracing kindness.

As to your entreaty to send one of your nationals to be accredited to my Celestial Court and to be in control of your country's trade with China, this request is contrary to all usage of my dynasty and cannot possibly be entertained. It is true that Europeans, in the service of the dynasty, have been permitted to live at Peking, but they are compelled to adopt Chinese dress, they are strictly confined to their own precincts and are never permitted to return home. You are presumably familiar with our dynastic regulations. Your proposed Envoy to my Court could not be placed in a position similar to that of European officials in Peking who are forbidden to leave China, nor could he, on the other hand, be allowed liberty of movement and the privilege of corresponding with his own country; so that you would gain nothing by his residence in our midst.

Moreover, Our Celestial dynasty possesses vast territories, and tribute missions from the dependencies are provided for by the Department for Tributary States, which ministers to their wants and exercises strict control over their movements. It would be quite impossible to leave them to their own devices. Supposing that your Envoy should come to our Court, his language and national dress differ from that of our people, and there would be no place in which he might reside. It may be suggested that he might imitate the Europeans permanently resident in Peking and adopt the dress and customs of China, but, it has never been our dynasty's wish to force people to do things unseemly and inconvenient. Besides, supposing I sent an Ambassador to reside in your country, how could you possibly make for him the requisite arrangements? Europe consists of many other nations besides your own: if each and all demanded to be represented at our Court, how could we possibly consent? The thing is utterly impracticable. How can our dynasty alter its whole procedure and regulations, established for more than a century, in order to meet your individual views? If it be said that your object is to exercise control over your country's trade, your nationals have had full liberty to trade at Canton for many a year, and have received the greatest consideration at our hands. Missions have been sent by Portugal and Italy, preferring similar requests. The Throne appreciated their sincerity and loaded them with favours, besides authorising measures to facilitate their trade with China. You are no doubt aware that, when my Canton merchant, Wu Chao-p'ing, was in debt to the foreign ships, I made the Viceroy advance the monies due, out of the provincial treasury, and ordered him to punish the culprit severely. Why then should foreign nations advance this utterly unreasonable request to be represented at my Court? Peking is nearly 10,000 *li* from Canton, and at such a distance what possible control could any British representative exercise?

If you assert that your reverence for Our Celestial dynasty fills you with a desire to acquire our civilisation, our ceremonies and code of laws differ so completely from your own that, even if your Envoy were able to acquire the rudiments of our civilisation, you could not possibly transplant our manners and customs to your alien soil. Therefore, however adept the Envoy might become, nothing would be gained thereby.

Swaying the wide world, I have but one aim in view, namely, to maintain a perfect governance and to fulfil the duties of the State; strange and costly objects do not interest me. If I have commanded that the tribute offerings sent by you, O King, are to be accepted, this was solely in consideration for the spirit which prompted you to dispatch them from afar. Our dynasty's majestic virtue has penetrated unto every country under Heaven, and Kings of all nations have offered their costly tribute by land and sea. As your Ambassador can see for himself, we possess all things. I set no value on objects strange or ingenious, and have no use for your country's manufactures. This then is my answer to your request to appoint a representative at my Court, a request contrary to our dynastic usage, which would only result in inconvenience to yourself. I have expounded my wishes in detail and have commanded your tribute Envoys to leave in peace on their homeward journey. It behoves you, O King, to respect my sentiments and to display even greater devotion and loyalty in the future, so that, by perpetual submission to our Throne, you may secure peace and prosperity for your country hereafter. Besides making gifts (of which I enclose a list) to each member of your Mission, I confer upon you, O King, valuable presents in excess of the number usually bestowed on such occasions, including silks and curios—a list of which is likewise enclosed. Do you reverently receive them and take note of my tender goodwill towards you! A special mandate.

(b)

You, O King from afar, have yearned after the blessings of our civilisation, and in your eagerness to come into touch with our converting influence have sent an Embassy across the sea bearing a memorial. I have already taken note of your respectful spirit of submission, have treated your mission with extreme favour and loaded it with gifts, besides issuing a mandate to you, O King, and honouring you with the bestowal of valuable presents. Thus has my indulgence been manifested.

Yesterday your Ambassador petitioned my Ministers to memorialize me regarding your trade with China, but his proposal is not consistent with our dynastic usage and cannot be entertained. Hitherto, all European nations, including your own country's barbarian merchants, have carried on their trade with Our Celestial Empire at Canton. Such has been the procedure for many years, although Our Celestial Empire possesses all things in prolific abundance and lacks no product within it own borders. There was therefore no need to import the manufactures of outside barbarians in exchange for our own produce. But as the tea, silk, and porcelain which the Celestial Empire produces are absolute necessities to European nations and to yourselves, we have permitted, as a signal mark of favour, that foreign *hongs* should be established at Canton, so that your wants might be supplied and your country thus participate in our beneficence. But your Ambassador has now put forward new requests which completely fail to recognise the Throne's principle to "treat strangers from afar with indulgence," and to exercise a pacifying control over barbarian tribes, the world over. Moreover, our dynasty, swaying the myriad races of the globe, extends the same benevolence towards all. Your England is not the only nation trading at Canton. If other nations, following your bad example, wrongfully importune my ear with further impossible requests, how will it be possible for me to treat them with easy indulgence? Nevertheless, I do not forget the lonely remoteness of your island, cut off from the world by intervening wastes of sea, nor do I overlook your excusable ignorance of the usages of Our Celestial Empire. I have consequently commanded my Ministers to enlighten your Ambassador on the subject, and have ordered the departure of the mission. But I have doubts that, after your Envoy's return he may fail to acquaint you with my view in detail or that he may be lacking in lucidity, so that I shall now proceed to take your requests *seriatim* and to issue my mandate on each question separately. In this way you will, I trust, comprehend my meaning.

1. Your Ambassador requests facilities for ships of your nation to call at Ningpo, Chusan, Tientsin and other places for purposes of trade. Until now trade with European nations has always been conducted at Macao, where the foreign *hongs* are established to store and sell foreign merchandise. Your nation has obediently complied with this regulation for years past without raising any objection. In none of the other ports named have *hongs* been established, so that even if your vessels were to proceed thither, they would have no means of disposing of their cargoes. Furthermore, no interpreters are available, so you would have no means of explaining your wants, and nothing but general inconvenience would result. For the future, as in the past, I decree that your request is refused and that the trade shall be limited to Macao.

2. The request that your merchants may establish a repository in the capital of my Empire for the storing and sale of your produce, in accordance with the precedent granted to Russia, is even more impracticable than the last. My capital is the hub and centre about which all quarters of the globe revolve. Its ordinances are most august and its laws are strict in the extreme. The subjects of our dependencies have never been allowed to open places of business in Peking. Foreign trade has hitherto been conducted at Macao, because it is conveniently near to the sea, and therefore an important gathering place for the ships of all nations sailing to and fro. If warehouses were established in Peking, the remoteness of your country lying far to the northwest of my capital, would render transport extremely difficult. Before Kiakhta was opened, the Russians were permitted to trade at Peking, but the accommodation furnished them was only temporary. As soon as Kiakhta was available, they were compelled to withdraw from Peking, which has been closed to their trade these many years. Their frontier trade at Kiakhta is on all fours with your trade at Macao. Possessing facilities at the latter place, you now ask for further privileges at Peking, although our dynasty observes the severest restrictions respecting the admission of foreigners within its boundaries, and has never permitted the subjects of dependencies to cross the Empire's barriers and settle at will amongst the Chinese people. This request is also refused.

3. Your request for a small island near Chusan, where your merchants may reside and goods be warehoused, arises from your desire to develop trade. As there are neither foreign *hongs* nor interpreters in or near Chusan, where none of your ships have ever called, such an island would be utterly useless for your purposes. Every inch of the territory of our Empire is marked on the map and the strictest vigilance is exercised over it all: even tiny islets and far-lying sandbanks are clearly defined as part of the provinces to which they belong. Consider, moreover, that England is not the only barbarian land which wishes to establish relations with our civilisation and trade with our Empire: supposing that other nations were all to imitate your evil example and beseech me to present them each and all with a site for trading purposes, how could I possibly comply. This also is a flagrant infringement of the usage of my Empire and cannot possibly be entertained.

4. The next request, for a small site in the vicinity of Canton city, where your barbarian merchants may lodge or, alternatively, that there be no longer any restrictions over their movements at Macao, has arisen from the following causes. Hitherto, the barbarian merchants of Europe have had a definite locality assigned to them at Macao for residence and trade, and have been forbidden to encroach an inch beyond the limits assigned to that locality. Barbarian merchants having business with the *hongs* have never been allowed to enter the city of Canton; by these measures, disputes between Chinese and barbarians are prevented, and a firm barrier is raised between my subjects and those of other nations. The present request is quite contrary to precedent; furthermore, European nations have been trading with Canton for a number of years and, as they make large profits, the number of traders is constantly increasing. How could it be possible to grant such a site to each country? The merchants of the foreign *hongs* are responsible to the local officials for the proceedings of barbarian merchants and they carry out periodical inspections. If these restrictions were withdrawn, friction would inevitably occur between the Chinese and your barbarian subjects, and the results would militate against the benevolent regard that I feel towards you. From every point of view, therefore, it is best that the regulations now in force should continue unchanged.

5. Regarding your request for remission or reduction of duties on merchandise discharged by your British barbarian merchants at Macao

and distributed throughout the interior, there is a regular tariff in force for barbarian merchant's goods, which applies equally to all European nations. It would be as wrong to increase the duty imposed on your nation's merchandise on the ground that the bulk of foreign trade is in your hands, as to make an exception in your case in the shape of specially reduced duties. In the future, duties shall be levied equitably without discrimination between your nation and any other, and, in order to manifest my regard, your barbarian merchants shall continue to be shown every consideration at Macao.

6. As to your request that your ships shall pay the duties leviable by tariff, there are regular rules in force at the Canton Custom house respecting the amounts payable, and since I have refused your request to be allowed to trade at other ports, this duty will naturally continue to be paid at Canton as heretofore.

7. Regarding your nation's worship of the Lord of Heaven, it is the same religion as that of other European nations. Ever since the beginning of history, sage Emperors and wise rulers have bestowed on China a moral system and inculcated a code, which from time immemorial has been religiously observed by the myriads of my subjects. There has been no hankering after heterodox doctrines. Even the European (missionary) officials in my capital are forbidden to hold intercourse with Chinese subjects; they are restricted within the limits of their appointed residences, and may not go about propagating their religion. The distinction between Chinese and barbarian is most strict, and your Ambassador's request that barbarians shall be given full liberty to disseminate their religion is utterly unreasonable.

It may be, O King, that the above proposals have been wantonly made by your Ambassador on his own responsibility, or peradventure you yourself are ignorant of our dynastic regulations and had no intention of transgressing them when you expressed these wild ideas and hopes. I have ever shown the greatest condescension to the tribute missions of all States which sincerely yearn after the blessings of civilisation, so as to manifest my kindly indulgence. I have even gone out of my way to grant any requests which were in any way consistent with Chinese usage. Above all, upon you, who live in a remote and inaccessible region, far across the spaces of ocean, but who have shown your submissive loyalty by sending this tribute mission, I have heaped benefits far in excess of those accorded to other nations. But the demands presented by your Embassy are not only a contravention of dynastic tradition, but would be utterly unproductive of good result to yourself, besides being quite impracticable. I have accordingly stated the facts to you in detail, and it is your bounden duty reverently to appreciate my feelings and to obey these instructions henceforward for all time, so that you may enjoy the blessings of perpetual peace. If, after the receipt of this explicit decree, you lightly give ear to the representations of your subordinates and allow your barbarian merchants to proceed to Chekiang and Tientsin, with the object of landing and trading there, the ordinances of my Celestial Empire are strict in the extreme, and the local officials, both civil and military, are bound reverently to obey the law of the land. Should your vessels touch shore, your merchants will assuredly never be permitted to land or to reside there, but will be subject to instant expulsion. In that event your barbarian merchants will have had a long journey for nothing. Do not say that you were not warned in due time! Tremblingly obey and show no negligence! A special mandate!

QUESTIONS

1. According to these documents, what did the British request and why did the emperor reject those requests?
2. In what ways do the edicts reflect Chinese misconceptions about the British and the West in general?
3. How do you think these edicts were received by the British king and his government? What might the British have found particularly objectionable?
4. What do these documents reveal about the mindset of China's rulers at the end of the eighteenth century? What problems might that attitude have created?

THE CARTAGENA MANIFESTO

Simón Bolívar

For three hundred years, Spain and Portugal ruled their enormous American empires with few serious challenges from people living in the colonies. But within less than two decades between 1808 and 1826, Brazil and most of Spanish America won independence, leaving Spain with just two islands, Cuba and Puerto Rico, and Portugal with nothing. From Mexico to Argentina, the new nations of Spanish and Portuguese America emerged.

Spanish Americans became disgruntled with colonial rule as a result of a series of administrative reforms instituted by a series of kings from the Bourbon royal family, who had taken over after the Hapsburg family had expired, which raised taxes and limited local autonomy. The increased taxes put pressure on the landowning indigenous population. The limited autonomy was perceived as discrimination against American-born Spaniards who could not obtain political influence commensurate with their wealth. The precipitating events of the independence movement were Napoleon's invasion of Spain in 1808 and his subsequent ouster of successive Bourbon kings.

Simón Bolívar (1783–1830) was the foremost leader of the independence movement in Spanish America. Wealthy and educated in Venezuela and Europe, Bolívar returned home from his extensive travels to participate in the independence movement in Caracas in 1810. He quickly became a leader of the rebellion against the Spanish. He fought for sixteen years, through a disheartening series of defeats before 1815 and then a series of hard-won battles from Venezuela to Peru. He earned his final victory December 9, 1824, at the

---

Reprinted from *Memorial to the Citizens of New Grenada by a Citizen of Caracas*, 1812.

Battle of Ayacucho in the Peruvian central Andes, thereby assuring independence for all of Spanish South America.

Written in December 1812, the Cartagena Manifesto was an effort on the part of Bolívar to explain how Venezuela's first attempt at an independent republic had failed. His hope was that neighboring New Granada (Colombia) would not suffer the same fate.

MEMORIAL TO THE CITIZENS OF NEW GRANADA
BY A CITIZEN OF CARACAS

[Pamphlet, printed 1813]

Cartagena de [las] Indias, December 15, 1812.

To spare New Granada the fate of Venezuela and to release the latter from its suffering are the objects which I have set for myself in this memorial. . . .

I am, Granadans, a son of unhappy Caracas, who miraculously escaped from amidst her physical and political ruins, and, ever faithful to the liberal and just system proclaimed by my country, I have come here to follow the banners of independence which so gloriously wave in these states.

Forgive me if I, inspired by patriotic zeal, take the liberty of addressing you, in order to sketch briefly the causes that brought Venezuela to its destruction. I flatter myself that the terrible and exemplary lessons which that defunct Republic has supplied may induce America to mend her ways and correct her shortcomings in unity, strength, and energy, which are apparent in her governments.

The most grievous error committed by Venezuela in making her start on the political stage was, as none can deny, her fatal adoption of the system of tolerance—a system long condemned as weak and inadequate by every man of common sense, yet tenaciously maintained with an unparalleled blindness to the very end. . . .

The codes consulted by our magistrates were not those which could teach them the practical science of government but were those devised by certain benevolent visionaries, who, creating fantastic republics in their imaginations, have sought to attain political perfection, assuming the perfectibility of the human race. Thus we were given philosophers for lead-

125

ers, philanthropy for legislation, dialectic for tactics, and sophists for soldiers. Through such a distortion of principles, the social order was thoroughly shaken, and from that time on the State made giant strides toward its general dissolution, which, indeed, shortly came to pass.

Thence was born an impunity toward crimes against the State. They were shamelessly committed by the malcontents, and particularly by our born and implacable enemies, the European Spaniards, who had schemingly remained in our country in order to keep it in continual turmoil and to foster whatever conspiracies our judges permitted them to organize, by always acquitting them even when their misdeeds were of such enormity as to endanger public welfare. . . .

Next came the firm opposition to raising seasoned, disciplined troops, prepared to take their place on the field of battle and indoctrinated with the desire to defend liberty with success and honor. Instead, innumerable undisciplined militia units were formed. The salaries paid the staff officers of these units exhausted the funds of the national treasury. Agriculture was destroyed because the farmers were torn from their homes; this brought odium upon the Government which had forced them to abandon their families and take up arms.

"Republics," said our statesmen, "have no need for hirelings to maintain their liberty. Every citizen will turn soldier when the enemy attacks us. . . ."

With such political thinking and inaccurate reasoning, they deceived the simple-minded; but they did not convince the judicious who clearly understood the immense difference between the peoples, times, and customs of those republics and ours. It is true that they did not pay standing armies, but that was because these did not exist in antiquity; the safety and the honor of their states was entrusted to their civic virtues, their austere habits, and their military qualities—traits which we are very far from possessing. As regards the modern nations which have thrown off the yoke of tyranny, it is well known that they have maintained the number of hardened veterans necessary to insure their security. . . .

What followed in Venezuela was bitter evidence of the error of her calculations. The militia that went to meet the enemy, not knowing how to handle arms and unaccustomed to discipline and obedience, was routed at the very beginning of the last campaign, notwithstanding the heroic and extraordinary efforts of their leaders to lead them to victory. This defeat caused general discouragement among soldiers and officers, for it is a military truth that only battle-hardened armies are capable of surmounting the first reverses of a campaign. The novice soldier believes all is lost when he has once been routed. Experience has not proved to him that bravery, skill, and perseverance can mend misfortune.

The subdividing of the province of Caracas, planned, discussed, and sanctioned by the Federal Congress, awakened and fomented bitter rivalry against the capital in the smaller cities and towns. . . . Flame of civil war was kindled in Valencia, and, even with the reduction of that city, it was never extinguished. . . .

The dissipation of the public taxes for frivolous and harmful purposes, and particularly on salaries for an infinite number of officeholders, secretaries, judges, magistrates, and provincial and federal legislators dealt the Republic a mortal blow, since it was obliged to seek recourse in the dangerous expedient of issuing paper money, with no other guarantee than the probable revenues and backing of the Confederation. This new money, in the eyes of most people, was a direct violation of property rights, because they felt that they were being deprived of objects of intrinsic value in exchange for others of uncertain and even problematical worth. The paper money roused discontent among the otherwise indifferent people of the interior; hence, they called upon the commandant of the Spanish troops to come and free them from a currency which they regarded with a horror greater than slavery.

But what weakened the Venezuelan government most was the federal form it adopted in keeping with the exaggerated precepts of the rights of man; this form by authorizing self-government, disrupts social contracts and reduces nations to anarchy. Such was the true state of the Confederation. Each province governed itself independently; and, following this example, each city demanded like powers, based on the practice of the provinces and on the theory that all men and all peoples are entitled to establish arbitrarily the form of government that pleases them.

The federal system, although the most perfect and the most capable of providing for human happiness in society, is, nevertheless, the most contrary to the interests of our infant states. Generally speaking, our fellow-citizens are not yet able to exercise their rights themselves in the fullest

127

measure, because they lack the political virtues that characterize true republicans—virtues that are not acquired under absolute governments, where the rights and duties of the citizen are not recognized. . . .

Caracas was made to suffer severely by the shortcomings of the Confederation, which, far from aiding it, exhausted its treasury and war supplies. When danger threatened, the Confederation abandoned the city to its fate without assisting it with even a small contingent. The Confederation, moreover, created new difficulties, for the rivalry which developed between the federal and the provincial authorities enabled the enemies to penetrate deep into the heart of the State and to occupy a large part of the province before the question as to whether federal or provincial troops should go out to repel them was settled. . . .

I believe that, unless we centralize our American governments, our enemies will gain every advantage. We will inevitably be involved in the horrors of civil strife and miserably defeated by that handful of bandits who infest our territories.

The popular elections held by the simple people of the country and by the scheming inhabitants of the city added a further obstacle to our practice of federation, because the former are so ignorant that they cast their votes mechanically and the latter so ambitious that they convert everything into factions. As a result, Venezuela never witnessed a free and proper election and the government was placed in the hands of men who were either inept, immoral, or opposed to the cause of independence. Party spirit determined everything and, consequently, caused us more disorganization than the circumstances themselves. Our division, not Spanish arms, returned us to slavery.

The earthquake of March 26, to be sure, was physically and morally destructive and can properly be termed the immediate cause of Venezuela's ruin; but this event could have happened without producing such fatal results had Caracas been governed at that time by a single authority, who, acting promptly and vigorously, could have repaired the damage without those hindrances and rivalries which retarded the effectiveness of the measures taken and allowed the evil to grow to such proportions that it is beyond remedy. . . .

Following the earthquake, ecclesiastical influences played a very considerable part in the insurgency of the villages and smaller towns, and in bringing enemies into the country, thereby sacrilegiously abusing the sanctity of their office in behalf of the fomenters of civil war. . . .

SIMÓN BOLÍVAR

QUESTIONS

1. What was the most crucial weakness of Venezuela's First Republic, according to Bolívar?
2. Why were popular elections not, in the opinion of Bolívar, successful?
3. What was the clergy's role in the failure of the independence movement in Venezuela in 1812?
4. Judging from Bolívar's analysis, why do you think that he was able to regroup and lead the independence movement to triumph?

BETWEEN THE ORINOCO AND THE AMAZON

Alexander von Humboldt

Alexander von Humboldt was born in Berlin in 1769 and was educated at the universities of Frankfurt, Göttingen, and Hamburg. His expertise in botany, zoology, geology, mineralogy, climatology, and ethnology made Humboldt one of the last great polymaths. He did research on magnetism and published his innovative ideas about plant geography during the 1790s, while still working for the Prussian State Mines. An inheritance allowed him to travel to the New World in 1799–1804 with his friend and French fellow-scientist Aimé Bonpland. Later journeys took him to Russia and central Asia. Hailed in the nineteenth century as one of the great scientist-explorers of his time, he is now acknowledged for his environmental and ecological insights. Humboldt died in 1859.

The Personal Narrative *of his travels in the New World formed part of the thirty volumes published between 1807 and 1834 describing the journey. The style was influenced by earlier scientific travel writers like Captain Cook, Louis Antoine de Bougainville, and Johann Reinhold Forster. Here he describes part of the arduous journey in 1800 that proved for the first time that the Orinoco and Amazon river systems were connected. The account shows his sharp scientific eye and his concern for European treatment of indigenous peoples.*

During the night we had left the Orinoco waters almost without realizing it. At sunrise we found ourselves in a new country, on the banks of a river whose name we had hardly heard mentioned, and which would lead us after a foot journey over Pimichín to the Río Negro on the Brazilian frontier. The father superior of the San Fernando mission said to us: 'First you must go up the Atabapo, then the Temi, and finally the Tuamini. If the black-water current is too strong to do this the guides will take you over flooded land through the jungle. In that deserted zone between the Orinoco and the Río Negro you will meet only two monks established there. In Javita you will find people to carry your canoe over land in four days to Caño Pimichín. If the canoe is not wrecked go straight down the Río Negro to the fort of San Carlos, then go up the Casiquiare and in a month you will reach San Fernando along the Upper Orinoco.' That was the plan drawn up for us, which we carried out, without danger, in thirty-three days. The bends are such in this labyrinth of rivers that without the map which I have drawn it would be impossible to picture the route we took. In the first part of this journey from east to west you find the famous bifurcations that have given rise to so many disputes, and whose location I was the first to establish through astronomic observations. One arm of the Orinoco, the Casiquiare,[1] running north to south, pours into the Guainia or Río Negro, which in turn joins the Marañon or Amazon.

No astronomical instruments had been brought along during the frontier expedition in this region, so with my chronometer, and by the meridional height of the stars, I established the exact location of San Baltasar de Atabapo, Javita, San Carlos de Río Negro, the Culimacarai rock and the Esmeralda mission. The map I drew has resolved any doubts about the reciprocal distances between the Christian outposts. When there is no other road but the tortuous and intricate river; when little villages lie hidden in thick jungle; when in a completely flat country with no mountains visible, you can read where you are on earth only by looking up to the sky.

The San Fernando missionary, with whom we stayed two days, lived in a village that appears slightly more prosperous than others we had stayed in on our journey, yet still had only 226 inhabitants.[2] We found some traces of agriculture; every Indian has his own cacao plantation, which gives a good crop by the fifth year but stops fruiting earlier than in the Aragua valleys. Around San Fernando there are some savannahs with good pasture but only some seven or eight cows remain from a vast herd left behind by the frontier expedition. The Indians are a little more civilized than in the other missions. Surprisingly, we came across an Indian blacksmith.

In San Fernando we were most struck by the *pihiguado* or *pirijao* palm, which gives the countryside its peculiar quality. Covered with thorns, its trunk reaches more than 60 feet high. The fruit of this tree is extraordinary; each bunch has some fifty to eighty; they are yellow, like apples, but turn purple on ripening, when they are 2 or 3 inches thick. Generally they fall off before the kernel develops. Of the eighty to ninety palm trees peculiar to the New World that I have described in my *Nova Genera plantarum aequinoctialem* (1815–25) none has such a fleshy fruit. The *pirijao* fruit yields a substance rather like flour, as yellow as egg yolk, slightly sweet and very nutritious. It is eaten like banana or sweet potato, cooked or baked in ashes, and is as healthy as it tastes good. Indians and missionaries vie in praising this magnificent palm, which could be called the peach palm. In these wild regions I was reminded of Linnaeus's assertion that the country of palm trees was man's first abode, and that man is essentially palmivorous.[3] When we examined what food the Indians stored in their huts we noticed that their diet depends as much on the fruit of the *pirijao* as on cassava and banana.

At San Fernando, and in the neighboring villages of San Baltasar and Javita, the missionaries live in attractive houses, covered in liana and surrounded by gardens. The tall *pirijao* were the most decorative part of the plantation. In our walks the head of the mission told us about his incursions up the Guaviare river. He reminded us how these journeys, undertaken for the 'conquest of souls', are eagerly anticipated by the Indians. All the Indians enjoy taking part, even old men and women. Under the pretext of recovering neophytes who have deserted the village, children of eight to ten are kidnapped and distributed among the missionary Indians as serfs, or *poitos*.

As soon as you enter the basin of the Atabapo river everything changes: the air, the colour of the water, the shape of the river-side trees. By day you no longer suffer the torment of mosquitoes; and their long-legged cousins the *zancudos* become rare at night. Beyond the San Fernando mission these nocturnal insects disappear altogether. The Orinoco waters are turbid, full of earthy matter, and in the coves give off a faint musky smell from the amount of dead crocodiles and other putrefying animals. To drink that water we had to filter it through a linen cloth. The waters of the Atabapo, on the other hand, are pure, taste good, are without smell, and appear brownish in reflected light and yellow under the sun.

The extreme purity of the black waters is confirmed by their transparency, and by the way they clearly reflect all the surrounding objects. The minutest fish are visible at a depth of 20 or 30 feet. It is easy to see the river bottom, which is not muddy but composed of a dazzlingly white granite or quartz sand. Nothing can be compared to the beauty of the Atabapo river banks, overloaded with vegetation, among which rise the palms with plumed leaves, reflected in the river water. The green of the reflected image seems as real as the object seen with your eyes.

Contrary to geographers, the Indians of San Fernando claim that the Orinoco rises from two rivers, the Guaviare and the Paragua. This latter name they give to the Upper Orinoco. Following their hypothesis they say the Casiquiare is not a branch of the Orinoco, but of the Paragua. If you look at my map you will see these names are quite arbitrary. It does not matter if you do not call the Orinoco the Paragua as long as you trace the rivers as they actually are in nature and do not separate rivers that form part of the same river system with mountain chains. The Paragua, or that part of the Orinoco east of the mouth of the Guaviare, has clearer, purer, more transparent water than the part of the Orinoco below San Fernando. The waters of the Guaviare are white and turbid and have the same taste, according to the Indians whose sense organs are very delicate and well tested, as the Orinoco waters near the Great Cataracts. 'Give me water from three or four great rivers of this country,' an old Indian from the Javita mission said, 'and I will tell you by tasting them where they come from; whether it is a white or black river, whether it is the Atabapo, Paragua or Guaviare.' European geographers are wrong not to admit to seeing things as Indians do, for they are the geographers of their own country.

APRIL 26TH. We advanced only 2 or 3 leagues, and spent the night on a rock near the Indian plantations or *conucos* of Guapasoso. As the river floods and spills over into the jungle, you lose sight of the banks and can moor only to a rock or small tableland rising above the water. In these granite rocks I found no cavity (druse), no crystallized substance, not even rock crystal, and no trace of pyrites or other metallic substances. I mention this detail on account of the chimerical ideas that have spread following Berrio's and Raleigh's voyages about 'the immense riches of the great and fine empire of Guiana'.[4]

In the Atabapo, above San Fernando, there are no longer any crocodiles; every now and then you come across some *bavas*, numerous freshwater dolphins, but no manatees. You would not find tapirs, nor araguato monkeys, nor howler monkeys, *zamuros*, or *guacharacas*, a kind of crested pheasant. However, enormous water snakes similar to boas are very common and endanger Indian bathers. From the first day we saw them swimming past our canoes, reaching 14 feet in length.

APRIL 27TH. The night was beautiful; black clouds crossed the sky with surprising speed. Guapasoso's latitude was 3.53' 55". The black waters served as my horizon. I was all the more delighted to make this observation as in the white-water rivers from the Apure to the Orinoco we had been cruelly bitten by mosquitoes, as Bonpland recorded the hours with the chronometer, and I myself adjusted the horizon. At two we left the Guapasoso *conucos*, going south and upstream as the river, at least that part of it free of trees, began to narrow. At sunrise it started to rain. In these forests we no longer heard the cries of the howler monkeys. Dolphins, or *toninas*, played by the side of our boat. At about midday we passed the mouth of the Ipurichapano river, and a little later the granite rock called Piedra del Tigre. We later regretted not resting near this rock as we had some problems trying to find a spot of dry land large enough upon which to light a fire and set up our hammocks and instruments.

APRIL 28TH. It poured with rain as soon as the sun set and we were worried about the damage to our collections. The poor missionary suffered one of his fever attacks and begged us to leave before midnight. After passing the Guarinuma rapids the Indians pointed out the ruins of the Mendaxari mission, abandoned some time back. On the east bank of the river, near the little rock of Kemarumo in the middle of Indian plantations, we saw a gigantic ceiba (the *Bombax ceiba*). We landed to measure it; it was some 120 feet high, with a diameter of 14 or 15 feet.

APRIL 29TH. The air was cooler, and without *zancudos*, but the clouds blocked out all the stars. I begin to miss the Lower Orinoco as the strong current slowed our progress. We stopped for most of the day, looking for plants. It was night when we reached the San Baltasar mission or, as the monks call it, *la divina pastora de Baltasar de Atabapo*. We lodged with a Catalan missionary, a lively and friendly man who, in the middle of the jungle, displayed the activities of his people. He had planted a wonderful orchard where European figs grew with persea, and lemon trees with mamey. The village was built with a regularity typical of Protestant Germany or America. Here we saw for the first time that white and spongy substance which I have made known as *dapicho* and *zapis*. We saw that this stuff was similar to elastic resin. But through sign language the Indians made us think that it came from under ground so we first thought that maybe it was a fossil rubber. A Poimisano Indian was sitting by a fire in the missionary hut transforming *dapicho* into black rubber. He had stuck several bits on to thin sticks and was roasting it by the fire like meat. As it melts and becomes elastic the *dapicho* blackens. The Indian then beat the black mass with a club made of Brazilwood and then kneaded the *dapicho* into small balls some 3 to 4 inches thick, and let them cool. The balls appear identical to rubber though the surface remains slightly sticky. At San Baltasar they are not used for the game of pelota that Indians play in Uruana and Encaramada but are cut up and used as more effective corks than those made from cork itself. In front of the Casa de los Solteros—the house where unmarried men lived—the missionary showed us a drum made from a hollow cylinder of wood. This drum was beaten with great lumps of *dapicho* serving as drumsticks. The drum has openings that could be blocked by hand to vary the sounds, and was hanging on two light supports. Wild Indians love noisy music. Drums and *botutos*, the baked-earth trumpets, are indispensable instruments when Indians decide to play music and make a show.

APRIL 30TH. We continued upstream on the Atabapo for five miles, then instead of following this river to its source, where it is called the Atacavi, we entered the Temi river. Before reaching this tributary, near the Guasacavi mouth, a granite outcrop on the west bank fixed our attention: it is called the rock of the Guahiba Indian woman, or the Mother Rock, the Piedra de la Madre. Father Zea could not explain its bizarre name, but a few weeks later another missionary told us a story that stirred up painful feelings. If, in these deserted places, man leaves hardly any traces behind him, it is doubly humiliating for a European to see in the name of a rock a memory of the moral degradation of whites that contrasts the virtue of a wild Indian with the barbarity of civilized men!

In 1797 the San Fernando missionary had led his men to the banks of the Guaviare river on one of those hostile incursions banned both by religion and Spanish law. They found a Guahiba mother with three children in a hut, two of whom were not yet adults. They were busy preparing cassava flour. Resistance was impossible; their father had gone out fishing, so the mother tried to run off with her children. She had just reached the savannah when the Indians, who hunt people the way whites hunt blacks in Africa, caught her. The mother and children were tied up and brought back to the river bank. The monks were waiting for this expedition to end, without suffering any of the dangers. Had the mother resisted the Indians would have killed her; anything is allowed in this hunting of souls (*conquista espiritual*), and it is especially children that are captured and treated as *poitos* or slaves in the Christian missions. They brought the prisoners to San Fernando, hoping that the mother would not find her way back by land to her home. Separated from those children who had gone fishing with their father the day she was kidnapped, this poor woman began to show signs of the deepest despair. She wanted to bring those children in the power of the missionaries back home, and several times ran off with them from the San Fernando village but the Indians hunted her down each time. After severely punishing her the missionary took the cruel decision of separating the mother from her two infants. She was led alone to a mission on the Río Negro, up the Atabapo river. Loosely tied up, she sat in the bow of the boat. She had not been told where she was going; but she guessed by the sun's position that she was being taken away from her house and native land. She managed to break her bonds and jumped into the water and swam to the river bank. The current pushed her to a bank of rock, which is named after her today. She climbed up and walked into the jungle. But the head of the mission ordered his Indians to follow and capture her. She was again caught by the evening. She was stretched out on the rock (the Piedra de la Madre) where she was beaten with manatee whips. Her hands tied up behind her back with the strong cords of the *mavacure*, she was then dragged to the Javita mission and thrown into one of the inns called *casas del rey*. It was the rainy season and the night was very dark. Impenetrable forests separate the Javita and San Fernando missions some

25 leagues apart in a straight line. The only known route was by river. Nobody ever tried to go by land from one mission to another, even if only a few leagues away. But this did not prevent a mother separated from her children. Her children were at San Fernando so she had to find them, rescue them from Christians, and bring them back to their father on the Guaviare. The Guahiba woman was not closely supervised in the inn. As her hands were bloodied the Javita Indians had loosened her bindings. With her teeth she managed to break the cords, and she disappeared into the night. On the fourth day she was seen prowling round the hut where her children were being kept at the San Fernando mission. 'This woman had just carried out,' added the monk telling us this sad story, 'something that the toughest Indian would not have even considered.' She had crossed the jungle in a season when the sky is continuously covered with cloud, when the sun appears only for a few minutes for days on end. Had she followed the flow of water? But flooding had forced her to walk far from the river, in the middle of jungles where the river is imperceptible. How many times must she have been blocked by thorny liana growing round trees! How many times must she have swum across streams! What on earth could this luckless woman have eaten during her four days' walk? She said that she had eaten only those large black ants called *vachacos* that climb up trees and hang resinous nests from branches. We pressed the missionary to tell us whether the Guahiba woman had finally enjoyed peace and happiness with her family. He did not want to satisfy our curiosity. But on our return from the Río Negro we learned that this Indian woman was not even left to recover from her wounds before she was again separated from her children, and sent to a mission on the Upper Orinoco. She died by refusing to eat food, as do all Indians when faced with great calamities.[5]

Such is the memory attached to this fatal rock called the Piedra de la Madre. If I have dawdled over this touching story of maternal love in an often vilified race, it is because I wanted to make public this story heard from monks to prove that even missions should obey laws.

Wherever the Temi forms bays the jungle is flooded for more than half a square league. To avoid the bends and shorten our journey the Indians leave the river bed and go south along paths or *sendas*, that is, canals, some 4 or 5 feet wide. The depth of the water rarely exceeds half a fathom. These *sendas* are formed in the flooded jungle like paths in dry land.

Whenever they could the Indians crossed from one mission to another along the same path in their pirogues. But as the passage is narrow the thick vegetation sometimes leads to surprises. An Indian stands in the bow with his machete, incessantly cutting branches blocking the canal. In the thickest part of the jungle we heard an odd noise. As the Indian cut at some branches a school of *toninas*—freshwater dolphins— surrounded our boat. The animals had hidden under branches of a ceiba and escaped through the flooded jungle, squirting up water and compressed air, living up to their name of 'blowers'. What a strange sight, inland, 300 to 400 leagues from the Orinoco and Amazon mouths!

MAY 1ST. . . .

The jungle between Javita and Caño Pimichín holds a quantity of gigantic trees: ocoteas, laurels, *curvana*, *jacio*, *iacifate*, with a red wood like Brazilwood, *guamufate*, the *Amyris caraña* and the *mani*. All these trees top 100 feet. As their trunks throw out branches more than 100 feet high we had trouble getting flowers and leaves. Though the ground was strewn with foliage we could not rely on the Indians to tell us from which tree or liana they came. In the midst of such natural riches, our herborizations caused us more regret than satisfaction. What we managed to collect seemed without interest in comparison with what we might have collected. It rained without a break for several months and Bonpland lost the greater part of the specimens he had dried with artificial heat. Usually Indians name trees by chewing the bark. They distinguish leaves better than flowers or fruit. Busy in locating timber for canoes they are inattentive to flowers. 'None of those tall trees have flowers or fruit,' they continually repeated. Like the botanists of antiquity, they denied what they had not bothered to observe. Tired by our questions they, in turn, made us impatient.

Every day we went into the jungle to see how our canoe was advancing over land. Twenty-three Indians were dragging it by placing logs as rollers. Usually this takes a day and a half, but our canoe was very large. As we also had to pass the cataracts a second time it was necessary to be very careful about not scraping it on the ground.

In this same jungle we at last were able to solve the problem of the supposed fossil rubber that the Indians call *dapicho*. The old Indian captain Javita led us to a small stream that runs into the Tuamini. He showed us how to dig some two to three feet deep into the muddy ground between the roots of two trees: the *jacio* and the *curvana*. The first is the hevea or siphonia of modern botany, which yields rubber; the second has pinnate leaves its juice is milky but very diluted and barely sticky. It appears that *dapicho* is formed when the latex oozes out from the roots, especially when the tree is very old and begins to decay inside its trunk. The bark and sapwood crack to achieve naturally what man himself must do to gather latex.

Four days had passed and our boat still had not reached the Pimichín river landing-stage. 'There is nothing you lack in my mission,' Father Cerezo said to us. 'There are bananas and fish; at night mosquitoes do not bite; and the longer you stay the more likely it is that you will be able to observe stars. If your boat is wrecked during the portage we will get you another one and I will enjoy living a few more weeks *con gente blanco y de razón* (with white and rational people).' Despite our impatience, we listened with interest to this missionary's stories confirming all that we had been told about the spiritual state of the Indians in that region. They live in isolated clans of forty to fifty people under a chief. They recognize a common cacique only in times of war with neighbors. Between these clans mutual mistrust is great, as even those who live near each other speak different languages. Such is the labyrinth of these rivers that families settled themselves without knowing what tribe lived nearest to them. In Spanish Guiana a mountain or a jungle just half a league wide separates clans who would need two days navigating along rivers to meet. In the impenetrable jungle of the torrid zone rivers increase the dismemberment of great nations, favor the transition of dialects into separate languages, and nourish distrust and national hatred. Men avoid each other because they do not understand each other, and hate because they fear.

When we carefully examine this wild part of America we imagine how it was in primitive times when the land was peopled in stages, and seem to be present at the birth of human societies. In the New World we do not see the progressive developments of civilization, those moments of rest, those stations in the lives of a people. Such is the wonderful fertility of nature that the Indian's field is a patch of land. To clear it means setting fire to branches. To farm means dropping a few seeds into the ground. However far back in time you go in thought in these dense jungles the Indians have got their food from the earth, but as this earth produces abundantly on a small patch, without much work, these people often change their homes along the river banks. Still today, the Orinoco Indians travel with their seeds, transporting what they cultivate (*conucos*), like the Arab does his tents.

. . .

MAY 6TH. We set off at dawn after inspecting the bottom of our canoe. We counted on our boat surviving another three hundred leagues of navigation down the Río Negro, up the Casiquiare and back down the Orinoco again to Angostura. The Pimichín is about as wide as the Seine in Paris but little trees that like water narrow the river so much that only a canal of some fifteen to twenty toises remains. This *caño* is navigable all year round. After following it for four hours we at last reached the Río Negro.

The morning was fresh and beautiful. For thirty-six days we had been locked up in a narrow canoe which was so unsteady that standing up suddenly from your seat would have capsized it. We had cruelly suffered from insect bites, but we had survived this unhealthy climate, and had crossed the many waterfalls and dykes that block the rivers and make the journey more dangerous than crossing the seas, without sinking. After all that we had endured, it gives me pleasure to speak of the joy we felt in having reached a tributary of the Amazon, of having passed the isthmus that separates the two great river systems. The uninhabited banks of the Casiquiare, covered in jungle, busied my imagination. In this interior of a new continent you get used to seeing man as not essential to the natural order. The earth is overloaded with vegetation: nothing prevents its development. An immense layer of mould manifests the uninterrupted action of organic forces. Crocodile and boa are the masters of the river; jaguar, peccary, the dante and monkeys cross the jungle without fear or danger, established there in an ancient heritage. This view of a living nature where man is nothing is both odd and sad. Here, in a fertile land, in an eternal greenness, you search in vain for traces of man; you feel you are carried into a different world from the one you were born into.

END NOTES

1. *whose location I was the first to establish . . . the Casiquiare:* Sailing down the Casiquiare was Humboldt's greatest exploratory achievement. The Casiquiare canal was known to La Condamine, but not actually explored by him. A.R. Wallace followed Humboldt's 'illustrious' trail from Brazil in 1851; see *Travels on the Rio Negro* (1853), chs. 8–10. For a modern trip, accompanied by Humboldt's travelogue, see Redmond O'Hanlon, *In Trouble Again: A Journey between the Orinoco and the Amazon* (London, 1988).
2. Here Humboldt interrupts his narrative by gathering together all his observations and readings about the San Fernando mission.
3. *Linnaeus's assertion . . . palmivorous:* Humboldt refers to Linnaeus, *Systema naturae,* in Latin, vol. 1 (1735), p. 24.
4. *Berrio's and Raleigh's . . . Guiana:* Humboldt cites Raleigh's 'pompously' titled *The Discovery of the Large, Rich and Beautiful Empire of Guiana* (London, 1596). Raleigh sailed for the Orinoco in 1595 and again in 1616. Antonio de Berrio's first expedition up the Orinoco in search of El Dorado was in 1586. He was guided by a Spanish soldier who had been taken there blindfolded, so he could not remember the way back. In 1590 Berrio, now governor of El Dorado, tried again. See Edward J. Goodman (1972), p. 80.
5. *Piedra de la Madre . . . great calamities:* Humboldt in this tale airs his age's sentimentalities about the 'sanctity of motherhood'. Redmond O'Hanlon retells this story in Helen Maria Williams's words in *In Trouble Again* (London, 1988), pp. 134–6.

QUESTIONS

1. How does Humboldt use all of his senses to learn about the lands and waters he travels through?
2. What, according to Humboldt, can Europeans learn from the Indians?
3. What account does Humboldt give of relations between the Indians and the missionaries who live among them? Why does he recount the story behind the "Mother Rock"?
4. What is the impact of water and rivers on Indian culture?

THE IRON LAW OF POPULATION GROWTH

Thomas Malthus

Thomas Malthus was born in Guilford, England, in 1766, the second and last son among eight siblings. In 1784 he was sent to Jesus College, Cambridge, and soon became an academic star. Malthus mastered the chief European languages, acquired a thorough knowledge of history, and attained high honors in mathematics. In 1788 he graduated and, like many educated men of his day, became a clergyman. It was in 1798 that Malthus's talents became known to the public. In that year he anonymously published his Essay on the Principle of Population. *The work was inspired by Malthus's interests in both mathematics and social observation. It is now recognized as Europe's first systematic study of population growth. The* Essay *achieved instant fame in some quarters, and instant notoriety in others. From 1799 until 1802, Malthus traveled in Europe, observing the varied social behavior on the Continent. In 1803 he published a longer and more scientific version of his* Essay. *Malthus became Britain's first professor of political economy in 1805 (at the East India College), and he continued to publish works on economic subjects. In 1811 Malthus initiated a correspondence with the famous economist David Ricardo. By this time he was himself a leading figure in the new discipline of political economy. Thomas Malthus died in 1834.*

Malthus's Essay on the Principle of Population *offers a scientific model of human population growth. Its central premise is that populations tend to grow geometrically (perhaps doubling every twenty-five years), and that food*

Reprinted from *Essay on the Principle of Population*, first published in 1798 and revised in 1803.

production can never keep pace with this growth. Populations are thus forced into equilibrium, either by deliberate effort or (more likely) by catastrophes such as famine. Efforts to improve the condition of an expanding lower class are, in Malthus's view, doomed to fail because they attempt to defy the iron law of population growth. Malthus thus opposed social legislation such as the English Poor Law. The pessimism of Malthus made him deeply unpopular in many quarters (Marx despised his work). But classical economists and later social Darwinians embraced the cold logic of the Malthusian system. Malthus's conclusions have been modified today in many particulars, but he remains the grandfather of modern population studies.

It is an obvious truth, which has been taken notice of by many writers, that population must always be kept down to the level of the means of subsistence; but no writer that the Author recollects has inquired particularly into the means by which this level is effected: and it is a view of these means which forms, to his mind, the strongest obstacle in the way to any very great future improvement of society. He hopes it will appear that, in the discussion of this interesting subject, he is actuated solely by a love of truth, and not by any prejudices against any particular set of men, or of opinions. He professes to have read some of the speculations on the future improvement of society in a temper very different from a wish to find them visionary, but he has not acquired that command over his understanding which would enable him to believe what he wishes, without evidence, or to refuse his assent to what might be unpleasing, when accompanied with evidence.

The view which he has given of human life has a melancholy hue, but he feels conscious that he has drawn these dark tints from a conviction that they are really in the picture, and not from a jaundiced eye or an inherent spleen of disposition.

. . .

The great and unlooked for discoveries that have taken place of late years in natural philosophy, the increasing diffusion of general knowledge from the extension of the art of printing, the ardent and unshackled spirit of inquiry that prevails throughout the lettered and even unlettered world, the new and extraordinary lights that have been thrown on political subjects which dazzle and astonish the understanding, and particularly that tremendous phenomenon in the political horizon, the French Revolution, which, like a blazing comet, seems destined either to inspire with fresh life and vigour, or to scorch up and destroy the shrinking inhabitants of the earth, have all concurred to lead many able men into the opinion that we were touching on a period big with the most important changes, changes that would in some measure be decisive of the future fate of mankind.

It has been said that the great question is now at issue, whether man shall henceforth start forwards with accelerated velocity towards illimitable, and hitherto unconceived improvement, or be condemned to a perpetual oscillation between happiness and misery, and after every effort remain still at an immeasurable distance from the wished-for goal.

Yet, anxiously as every friend of mankind must look forwards to the termination of this painful suspense, and eagerly as the inquiring mind would hail every ray of light that might assist its view into futurity, it is much to be lamented that the writers on each side of this momentous question still keep far aloof from each other. Their mutual arguments do not meet with a candid examination. The question is not brought to rest on fewer points, and even in theory scarcely seems to be approaching to a decision.

The advocate for the present order of things is apt to treat the sect of speculative philosophers either as a set of artful and designing knaves who preach up ardent benevolence and draw captivating pictures of a happier state of society only the better to enable them to destroy the present establishments and to forward their own deep-laid schemes of ambition, or as wild and mad-headed enthusiasts whose silly speculations and absurd paradoxes are not worthy the attention of any reasonable man.

The advocate for the perfectibility of man, and of society, retorts on the defender of establishments a more than equal contempt. He brands him as the slave of the most miserable and narrow prejudices; or as the defender of the abuses of civil society only because he profits by them. He paints him either as a character who prostitutes his understanding to his interest, or as one whose powers of mind are not of a size to grasp any thing great and noble, who cannot see above five yards before him, and who must therefore be utterly unable to take in the views of the enlightened benefactor of mankind.

144

In this unamicable contest the cause of truth cannot but suffer. The really good arguments on each side of the question are not allowed to have their proper weight. Each pursues his own theory, little solicitous to correct or improve it by an attention to what is advanced by his opponents.

The friend of the present order of things condemns all political speculations in the gross. He will not even condescend to examine the grounds from which the perfectibility of society is inferred. Much less will he give himself the trouble in a fair and candid manner to attempt an exposition of their fallacy.

The speculative philosopher equally offends against the cause of truth. With eyes fixed on a happier state of society, the blessings of which he paints in the most captivating colors, he allows himself to indulge in the most bitter invectives against every present establishment, without applying his talents to consider the best and safest means of removing abuses and without seeming to be aware of the tremendous obstacles that threaten, even in theory, to oppose the progress of man towards perfection.

It is an acknowledged truth in philosophy that a just theory will always be confirmed by experiment. Yet so much friction, and so many minute circumstances occur in practice, which it is next to impossible for the most enlarged and penetrating mind to foresee, that on few subjects can any theory be pronounced just, till all the arguments against it have been maturely weighed and clearly and consistently refuted.

I have read some of the speculations on the perfectibility of man and of society with great pleasure. I have been warmed and delighted with the enchanting picture which they hold forth. I ardently wish for such happy improvements. But I see great, and, to my understanding, unconquerable difficulties in the way to them. These difficulties it is my present purpose to state, declaring, at the same time, that so far from exulting in them, as a cause of triumph over the friends of innovation, nothing would give me greater pleasure than to see them completely removed.

. . .

I think I may fairly make two postulata.

First, That food is necessary to the existence of man.

Secondly, That the passion between the sexes is necessary and will remain nearly in its present state.

These two laws, ever since we have had any knowledge of mankind, appear to have been fixed laws of our nature, and, as we have not hitherto seen any alteration in them, we have no right to conclude that they will ever cease to be what they now are, without an immediate act of power in that Being who first arranged the system of the universe, and for the advantage of his creatures, still executes, according to fixed laws, all its various operations.

. . .

Assuming then my postulata as granted, I say, that the power of population is indefinitely greater than the power in the earth to produce subsistence for man.

Population, when unchecked, increases in a geometrical ratio. Subsistence increases only in an arithmetical ratio. A slight acquaintance with numbers will shew the immensity of the first power in comparison of the second.

By that law of our nature which makes food necessary to the life of man, the effects of these two unequal powers must be kept equal.

This implies a strong and constantly operating check on population from the difficulty of subsistence. This difficulty must fall somewhere and must necessarily be severely felt by a large portion of mankind.

. . .

To remedy the frequent distresses of the common people, the poor laws of England have been instituted; but it is to be feared, that though they may have alleviated a little the intensity of individual misfortune, they have spread the general evil over a much larger surface. It is a subject often started in conversation and mentioned always as a matter of great surprise that, notwithstanding the immense sum that is annually collected for the poor in England, there is still so much distress among them. Some think that the money must be embezzled, others that the churchwardens and overseers consume the greater part of it in dinners. All agree that somehow or other it must be very ill-managed. In short the fact that nearly three millions are collected annually for the poor and yet that their distresses are not removed is the subject of continual astonishment. But a man who sees a little below the surface of things would be very much more astonished if the fact were otherwise than it is observed to be, or even if a collection universally of eighteen shillings in the pound, instead of four, were materially to alter it. I will state a case which I hope will elucidate my meaning.

Suppose that by a subscription of the rich the eighteen pence a day which men earn now was made up five shillings, it might be imagined, perhaps, that they would then be able to live comfortably and have a piece of meat every day for their dinners. But this would be a very false conclusion. The transfer of three shillings and sixpence a day to every laborer would not increase the quantity of meat in the country. There is not at present enough for all to have a decent share. What would then be the consequence? The competition among the buyers in the market of meat would rapidly raise the price from sixpence or sevenpence, to two or three shillings in the pound, and the commodity would not be divided among many more than it is at present. When an article is scarce, and cannot be distributed to all, he that can shew the most valid patent, that is, he that offers most money, becomes the possessor. If we can suppose the competition among the buyers of meat to continue long enough for a greater number of cattle to be reared annually, this could only be done at the expense of the corn, which would be a very disadvantagous exchange, for it is well known that the country could not then support the same population, and when subsistence is scarce in proportion to the number of people, it is of little consequence whether the lowest members of the society possess eighteen pence or five shillings. They must at all events be reduced to live upon the hardest fare and in the smallest quantity.

It will be said, perhaps, that the increased number of purchasers in every article would give a spur to productive industry and that the whole produce of the island would be increased. This might in some degree be the case. But the spur that these fancied riches would give to population would more than counterbalance it, and the increased produce would be to be divided among a more than proportionably increased number of people. All this time I am supposing that the same quantity of work would be done as before. But this would not really take place. The receipt of five shillings a day, instead of eighteen pence, would make every man fancy himself comparatively rich and able to indulge himself in many hours or days of leisure. This would give a strong and immediate check to productive industry, and, in a short time, not only the nation would be poorer, but

147

the lower classes themselves would be much more distressed than when they received only eighteen pence a day.

A collection from the rich of eighteen shillings in the pound, even if distributed in the most judicious manner, would have a little the same effect as that resulting from the supposition I have just made, and no possible contributions or sacrifices of the rich, particularly in money, could for any time prevent the recurrence of distress among the lower members of society, whoever they were. Great changes might, indeed, be made. The rich might become poor, and some of the poor rich, but a part of the society must necessarily feel a difficulty of living, and this difficulty will naturally fall on the least fortunate members.

It may at first appear strange, but I believe it is true, that I cannot by means of money raise a poor man and enable him to live much better than he did before, without proportionably depressing others in the same class. If I retrench the quantity of food consumed in my house, and give him what I have cut off, I then benefit him, without depressing any but myself and family, who, perhaps, may be well able to bear it. If I turn up a piece of uncultivated land, and give him the produce, I then benefit both him and all the members of the society, because what he before consumed is thrown into the common stock, and probably some of the new produce with it. But if I only give him money, supposing the produce of the country to remain the same, I give him a title to a larger share of that produce than formerly, which share he cannot receive without diminishing the shares of others. It is evident that this effect, in individual instances, must be so small as to be totally imperceptible; but still it must exist, as many other effects do, which, like some of the insects that people the air, elude our grosser perceptions.

Supposing the quantity of food in any country to remain the same for many years together, it is evident that this food must be divided according to the value of each man's patent, or the sum of money that he can afford to spend on this commodity so universally in request. It is a demonstrative truth, therefore, that the patents of one set of men could not be increased in value without diminishing the value of the patents of some other set of men. If the rich were to subscribe and give five shillings a day to five hundred thousand men without retrenching their own tables, no doubt can exist, that as these men would naturally live more at their ease and consume a greater quantity of provisions, there would be less food remaining to

148

divide among the rest, and consequently each man's patent would be diminished in value or the same number of pieces of silver would purchase a smaller quantity of subsistence. (Mr Godwin calls the wealth that a man receives from his ancestors a mouldy patent. It may, I think, very properly be termed a patent, but I hardly see the propriety of calling it a mouldy one, as it is an article in such constant use.)

An increase of population without a proportional increase of food will evidently have the same effect in lowering the value of each man's patent. The food must necessarily be distributed in smaller quantities, and consequently a day's labor will purchase a smaller quantity of provisions. An increase in the price of provisions would arise either from an increase of population faster than the means of subsistence, or from a different distribution of the money of the society. The food of a country that has been long occupied, if it be increasing, increases slowly and regularly and cannot be made to answer any sudden demands, but variations in the distribution of the money of a society are not infrequently occurring, and are undoubtedly among the causes that occasion the continual variations which we observe in the price of provisions.

The poor laws of England tend to depress the general condition of the poor in these two ways. Their first obvious tendency is to increase population without increasing the food for its support. A poor man may marry with little or no prospect of being able to support a family in independence. They may be said therefore in some measure to create the poor which they maintain, and as the provisions of the country must, in consequence of the increased population, be distributed to every man in smaller proportions, it is evident that the labor of those who are not supported by parish assistance will purchase a smaller quantity of provisions than before and consequently more of them must be driven to ask for support.

Secondly, the quantity of provisions consumed in workhouses upon a part of the society that cannot in general be considered as the most valuable part diminishes the shares that would otherwise belong to more industrious and more worthy members, and thus in the same manner forces more to become dependent. If the poor in the workhouses were to live better than they now do, this new distribution of the money of the society would tend more conspicuously to depress the condition of those out of the workhouses by occasioning a rise in the price of provisions.

Fortunately for England, a spirit of independence still remains among the peasantry. The poor laws are strongly calculated to eradicate this spirit. They have succeeded in part, but had they succeeded as completely as might have been expected their pernicious tendency would not have been so long concealed.

Hard as it may appear in individual instances, dependent poverty ought to be held disgraceful. Such a stimulus seems to be absolutely necessary to promote the happiness of the great mass of mankind, and every general attempt to weaken this stimulus, however benevolent its apparent intention, will always defeat its own purpose. If men are induced to marry from a prospect of parish provision, with little or no chance of maintaining their families in independence, they are not only unjustly tempted to bring unhappiness and dependence upon themselves and children, but they are tempted, without knowing it, to injure all in the same class with themselves. A laborer who marries without being able to support a family may in some respects be considered as an enemy to all his fellow-laborers.

I feel no doubt whatever that the parish laws of England have contributed to raise the price of provisions and to lower the real price of labor. They have therefore contributed to impoverish that class of people whose only possession is their labor. It is also difficult to suppose that they have not powerfully contributed to generate that carelessness and want of frugality observable among the poor, so contrary to the disposition frequently to be remarked among petty tradesmen and small farmers. The laboring poor, to use a vulgar expression, seem always to live from hand to mouth. Their present wants employ their whole attention, and they seldom think of the future. Even when they have an opportunity of saving they seldom exercise it, but all that is beyond their present necessities goes, generally speaking, to the ale-house. The poor laws of England may therefore be said to diminish both the power and the will to save among the common people, and thus to weaken one of the strongest incentives to sobriety and industry, and consequently to happiness.

It is a general complaint among master manufacturers that high wages ruin all their workmen, but it is difficult to conceive that these men would not save a part of their high wages for the future support of their families, instead of spending it in drunkenness and dissipation, if they did not rely on parish assistance for support in case of accidents. And that the poor employed in manufactures consider this assistance as a reason why they may spend all the wages they earn and enjoy themselves while they can appears to be evident from the number of families that, upon the failure of any great manufactory, immediately fall upon the parish, when perhaps the wages earned in this manufactory while it flourished were sufficiently above the price of common country labour to have allowed them to save enough for their support till they could find some other channel for their industry.

A man who might not be deterred from going to the ale-house from the consideration that on his death, or sickness, he should leave his wife and family upon the parish might yet hesitate in thus dissipating his earnings if he were assured that, in either of these cases, his family must starve or be left to the support of casual bounty. In China, where the real as well as nominal price of labor is very low, sons are yet obliged by law to support their aged and helpless parents. Whether such a law would be advisable in this country I will not pretend to determine. But it seems at any rate highly improper, by positive institutions, which render dependent poverty so general, to weaken that disgrace, which for the best and most humane reasons ought to attach to it.

The mass of happiness among the common people cannot but be diminished when one of the strongest checks to idleness and dissipation is thus removed, and when men are thus allured to marry with little or no prospect of being able to maintain a family in independence. Every obstacle in the way of marriage must undoubtedly be considered as a species of unhappiness.

. . .

The poor laws of England were undoubtedly instituted for the most benevolent purpose, but there is great reason to think that they have not succeeded in their intention. They certainly mitigate some cases of very severe distress which might otherwise occur, yet the state of the poor who are supported by parishes, considered in all its circumstances, is very far from being free from misery. But one of the principal objections to them is that for this assistance which some of the poor receive, in itself almost a doubtful blessing, the whole class of the common people of England is subjected to a set of grating, inconvenient, and tyrannical laws, totally inconsistent with the genuine spirit of the constitution. The whole business of settlements, even in its present amended state, is utterly contradictory to all ideas of freedom. The parish persecution of men whose families are likely to become chargeable, and of poor women who are near lying-in, is a most disgraceful and disgusting tyranny. And the obstructions continually occasioned in the market of labor by these laws have a constant tendency to add to the difficulties of those who are struggling to support themselves without assistance.

These evils attendant on the poor laws are in some degree irremediable. If assistance is to be distributed to a certain class of people, a power must be given somewhere of discriminating the proper objects and of managing the concerns of the institutions that are necessary, but any great interference with the affairs of other people is a species of tyranny, and in the common course of things the exercise of this power may be expected to become grating to those who are driven to ask for support. The tyranny of Justices, Churchwardens, and Overseers, is a common complaint among the poor, but the fault does not lie so much in these persons, who probably, before they were in power, were not worse than other people, but in the nature of all such institutions.

The evil is perhaps gone too far to be remedied, but I feel little doubt in my own mind that if the poor laws had never existed, though there might have been a few more instances of very severe distress, yet that the aggregate mass of happiness among the common people would have been much greater than it is at present.

QUESTIONS

1. Why was Malthus not "an advocate for the perfectibility of man"? What was his view of the future?
2. What are Malthus's two postulata? What makes them laws, as he calls them? What are the consequences of the operation of these two laws?
3. Why does Malthus believe that England's poor laws have made matters worse rather than better? Why would raising wages not help the working poor, according to Malthus?
4. What moral assumptions underlie Malthus's view of humans generally and of the poor in particular? Where do these assumptions show themselves?

COMMISSIONER LIN'S LETTER TO THE QUEEN

Lin Zexu

After hotly debating what to do about the increasing flow of illegal opium into China from British India, the Daoguang emperor (r. 1821–1850) decided to crack down on the smuggling trade and the corruption that allowed it to flourish. He appointed respected scholar-official Lin Zexu (Lin Tse-hsu, 1785–1850) his Imperial Commissioner to lead the effort. Commissioner Lin arrived in the city of Canton—the center of foreign trade—in March 1939 with a mandate to wipe out China's opium problem. Lin implemented a comprehensive plan that sought to cure those who smoked opium; punish those who sold and distributed it; and eliminate the foreign source of the drug.

For the British, Chinese restrictions on the opium trade were only part of a larger problem. British merchants wanted full access to the rich markets of China, particularly the tea-growing regions, but the Qing Dynasty (1644–1911) had confined foreign traders since the late 1700s to the port of Canton (Guangzhou) in Guangdong (Kwangtung) Province, where many restrictions limited their movements and their ability to do business. The new anti-opium campaign brought dissatisfaction on both sides to a head. Commissioner Lin took his charge seriously, and when negotiations with Captain Charles Elliot, British Superintendent of Trade, failed to produce results he desired, Lin resorted to force, blockading the opium merchants in their warehouses until Elliot ordered the handover of the stockpiled drug. The

Reprinted from Lin Zexu's July 1839 letter to Queen Victoria, published in *Ch'ou-pan i-wu shih-mo (A Complete Account of the Management of Barbarian Affairs)* of the Tao-kuang period, 1836–1850.

Chinese destroyed more than twenty thousand chests of the lucrative com-
modity (a chest contained from 130 lbs to 170 lbs of opium), but Elliot's order
made the British government liable for compensating the merchants for their
loss. The British also objected to subjecting their citizens to what they saw as
overly harsh, barbaric Chinese law, particularly because opium smuggling
was now a capital crime.

It was at this point that Lin composed his famous missive to Queen
Victoria, and it is quite revealing of the mindset of the Chinese government
and Chinese officialdom at the time. The letter was never delivered, allegedly
because it was not submitted according to British protocol, but its moralistic,
condescending tone was not likely to have garnered results. The Opium War
(1839–1842) that erupted after Lin's actions resulted in a humiliating defeat
for the Chinese, and revealed the deficiencies of its military. Lin was sacked
and exiled. However, his talents were still recognized and he was called back
to service and died en route to a new post.

LIN TSE-HSÜ'S MORAL ADVICE TO QUEEN VICTORIA, 1839[1]

A communication: magnificently our great Emperor soothes and paci-
fies China and the foreign countries, regarding all with the same kindness.
If there is profit, then he shares it with the peoples of the world; if there is
harm, then he removes it on behalf of the world. This is because he takes
the mind of heaven and earth as his mind.

The kings of your honorable country by a tradition handed down from
generation to generation have always been noted for their politeness and
submissiveness. We have read your successive tributary memorials saying,
"In general our countrymen who go to trade in China have always received
His Majesty the Emperor's gracious treatment and equal justice," and so
on. Privately we are delighted with the way in which the honorable rulers
of your country deeply understand the grand principles and are grateful for
the Celestial grace. For this reason the Celestial Court in soothing those
from afar has redoubled its polite and kind treatment. The profit from trade
has been enjoyed by them continuously for two hundred years. This is the
source from which your country has become known for its wealth.

But after a long period of commercial intercourse, there appear among
the crowd of barbarians both good persons and bad, unevenly.

154

Consequently there are those who smuggle opium to seduce the Chinese people and so cause the spread of the poison to all provinces. Such persons who only care to profit themselves, and disregard their harm to others, are not tolerated by the laws of heaven and are unanimously hated by human beings. His Majesty the Emperor, upon hearing of this, is in a towering rage. He has especially sent me, his commissioner, to come to Kwangtung, and together with the governor-general and governor jointly to investigate and settle this matter.

All those people in China who sell opium or smoke opium should receive the death penalty. If we trace the crime of those barbarians who through the years have been selling opium, then the deep harm they have wrought and the great profit they have usurped should fundamentally justify their execution according to law. We take into consideration, however, the fact that the various barbarians have still known how to repent their crimes and return to their allegiance to us by taking the 20,183 chests[2] of opium from their storeships and petitioning us, through their consular officer [superintendent of trade], Elliot, to receive it. It has been entirely destroyed and this has been faithfully reported to the Throne in several memorials by this commissioner and his colleagues.

Fortunately we have received a specially extended favor from His Majesty the Emperor, who considers that for those who voluntarily surrender there are still some circumstances to palliate their crime, and so for the time being he has magnanimously excused them from punishment. But as for those who again violate the opium prohibition, it is difficult for the law to pardon them repeatedly. Having established new regulations, we presume that the ruler of your honorable country, who takes delight in our culture and whose disposition is inclined towards us, must be able to instruct the various barbarians to observe the law with care. It is only necessary to explain to them the advantages and disadvantages and then they will know that the legal code of the Celestial Court must be absolutely obeyed with awe.

We find that your country is sixty or seventy thousand *li* [three *li* make one mile, ordinarily] from China. Yet there are barbarian ships that strive to come here for trade for the purpose of making a great profit. The wealth of China is used to profit the barbarians. That is to say, the great profit made by barbarians is all taken from the rightful share of China. By what right do they then in return use the poisonous drug to injure the Chinese people? Even though the barbarians may not necessarily intend to do us harm, yet in coveting profit to an extreme, they have no regard for injuring others. Let us ask, where is your conscience? I have heard that the smoking of opium is very strictly forbidden by your country; that is because the harm caused by opium is clearly understood. Since it is not permitted to do harm to your own country, then even less should you let it be passed on to the harm of other countries—how much less to China! Of all that China exports to foreign countries, there is not a single thing which is not beneficial to people: they are of benefit when eaten, or of benefit when used, or of benefit when resold: all are beneficial. Is there a single article from China which has done any harm to foreign countries? Take tea and rhubarb, for example; the foreign countries cannot get along for a single day without them. If China cuts off these benefits with no sympathy for those who are to suffer, then what can the barbarians rely upon to keep themselves alive? Moreover the woolens, camlets, and longells [i.e., textiles] of foreign countries cannot be woven unless they obtain Chinese silk. If China, again, cuts off this beneficial export, what profit can the barbarians expect to make? As for other foodstuffs, beginning with candy, ginger, cinnamon, and so forth, and articles for use, beginning with silk, satin, chinaware, and so on, all the things that must be had by foreign countries are innumerable. On the other hand, articles coming from the outside to China can only be used as toys. We can take them or get along without them. Since they are not needed by China, what difficulty would there be if we closed the frontier and stopped the trade? Nevertheless our Celestial Court lets tea, silk, and other goods be shipped without limit and circulated everywhere without begrudging it in the slightest. This is for no other reason but to share the benefit with the people of the whole world.

The goods from China carried away by your country not only supply your own consumption and use, but also can be divided up and sold to other countries, producing a triple profit. Even if you do not sell opium, you still have this threefold profit. How can you bear to go further, selling products injurious to others in order to fulfill your insatiable desire?

Suppose there were people from another country who carried opium for sale to England and seduced your people into buying and smoking it; certainly your honorable ruler would deeply hate it and be bitterly aroused. We have heard heretofore that your honorable ruler is kind and benevolent. Naturally you would not wish to give unto others what you yourself do not want. We have also heard that the ships coming to Canton have all had regulations promulgated and given to them in which it is stated that it is not permitted to carry contraband goods. This indicates that the administrative orders of your honorable rule have been originally strict and clear. Only because the trading ships are numerous, heretofore perhaps they have not been examined with care. Now after this communication has been dispatched and you have clearly understood the strictness of the prohibitory laws of the Celestial Court, certainly you will not let your subjects dare again to violate the law.

We have further learned that in London, the capital of your honorable rule, and in Scotland (Su-ko-lan), Ireland (Ai-lun), and other places, originally no opium has been produced. Only in several places of India under your control such as Bengal, Madras, Bombay, Patna, Benares, and Malwa has opium been planted from hill to hill, and ponds[3] have been opened for its manufacture. For months and years work is continued in order to accumulate the poison. The obnoxious odor ascends, irritating heaven and frightening the spirits. Indeed you, O King, can eradicate the opium plant in these places, hoe over the fields entirely, and sow in its stead the five grains [i.e., millet, barley, wheat, etc.]. Anyone who dares again attempt to plant and manufacture opium should be severely punished. This will really be a great, benevolent goverment policy that will increase the common weal and get rid of evil. For this, Heaven must support you and the spirits must bring you good fortune, prolonging your old age and extending your descendants. All will depend on this act.

As for the barbarian merchants who come to China, their food and drink and habitation are all received by the gracious favor of our Celestial Court. Their accumulated wealth is all benefit given with pleasure by our Celestial Court. They spend rather few days in their own country but more time in Canton. To digest clearly the legal penalties as an aid to instruction has been a valid principle in all ages. Suppose a man of another country comes to England to trade, he still has to obey the English laws; how much more should he obey in China the laws of the Celestial Dynasty?

Now we have set up regulations governing the Chinese people. He who sells opium shall receive the death penalty and he who smokes it also the death penalty. Now consider this: if the barbarians do not bring opium, then how can the Chinese people resell it, and how can they smoke it? The fact is that the wicked barbarians beguile the Chinese people into a death trap. How then can we grant life only to these barbarians? He who takes the life of even one person still has to atone for it with his own life; yet is the harm done by opium limited to the taking of one life only? Therefore in the new regulations, in regard to those barbarians who bring opium to China, the penalty is fixed at decapitation or strangulation. This is what is called getting rid of a harmful thing on behalf of mankind.

Moreover we have found that in the middle of the second month of this year [April 9] Consul [Superintendent] Elliot of your nation, because the opium prohibition law was very stern and severe, petitioned for an extension of the time limit. He requested a limit of five months for India and its adjacent harbors and related territories, and ten months for England proper, after which they would act in conformity with the new regulations. Now we, the commissioner and others, have memorialized and have received the extraordinary Celestial grace of His Majesty the Emperor, who has redoubled his consideration and compassion. All those who within the period of the coming one year (from England) or six months (from India) bring opium to China by mistake, but who voluntarily confess and completely surrender their opium, shall be exempt from their punishment. After this limit of time, if there are still those who bring opium to China then they will plainly have committed a wilful violation and shall at once be executed according to law, with absolutely no clemency or pardon. This may be called the height of kindness and the perfection of justice.

Our Celestial Dynasty rules over and supervises the myriad states, and surely possesses unfathomable spiritual dignity. Yet the Emperor cannot bear to execute people without having first tried to reform them by instruction. Therefore he especially promulgates these fixed regulations. The barbarian merchants of your country, if they wish to do business for a prolonged period, are required to obey our statutes respectfully and to cut off permanently the source of opium. They must by no means try to test the effectiveness of the law with their lives. May you, O King, check your wicked and sift your vicious people before they come to China, in order to guarantee the peace of your nation, to show further the sincerity of your politeness and submissiveness, and to let the two countries enjoy together the blessings of peace. How fortunate, how fortunate indeed! After receiving this dispatch will you immediately give us a prompt reply regarding the details and circumstances of your cutting off the opium traffic. Be sure not to put this off. The above is what has to be communicated. [Vermilion endorsement:] This is appropriately worded and quite comprehensive *(Te-t'i chou-tao).*

END NOTES

1. From IWSM-TK, 7.33-36b, enclosed in an edict of August 27, 1839 (not translated here). This source omits a postscript which appears in Lin's political writings (*Lin Wen-chung-kung cheng-shu,* part II, 4.16–20). CSL (324.25b–26) reproduces the covering edict of August 27, but not the communication here translated. An English translation (not followed here) is in the *Chinese Repository*, 8.10: 497–503 (Feb. 1840); a briefer popularized version in *ibid.*, 8.1: 9–12 (May 1839); and a Dutch translation in G. W. Overdijkink, *Lin Tse-hsü,* pp. 148–151.
2. The *Lin Wen-chung-kung cheng-shu* version is 20,283 chests.
3. Here the text of *Lin Wen-chung-kung cheng-shu* is followed; while the IWSM version is *ti*, meaning "ground."

    Lin Tse-hsü's letter to Queen Victoria (1839), in IWSM-TK, 24–27
    Ch'ou-pan i-wu shih-mo
    TK = Tao-Kuang Period (1836-1850)
    (A Complete Account of the Management of Barbarian Affairs)

QUESTIONS

1. In his letter, what does Lin ask Queen Victoria to do about the opium trade between British India and China? What is China's plan to eliminate the trade?
2. What are the key points in Lin's argument against the trade?
3. In what ways does Lin's letter reveal Chinese misconceptions about Great Britain? About China's strength and status in the world?
4. If Queen Victoria had received this letter, how do you think she would have reacted? Why?

MINUTE ON INDIAN EDUCATION

Thomas Babington Macaulay

Thomas Babington Macaulay (1800–1859), was a prominent progressive politician of nineteenth century England. He was a member of the Whig party and was elected several times to be a member of the British parliament, often on the side of reform, progress, and the democratization of British society. He served in the Supreme Council of India between 1834 and 1838, and initiated a series of legal and social reforms of the colonial government in India. He became known widely as a brilliant essayist, speaker, and eventually writer of the History of England, *which sold very widely, surpassed in sales only by Charles Dickens and Walter Scott.*

This memorandum, addressed to the governor-general of India, William Bentinck, proved to be an extremely influential and controversial proposal for reforming the education of Indians. This "minute" (i.e., a brief note or recommendation) intervened in the debate between "orientalists," who felt that education in India should support vernacular languages and promote local forms of learning, and "anglicists," who felt that education in India should be conducted in English, which they felt was a more rational and scientific language and imparted modern knowledge. Shortly after this minute was issued in 1835, the official language of the colonial government was changed to English, replacing Persian, which was the standard Mughal court language. In this minute, Macaulay made his now-famous pronouncement, "I have never

Reprinted from *Indian Education: Minute of the 2nd of February*, 1835.

found one among [the orientalists] who could deny that a single shelf of a good European library was worth the whole native literature of India and Arabia." Although the minute diminished the value of Arabic, Sanskrit, and vernacular learning, Macaulay was careful to compliment the ability of intelligent Indians to master the English language in order to bring rational and progressive practices to India.

MINUTE OF THE 2ND OF FEBRUARY, 1835

[On his arrival in India, as a Member of the Supreme Council, Macaulay was appointed President of the Committee of Public Instruction, which he found irreconcilably split into two factions: the orientalists and those who wanted to teach the Indians Western learning. He addressed this minute to the Governor General, Lord Bentinck, who, on 7 March, pronounced in favor of "the promotion of European literature and science among the natives of India."]

As it seems to be the opinion of some of the gentlemen who compose the Committee of Public Instruction, that the course which they have hitherto pursued was strictly prescribed by the British Parliament in 1813, and as, if that opinion be correct, a legislative act will be necessary to warrant a change, I have thought it right to refrain from taking any part in the preparation of the adverse statements which are now before us, and to reserve what I had to say on the subject till it should come before me as a member of the Council of India.

It does not appear to me that the Act of Parliament can, by any art of construction, be made to bear the meaning which has been assigned to it. It contains nothing about the particular languages or sciences which are to be studied. A sum is set apart "for the revival and promotion of literature and the encouragement of the learned natives of India, and for the introduction and promotion of a knowledge of the sciences among the inhabitants of the British territories." It is argued, or rather taken for granted, that by literature, the Parliament can have meant only Arabic and Sanscrit literature, that they never would have given the honorable appellation of "a learned native" to a native who was familiar with the poetry of Milton, the Metaphysics of Locke, and the Physics of Newton; but that they meant to designate by that name only such persons as might have studied in the

161

sacred books of the Hindoos all the uses of cusa-grass, and all the mysteries of absorption into the Deity. This does not appear to be a very satisfactory interpretation. To take a parallel case; suppose that the Pacha of Egypt, a country once superior in knowledge to the nations of Europe, but now sunk far below them, were to appropriate a sum for the purpose of "reviving and promoting literature, and encouraging learned natives of Egypt," would anybody infer that he meant the youth of his pachalic to give years to the study of hieroglyphics, to search into all the doctrines disguised under the fable of Osiris, and to ascertain with all possible accuracy the ritual with which cats and onions were anciently adored? Would he be justly charged with inconsistency, if, instead of employing his young subjects in deciphering obelisks, he were to order them to be instructed in the English and French languages, and in all the sciences to which those languages are the chief keys?

The words on which the supporters of the old system rely do not bear them out, and other words follow which seem to be quite decisive on the other side. This lac of rupees is set apart, not only for "reviving literature in India," the phrase on which their whole interpretation is founded, but also for "the introduction and promotion of a knowledge of the sciences among the inhabitants of the British territories,"—words which are alone sufficient to authorize all the changes for which I contend.

If the Council agree in my construction, no legislative Act will be necessary. If they differ from me, I will prepare a short Act rescinding that clause of the Charter of 1813, from which the difficulty arises.

The argument which I have been considering, affects only the form of proceeding. But the admirers of the Oriental system of education have used another argument, which, if we admit it to be valid, is decisive against all change. They conceive that the public faith is pledged to the present system, and that to alter the appropriation of any of the funds which have hitherto been spent in encouraging the study of Arabic and Sanscrit, would be downright spoliation. It is not easy to understand by what process of reasoning they can have arrived at this conclusion. The grants which are made from the public purse for the encouragement of literature differed in no respect from the grants which are made from the same purse for other objects of real or supposed utility. We found a sanatarium on a spot which we suppose to be healthy. Do we thereby pledge ourselves to keep a sanatarium there, if the result should not answer our expectation? We commence the erection of a pier. Is it a violation of the public faith to stop the works, if we afterwards see reason to believe that the building will be useless? The rights of property are undoubtedly sacred. But nothing endangers those rights so much as the practice, now unhappily too common, of attributing them to things to which they do not belong. Those who would impart to abuses the sanctity of property are in truth imparting to the institution of property the unpopularity and the fragility of abuses. If the Government has given to any person a formal assurance; nay, if the Government has excited in any person's mind a reasonable expectation that he shall receive a certain income as a teacher or a learner of Sanscrit or Arabic, I would respect that person's pecuniary interests—I would rather err on the side of liberality to individuals than suffer the public faith to be called in question. But to talk of a Government pledging itself to teach certain languages and certain sciences, though those languages may become useless, though those sciences may be exploded, seems to me quite unmeaning. There is not a single word in any public instructions, from which it can be inferred that the Indian Government ever intended to give any pledge on this subject, or ever considered the destination of these funds as unalterably fixed. But had it been otherwise, I should have denied the competence of our predecessors to bind us by any pledge on such a subject. Suppose that a Government had in the last century enacted in the most solemn manner that all its subjects should, to the end of time, be inoculated for the smallpox: would that Government be bound to persist in the practice after Jenner's discovery? These promises, of which nobody claims the performance, and from which nobody can grant a release; these vested rights, which vest in nobody; this property without proprietors; this robbery, which makes nobody poorer, may be comprehended by persons of higher faculties than mine—I consider this plea merely as a set form of words, regularly used both in England and in India, in defense of every abuse for which no other plea can be set up.

I hold this lac of rupees to be quite at the disposal of the Governor General in Council, for the purpose of promoting learning in India, in any way which may be thought most advisable. I hold his Lordship to be quite as free to direct that it shall no longer be employed in encouraging Arabic and Sanscrit, as he is to direct that the reward for killing tigers in Mysore shall be diminished, or that no more public money shall be expended on the chanting at the cathedral.

We now come to the gist of the matter. We have a fund to be employed as Government shall direct for the intellectual improvement of the people of this country. The simple question is, what is the most useful way of employing it?

All parties seem to be agreed on one point, that the dialects commonly spoken among the natives of this part of India, contain neither literary nor scientific information, and are, moreover, so poor and rude that, until they are enriched from some other quarter, it will not be easy to translate any valuable work into them. It seems to be admitted on all sides, that the intellectual improvement of those classes of the people who have the means of pursuing higher studies can at present be effected only by means of some language not vernacular amongst them.

What then shall that language be? One-half of the Committee maintain that it should be the English. The other half strongly recommend the Arabic and Sanscrit. The whole question seems to me to be, which language is the best worth knowing?

I have no knowledge of either Sanscrit or Arabic.—But I have done what I could to form a correct estimate of their value. I have read translations of the most celebrated Arabic and Sanscrit works. I have conversed both here and at home with men distinguished by their proficiency in the Eastern tongues. I am quite ready to take the Oriental learning at the valuation of the Orientalists themselves. I have never found one among them who could deny that a single shelf of a good European library was worth the whole native literature of India and Arabia. The intrinsic superiority of the Western literature is, indeed, fully admitted by those members of the Committee who support the Oriental plan of education.

It will hardly be disputed, I suppose, that the department of literature in which the Eastern writers stand highest is poetry. And I certainly never met with any Orientalist who ventured to maintain that the Arabic and Sanscrit poetry could be compared to that of the great European nations. But when we pass from works of imagination to works in which facts are recorded, and general principles investigated, the superiority of the Europeans becomes absolutely immeasurable. It is, I believe, no exaggeration to say, that all the historical information which has been collected from all the books written in the Sanscrit language is less valuable than what may be found in the most paltry abridgments used at preparatory schools in England. In every branch of physical or moral philosophy, the relative position of the two nations is nearly the same.

How, then, stands the case? We have to educate a people who cannot at present be educated by means of their mother-tongue. We must teach them some foreign language. The claims of our own language it is hardly necessary to recapitulate. It stands preeminent even among the languages of the west. It abounds with works of imagination not inferior to the noblest which Greece has bequeathed to us; with models of every species of eloquence; with historical compositions, which, considered merely as narratives, have seldom been surpassed, and which, considered as vehicles of ethical and political instruction, have never been equalled; with just and lively representations of human life and human nature; with the most profound speculations on metaphysics, morals, government, jurisprudence, and trade; with full and correct information respecting every experimental science which tends to preserve the health, to increase the comfort, or to expand the intellect of man. Whoever knows that language has ready access to all the vast intellectual wealth, which all the wisest nations of the earth have created and hoarded in the course of ninety generations. It may safely be said, that the literature now extant in that language is of far greater value than all the literature which three hundred years ago was extant in all the languages of the world together. Nor is this all. In India, English is the language spoken by the ruling class. It is spoken by the higher class of natives at the seats of Government. It is likely to become the language of commerce throughout the seas of the East. It is the language of two great European communities which are rising, the one in the south of Africa, the other in Australasia; communities which are every year becoming more important, and more closely connected with our Indian empire. Whether we look at the intrinsic value of our literature, or at the particular situation of this country, we shall see the strongest reason to think that, of all foreign tongues, the English tongue is that which would be the most useful to our native subjects.

The question now before us is simply whether, when it is in our power to teach this language, we shall teach languages in which, by universal confession, there are no books on any subject which deserve to be compared to our own; whether, when we can teach European science, we shall teach systems which, by universal confession, whenever they differ from those of Europe, differ for the worse; and whether, when we can patronize sound Philosophy and true History, we shall countenance, at the public expense, medical doctrines, which would disgrace an English farrier,—Astronomy, which would move laughter in girls at an English boarding school,—History, abounding with kings thirty feet high, and reigns thirty thousand years long,—and Geography, made up of seas of treacle and seas of butter.

We are not without experience to guide us. History furnishes several analogous cases, and they all teach the same lesson. There are in modern times, to go no further, two memorable instances of a great impulse given to the mind of a whole society,—of prejudices overthrown,—of knowledge diffused,—of taste purified,—of arts and sciences planted in countries which had recently been ignorant and barbarous.

The first instance to which I refer, is the great revival of letters among the Western nations at the close of the fifteenth and the beginning of the sixteenth century. At that time almost every thing that was worth reading was contained in the writings of the ancient Greeks and Romans. Had our ancestors acted as the Committee of Public Instruction has hitherto acted; had they neglected the language of Cicero and Tacitus; had they confined their attention to the old dialects of our own island; had they printed nothing and taught nothing at the universities but Chronicles in Anglo-Saxon, and Romances in Norman-French, would England have been what she now is? What the Greek and Latin were to the contemporaries of More and Ascham, our tongue is to the people of India. The literature of England is now more valuable than that of classical antiquity. I doubt whether the Sanscrit literature be as valuable as that of our Saxon and Norman progenitors. In some departments,—in History, for example, I am certain that it is much less so.

Another instance may be said to be still before our eyes. Within the last hundred and twenty years, a nation which has previously been in a state as barbarous as that in which our ancestors were before the crusades, has gradually emerged from the ignorance in which it was sunk, and has taken its place among civilized communities.—I speak of Russia. There is now in that country a large educated class, abounding with persons fit to serve the state in the highest functions, and in no wise inferior to the most accomplished men who adorn the best circles of Paris and London. There is reason to hope that this vast empire, which in the time of our grandfathers was probably behind the Punjab, may, in the time of our grand-children, be pressing close on France and Britain in the career of improve-ment. And how was this change effected? Not by flattering national prej-udices: not by feeding the mind of the young Muscovite with the old women's stories which his rude fathers had believed: not by filling his head with lying legends about St. Nicholas: not by encouraging him to study the great question, whether the world was or was not created on the 13th of September: not by calling him "a learned native," when he has mastered all these points of knowledge: but by teaching him those foreign languages in which the greatest mass of information had been laid up, and thus putting all that information within his reach. The languages of Western Europe civilized Russia. I cannot doubt that they will do for the Hindoo what they have done for the Tartar.

And what are the arguments against that course which seems to be alike recommended by theory and by experience? It is said that we ought to secure the co-operation of the native public, and that we can do this only by teaching Sanscrit and Arabic.

I can by no means admit that when a nation of high intellectual attain-ments undertakes to superintend the education of a nation comparatively ignorant, the learners are absolutely to prescribe the course which is to be taken by the teachers. It is not necessary, however, to say any thing on this subject. For it is proved by unanswerable evidence that we are not at pres-ent securing the cooperation of the natives. It would be bad enough to con-sult their intellectual taste at the expense of their intellectual health. But we are consulting neither,—we are withholding from them the learning for which they are craving, we are forcing on them the mock-learning which they nauseate.

This is proved by the fact that we are forced to pay our Arabic and Sanscrit students, while those who learn English are willing to pay us. All the declamations in the world about the love and reverence of the natives for their sacred dialects will never, in the mind of any impartial person, outweigh the undisputed fact, that we cannot find, in all our vast empire, a single student who will let us teach him those dialects unless we will pay him.

I have now before me the accounts of the Madrassa for one month,—the month of December, 1833. The Arabic students appear to have been seventy-seven in number. All receive stipends from the public. The whole amount paid to them is above 500 rupees a month. On the other side of the account stands the following item: Deduct amount realized from the out-students of English for the months of May, June and July last, 103 rupees.

I have been told that it is merely from want of local experience that I am surprised at these phenomena, and that it is not the fashion for students in India to study at their own charges. This only confirms me in my opinion. Nothing is more certain than that it never can in any part of the world be necessary to pay men for doing what they think pleasant and profitable. India is no exception to this rule. The people of India do not require to be paid for eating rice when they are hungry, or for wearing woollen cloth in the cold season. To come nearer to the case before us, the children who learn their letters and a little elementary Arithmetic from the village school-master are not paid by him. He is paid for teaching them. Why then is it necessary to pay people to learn Sanscrit and Arabic? Evidently because it is universally felt that the Sanscrit and Arabic are languages, the knowledge of which does not compensate for the trouble of acquiring them. On all such subjects the state of the market is the decisive test.

Other evidence is not wanting, if other evidence were required. A petition was presented last year to the Committee by several ex-students of the Sanscrit College. The petitioners stated that they had studied in the college ten or twelve years; that they had made themselves acquainted with Hindoo literature and science; that they had received certificates of proficiency: and what is the fruit of all this! "Notwithstanding such testimonials,' they say, "we have but little prospect of bettering our condition without the kind assistance of your Honorable Committee, the indifference with which we are generally looked upon by our countrymen leaving no hope of encouragement and assistance from them." They therefore beg that they may be recommended to the Governor General for places under the Government, not places of high dignity or emolument, but such as may just enable them to exist. "We want means," they say, "for a decent living, and for our progressive improvement, which, however, we cannot obtain without the assistance of Government, by whom we have been educated and maintained from childhood." They conclude by representing, very pathetically, that they are sure that it was never the intention of Government, after behaving so liberally to them during their education, to abandon them to destitution and neglect.

I have been used to see petitions to Government for compensation. All these petitions, even the most unreasonable of them, proceeded on the supposition that some loss had been sustained—that some wrong had been inflicted. These are surely the first petitioners who ever demanded compensation for having been educated gratis,—for having been supported by the public during twelve years, and then sent forth into the world well furnished with literature and science. They represent their education as an injury which gives them a claim on the Government for redress, as an injury for which the stipends paid to them during the infliction were a very inadequate compensation. And I doubt not that they are in the right. They have wasted the best years of life in learning what procures for them neither bread nor respect. Surely we might, with advantage, have saved the cost of making these persons useless and miserable; surely, men may be brought up to be burdens to the public and objects of contempt to their neighbors at a somewhat smaller charge to the state. But such is our policy. We do not even stand neuter in the contest between truth and falsehood. We are not content to leave the natives to the influence of their own hereditary prejudices. To the natural difficulties which obstruct the progress of sound science in the East, we add fresh difficulties of our own making. Bounties and premiums, such as ought not to be given even for the propagation of truth, we lavish on false taste and false philosophy.

By acting thus we create the very evil which we fear. We are making that opposition which we do not find. What we spend on the Arabic and Sanscrit colleges is not merely a dead loss to the cause of truth; it is bounty-money paid to raise up champions of error. It goes to form a nest, not merely of helpless place-hunters, but of bigots prompted alike by passion and by interest to raise a cry against every useful scheme of education. If there should be any opposition among the natives to the change which I recommend, that opposition will be the effect of our own system. It will be headed by persons supported by our stipends and trained in our colleges. The longer we persevere in our present course, the more formidable will that opposition be. It will be every year reinforced by recruits whom we are paying. From the native society left to itself, we have no difficulties to apprehend; all the murmuring will come from that oriental interest which we have, by artificial means, called into being, and nursed into strength.

There is yet another fact, which is alone sufficient to prove that the feeling of the native public, when left to itself, is not such as the supporters of the old system represent it to be. The Committee have thought fit to lay out above a lac of rupees in printing Arabic and Sanscrit books. Those books find no purchasers. It is very rarely that a single copy is disposed of. Twenty-three thousand volumes, most of them folios and quartos, fill the libraries, or rather the lumber-rooms, of this body. The Committee contrive to get rid of some portion of their vast stock of oriental literature by giving books away. But they cannot give so fast as they print. About twenty thousand rupees a year are spent in adding fresh masses of waste paper to a hoard which, I should think, is already sufficiently ample. During the last three years, about sixty thousand rupees have been expended in this manner. The sale of Arabic and Sanscrit books, during those three years, has not yielded quite one thousand rupees. In the mean time the Schoolbook Society is selling seven or eight thousand English volumes every year, and not only pays the expenses of printing, but realizes a profit of 20 percent, on its outlay.

The fact that the Hindoo law is to be learned chiefly from Sanscrit books, and the Mahomedan law from Arabic books, has been much insisted on, but seems not to bear at all on the question. We are commanded by Parliament to ascertain arid digest the laws of India. The assistance of a law Commission has been given to us for that purpose. As soon as the code is promulgated, the Shasster and the Hedaya will be useless to a Moonsiff or Sudder Ameen. I hope and trust that before the boys who are now entering at the Madrassa and the Sanscrit college have completed their studies, this great work will be finished. It would be manifestly absurd to educate the rising generation with a view to a state of things which we mean to alter before they reach manhood.

But there is yet another argument which seems even more untenable. It is said that the Sanscrit and Arabic are the languages in which the sacred books of a hundred millions of people are written, and that they are, on

170

that account, entitled to peculiar encouragement. Assuredly it is the duty of the British Government in India to be not only tolerant, but neutral on all religious questions. But to encourage the study of a literature admitted to be of small intrinsic value, only because that literature inculcates the most serious errors on the most important subjects, is a course hardly reconcileable with reason, with morality, or even with that very neutrality which ought, as we all agree, to be sacredly preserved. It is confessed that a language is barren of useful knowledge. We are to teach it because it is fruitful of monstrous superstitions. We are to teach false History, false Astronomy, false Medicine, because we find them in company with a false religion. We abstain, and I trust shall always abstain, from giving any public encouragement to those who are engaged in the work of converting natives to Christianity. And while we act thus, can we reasonably and decently bribe men out of the revenues of the state to waste their youth in learning how they are to purify themselves after touching an ass, or what text of the Vedas they are to repeat to expiate the crime of killing a goat?

It is taken for granted by the advocates of Oriental learning, that no native of this country can possibly attain more than a mere smattering of English. They do not attempt to prove this; but they perpetually insinuate it. They designate the education which their opponents recommend as a mere spelling book education. They assume it as undeniable, that the question is between a profound knowledge of Hindoo and Arabian literature and science on the one side, and a superficial knowledge of the rudiments of English on the other. This is not merely an assumption, but an assumption contrary to all reason and experience. We know that foreigners of all nations do learn our language sufficiently to have access to all the most abstruse knowledge which it contains, sufficiently to relish even the more delicate graces of our most idiomatic writers. There are in this very town natives who are quite competent to discuss political or scientific questions with fluency and precision in the English language. I have heard the very question on which I am now writing discussed by native gentlemen with a liberality and an intelligence which would do credit to any member of the Committee of Public Instruction. Indeed it is unusual to find, even in the literary circles of the continent, any foreigner who can express himself in English with so much facility and correctness as we find in many Hindoos. Nobody, I suppose, will contend that English is so difficult to a Hindoo as Greek to an Englishman. Yet an intelligent English youth, in a much smaller number of years than our unfortunate pupils pass at the Sanscrit college, becomes able to read, to enjoy, and even to imitate, not unhappily, the compositions of the best Greek Authors. Less than half the time which enables an English youth to read Herodotus and Sophocles, ought to enable a Hindoo to read Hume and Milton.

To sum up what I have said, I think it clear that we are not fettered by the Act of Parliament of 1813; that we are not fettered by any pledge expressed or implied; that we are free to employ our funds as we choose; that we ought to employ them in teaching what is best worth knowing; that English is better worth knowing than Sanscrit or Arabic; that the natives are desirous to be taught English, and are not desirous to be taught Sanscrit or Arabic; that neither as the languages of law, nor as the languages of religion, have the Sanscrit and Arabic any peculiar claim to our engagement; that it is possible to make natives of this country thoroughly good English scholars, and that to this end our efforts ought to be directed.

In one point I fully agree with the gentlemen to whose general views I am opposed. I feel with them, that it is impossible for us, with our limited means, to attempt to educate the body of the people. We must at present do our best to form a class who may be interpreters between us and the millions whom we govern; a class of persons, Indian in blood and color, but English in taste, in opinions, in morals, and in intellect. To that class we may leave it to refine the vernacular dialects of the country, to enrich those dialects with terms of science borrowed from the Western nomenclature, and to render them by degrees fit vehicles for conveying knowledge to the great mass of the population.

I would strictly respect all existing interests. I would deal even generously with all individuals who have had fair reason to expect a pecuniary provision. But I would strike at the root of the bad system which has hitherto been fostered by us. I would at once stop the printing of Arabic and Sanscrit books, I would abolish the Madrassa and the Sanscrit college at Calcutta. Benares is the great seat of Brahmanical learning; Delhi, of Arabic learning. If we retain the Sanscrit college at Benares and the Mahometan college at Delhi, we do enough, and much more than enough in my opinion, for the Eastern languages. If the Benares and Delhi colleges should be retained, I would at least recommend that no stipends shall be given to any students who may hereafter repair thither, but that the people shall be left to make their own choice between the rival systems of education without being bribed by us to learn what they have no desire to know. The funds which would thus be placed at our disposal would enable us to give larger encouragement to the Hindoo college at Calcutta, and to establish in the principal cities throughout the Presidencies of Fort William and Agra schools in which the English language might be well and thoroughly taught.

If the decision of his Lordship in Council should be such as I anticipate, I shall enter on the performance of my duties with the greatest zeal and alacrity. If, on the other hand, it be the opinion of the Government that the present system ought to remain unchanged, I beg that I may be permitted to retire from the chair of the Committee. I feel that I could not be of the smallest use there—I feel, also, that I should be lending my countenance to what I firmly believe to be a mere delusion. I believe that the present system tends, not to accelerate the progress of truth, but to delay the natural death of expiring errors. I conceive that we have at present no right to the respectable name of a Board of Public Instruction. We are a Board for wasting public money, for printing books which are of less value than the paper on which they are printed was while it was blank; for giving artificial encouragement to absurd history, absurd metaphysics, absurd physics, absurd theology; for raising up a breed of scholars who find their scholarship an encumbrance and a blemish, who live on the public while they are receiving their education, and whose education is so utterly useless to them that when they have received it they must either starve or live on the public all the rest of their lives. Entertaining these opinions, I am naturally desirous to decline all share in the responsibility of a body, which unless it alters its whole mode of proceeding, I must consider not merely as useless, but as positively noxious.

QUESTIONS

1. How does Macaulay think that learning English will benefit elite Indians?

2. Does Macaulay think that the British government has a responsibility to promote Arabic and Sanskrit learning? Why does he feel this way, and what evidence does he provide for his arguments?

3. What is the relationship between language and rational thinking? More specifically, in what ways does Macaulay think that the English language reflected the characteristics of British and European thinking?

4. What does Macaulay envision when he says, "We must at present do our best to form a class who may be interpreters between us and the millions whom we govern; a class of persons, Indian in blood and colour, but English in taste, in opinions, in morals, and in intellect"?

THE CAUSES OF THE INDIAN REVOLT (1858)

Syed Ahmed Khan

Syed Ahmed Khan (1817–1898) was one of the most prominent thinkers of his day. Born into a noble Muslim family, he witnessed the decline of the Mughal Empire and the British takeover of India. Although the British East India Company had ruled India in principle for years beforehand, it was in the wake of the 1857 revolt that the British crown began to rule directly, and openly. Syed Ahmed Khan wrote The Causes of the Indian Revolt *in response to the events of 1857.*

From 1857 to 1858, armed rebellions and uprisings broke out in the northern and central parts of India; British and Indians alike committed many atrocities. The conflict began with the sepoys, or Indian soldiers serving under British command. For this reason the 1857 revolt is also called the Sepoy Mutiny. Although the sepoys were both Muslim and Hindu, the British blamed Muslims for inciting the rebellion, and after it was put down, punished them severely. In The Causes of the Indian Revolt, *Syed Ahmed Khan sought to dispel the idea that the Muslims should bear primary responsibility for the events of 1857 and 1858. He enumerated the real causes of the revolt, which he believed to be the following: a misunderstanding on the part of Indians about the real intentions of the British in India; the promotion of laws, policies, and procedures that were contrary to the practices and culture of the people; British ignorance of their subjects; the poor conditions in which the ordinary*

*people lived; and the government's failure to manage the sepoy army effi-
ciently. Even more important, the British government did not listen to the
voices of the people it governed, and until it took steps to do so, Syed Ahmed
argued, it would never be able to rule effectively. Written for, and read primarily by, British officials,* The Causes of the Indian Revolt *had a significant
influence on subsequent British policy.*

The Causes of the Indian Revolt *marked Syed Ahmed Khan's entry into
public life. From that point forward, he dedicated himself to the service of the
Indian Muslims by encouraging progressive thinking among them, defending
them against the attacks of Christian missionaries, and highlighting Muslim
concerns before the British government in India. One of the lasting monu-
ments to his efforts is the Anglo-Oriental Muhammadan College which he
founded, now called Aligarh Muslim University.*

IN THE NAME OF GOD, THE MERCIFUL, THE COMPASSIONATE

> *"Obedience and submission become the servant;*
> *Forgiveness is the attribute of God:*
> *If I should do amiss*
> *Reward me as seemeth right in Thine eyes."*

Since I began this Essay on the causes of the Rebellion in Hindustan,
I have been tempted to keep silence on the events of the past, and even to
wish my remembrance of them should be blotted out. The proclamation
issued by Her Majesty contains such ample redress for every grievance
which led up to that revolt, that a man writing on the subject feels his pen
fall from his hands. Why enter further into the matter when the cause of
all the dissatisfaction has been discovered and provided against? Yet I
think that loyal men, and such as really wish well to their Government,
should not content themselves with reflection: but explain with all possible fidelity, their views on the origin of this rebellion. Although, therefore,
the causes of complaint have been met, and the grievances redressed, I
think it my duty to record my opinion on the subject. That many well-
informed, able, and experienced men have written on the causes of the dis-
turbance, I know; but I am not aware that any native of the country has

hitherto been among their number. I venture therefore, publicly to express my opinion.

What were the causes of the Rebellion in Hindustan?

Before answering this question, let us ask what is the meaning of the word, Rebellion. To fight against the Government, to aid and assist those who are resisting the authority of Government, to set at nought, and disobey the orders of Government with a view to resist its authority, or with contempt, and disrespect to infringe the rights of Government, and disregard its prerogations in any, or in all of these, I take it that Rebellion consists.

Definition of 'Rebellion exemplified with instances.

Let us clearly recapitulate the above.

1. To fight with or oppose, the servants or subjects of Government.
2. To neglect, and set at naught the Orders of government with a view to resist its authority.
3. To aid and assist or in any way take part with those who are in open opposition to Government.
4. To shew a turbulent disposition, and such as is likely to lead to lawless riot, and disregard of the authority of Government.
5. To swerve at heart from respect and loyalty to the Government; and in times of trouble, to withhold from it an active support.

In that sad year, 1857, there was not one of these forms of rebellion which did not find a place. There are but few men in truth even amongst the best of us, who may not be connected under the latter head; which though in appearance of little import, is in reality of no small weight.

The primary causes of rebellion are, I fancy, everywhere the same. It invariably results from the existence of a policy obnoxious to the dispositions, aims, habits, and views, of those by whom the rebellion is brought about.

Why it is resorted to.

From this it follows that widely spread disaffection cannot spring from any solitary, or local cause. Universal rebellion must rise from universal grounds for discontent or from streams, deriving from many different sources, but finally merging into one wide-spreading turbulent water.

As regards the Rebellion of 1857, the fact is that for a long period, many grievances had been rankling in the hearts of the people. In course of time, a vast store of explosive material had been collected. It wanted but the application of a match to light it, and that match was applied by the Mutinous army.

The Rebellion of 1857 did not originate from a single cause but from a complication of causes.

In the course of the year 1858, and almost simultaneously with the outbreak, chappaties were passed from hand to hand in many districts. Cholera happened at that time to be raging in Hindustan. Some have imagined that these chappaties were used as a kind of Talisman to keep off the Cholera, the superstitious Hindustanees being in the habit of using such talismans. The fact is that even at the present day we do not know what caused the distribution of those chappaties. We may be very sure, however, that they could never have been used with the object of spreading a conspiracy. We have, in Hindustan, I know, a custom of passing messages from tongue to tongue in this way; but with these chappaties there was no such message passed. Had there been, it would have been sure to have leaked out; known as it would have become to every native, to all races and tribes, and to men holding every kind of opinion. The manner in which the rebellion spread, first here, then there, now breaking out in this place and now in that, is alone good proof that there existed no wide-spread conspiracy.

The distribution of 'Chappaties', had not league for its object.

CAUSE I.

Ignorance on the part of the people, that is, misapprehension of the intentions of Government.

I would here say that I do not wish it to be understood that the views of Government were in reality such as have been imputed to them, I only wish to say that they were misconstrued by the people, and that this misconstruction harried on

Misunderstanding on the part of the Indians.

178

the rebellion. Had there been a native of Hindustan in the Legislative Council, the people would never have fallen into such errors.

Interference in matters of religion. There is not the smallest doubt that

Apprehension of interfer-
ence of Government with
the religious customs of
the Indians.

all men whether ignorant, well-informed, whether high or low, felt a firm conviction that the English Government was bent on interfering with their religion, and with their old established customs. They believed that Government intended to force the Christian religion and foreign customs upon Hindu and Mussulman alike. This was the chief among the secondary causes of the rebellion. It was believed by everyone that Government was slowly but surely developing its plans. Every step it was thought was being taken with the most extreme caution. Hence it is that men said that Government does not speak of proselytising Muhammadans summarily, and by force; but it will throw off the veil as it feels itself stronger, and will act with greater decision. Events, as I shall presently shew, increased and strengthened this conviction. Men never thought that our Government would openly compel them to change their religion. The idea was that indirect steps would be taken, such as doing away with the study of Arabic and Sanscrit, and reducing the people to ignorance and poverty. In this way, it was supposed, the people would be deprived of a knowledge of the principles of their own faith, and their attention turned to books containing the principles of the Christian Creed. It was supposed that Government would then work on the cupidity, and poverty of its subjects and on condition of their abjuring their faith, offer them employment in its own service.

In the year 1837, the year of the great drought, the step which was

Mention of the
Secundra Orphan
Asylum.

taken rearing orphans in the principles of the Christian faith, was looked upon throughout the N.W.P. as an example of the schemes of Government. It was supposed that when Government had similarly brought all Hindustanees to a pitch of ignorance and poverty, it would convert them to its own creed. The Hindustanees used, as I have said, to feel an increasing dismay at the annexation of each successive country by the Hon'ble East India Company. But I assert without fear of contradiction that this feeling arose solely from the belief in their minds, that as the power of Government increased, and there no longer remained foreign enemies to fight against, or internal troubles to quell, it would turn its attention inwards and carry out a more systematic interference with their creed and religious observances.

In the first days of British rule in Hindustan, there used to be less talk than at present on the subject of religion. Discussion on this point has been increasing day by day and has now reached its climax. I do not say that Government has interfered in these matters; but it has been the general opinion that all that was done was according to the instructions and hints of Government, and was by no means displeasing to it. It has been commonly believed that Government appointed Missionaries and maintained them at its own cost. It has been supposed that Government, and the officers of Government throughout the country were in the habit of giving large sums of money to these Missionaries with the intention of covering their expenses, enabling them to distribute books, and in everyway aiding them. Many covenanted officers, and many Military men have been in the habit of talking to their subordinates about religion; some of them would bid their servants come to their houses, and listen to the preaching of Missionaries, and thus it happened that in the course of time no man felt sure that his creed would last even his own life time.

Religious discussions being carried out to a great height during the present time.

The covenanted officers, assumed the Missionary functions.

The Missionaries moreover introduced a new system of preaching. They took to printing and circulating controversial tracts, in the shape of questions and answers. Men of a different faith were spoken of in those tracts in a most offensive and irritating way. In Hindustan these things have always been managed very differently. Every man in this country, preaches and explains his views in his own mosque, or his own house. If anyone wishes to listen to him, he can go to the mosque, or house, and hear what he has to say. But the Missionaries' plan was exactly the opposite. They used to attend places of public resort, markets for instance, and fairs

Preaching of the Gospel by the Missionaries.

where men of different creeds were collected together, and used to begin preaching there. It was only from fear of the authorities that no one bid them be off about their business. In some districts the Missionaries were actually attended by policemen from the station. And then the Missionaries did not confine themselves to explaining the doctrines of their own books. In violent and unmeasured language they attacked the followers and the holy places of other creeds; annoying, and insulting beyond expression the feelings of those who listened to them. In this way, too, the seeds of discontent were sown deep in the hearts of the people.

Then Missionary schools were started in which the principles of the Christian faith were taught. Men said it was by the order of Government. In some districts covenanted officers of high position and of great influence used to visit the schools and encourage the people to attend them; examinations were held in books which taught the tenets of the Christian religion. Lads who attended the schools used to be asked such questions as the following 'Who is your God?' 'Who is your Redeemer?' and these questions they were obliged to answer agreeably to the Christian belief; prizes being given accordingly. This again added to the prevailing ill-will. But it may be said with some justice, 'If the people were not satisfied with this course of education, why did they let their children go to the schools?' The fact is that we have here no question of like or dislike. On the contrary we must account for this by the painfully degraded and ignorant state of the people. They believed that if their children were entered at the schools, they might have employment given them by Government, and be enabled to find some means of subsistence. Hence they put up with a state of affairs in reality disagreeable enough to them. But it must not be thought that they ever liked those schools.

The establishment of Missionary Schools and the covenanted officers attending examination at them.

Village Schools.

When the village schools were established, the general belief was that they were instituted solely with the view of teaching the doctrines of Jesus. The Pergunnah visitors, and deputy inspectors, who use to go from village to village, and town to town advising the people to enter their children at these schools, got the nick-name of Native Clergyman. When the Pergunnah visitor, or Deputy Inspector entered any village the people used to say that the Native Clergyman had come. Their sole idea was that these were Christian schools, established with the view of converting them. Well-informed men, although they did not credit this, saw nevertheless that in these schools nothing but Urdu was taught. They were afraid that boys while reading only Urdu would forget the tenets of their own faith, and that they would thus drift into Christianity. They believed also, that Government wished such books as bore upon the doctrines of the former religions of Hindustan, to fall into entire disuse. This was to be done with the view of ensuring the spread of Christianity. In many of the Eastern districts of Hindustan where these schools were established, boys were entered at them by compulsion, and by compulsion only. It was currently reported that all this was in pursuance of the orders of Government.

There was at the same time a great deal of talk in Hindustan about female education, Man believed it to be the wish of Government, that girls should attend, and be taught at these schools, and leave off the habit of sitting veiled. Anything more obnoxious than this to the feelings of the Hindustanees cannot be conceived. In some districts the practice was actually intro-duced. The Pergunnah visitors and Deputy Inspectors hoped by enforcing the attendance of girls, to gain credit with their Superior. In every way, therefore, right or wrong, they tried to carry out their object. Here then was another cause of discontent among the people, through which they became confirmed in error.

The Introduction of female education.

The large colleges, established in the towns, were from the first a source of suspicion. At the time of their establishment Shah Abdulazeez, a celebrated Moulvie of Hindustan was alive. The Muhammadans asked him for a Futwah on the subject. His answer was distinct. 'Go,' he said, 'Read in the English colleges, and learn the English tongue. The laws of Islam admit it.' Acting on this opinion the Muhammadans did not hesitate to enter these colleges. At that time, how-

Alterations in the usual system of education in large Colleges.

ever, the colleges were conducted on a principle widely different from that which is at present adopted. Arabic, Persian, Sanskrit, and English were equally taught. The 'Fickah,' 'Hadees' and other such books were read. Examinations were held in the 'Fickah' for which certificates of proficiency were given. Religion was not in any way thrust forward. The professors were men of worth and weight: all Scholars of great reputation, wide knowledge and sound moral character. But all this has been changed. The study of Arabic is little thought of. The 'Fickah' and 'Hadees' were suddenly dropped. Persian is almost entirely neglected. Books and methods of teaching have been changed. But the study of Urdu and of English has greatly increased. All this has tended to strengthen the idea that Government wished to wipe out the religions which it found in Hindustan. The professors are no longer men of weight or acquirements. Students at the college, in whom people have not gained confidence, have for sometime past been appointed professors. And hence it is that throughout the country these colleges have fallen into disrepute.

The issue of Government proclamations on the subject admitting Government College English students to appointments in preference to other candidates.

Such was the state of the village schools and the colleges. Such the general feeling of distrust throughout the country as to the views of Government about conversion, when a proclamation was issued by Government to the following effect, Whoever had studied and passed an examination in certain Sciences, and in the English language, and had received a certificate to that effect, was to be considered as having prior claims for employment in the Public Service. Petty appointments were granted on the production of certificates from the Deputy Inspectors: the very men who had hitherto been nicknamed Native Clergymen. This came as a blow to every one. Suspicion increased tenfold. The rumour again arose that Government wished to deprive the

Hindustanees of all means of subsistence and by impoverishing them gradually, to substitute its own religion in the place of theirs.

CAUSE IV.

Neglect in matters which should have received consideration from Government.

Neglect in matters which should have received consideration of Government.

I will now proceed to shew what duties Government ought to have fulfilled and which it did not fulfil.

I feel it most necessary to say that which is in my heart and which I believe to be true even at the risk of its being distasteful to many of the ruling races. What I am now going to treat of is that which if only done in a right way will attract even wild animals, causing them to love instead of to dread, and which therefore will, in a much greater degree, attract men. I cannot here state at length what the benefits of friendship, intercourse and sympathy are, but I maintain that the maintenance of friendly relations between the Governors and the governed is far more necessary than between individuals, private friendships only affect a few, friendship and good feeling between a Government and its subjects affects a nation. As in private friendships two persons are united by the bond of common friendship, so also should a Government and its people be knit together in like manner. *The people and the Government* I may liken to a tree, the latter being the root and the former the growth of that root. As the root is so will the tree be. What! Was such intimacy impossible under this Government? Most certainly not. We have numerous instances in which foreigners and natives of countries have been brought in contact with each other and of their becoming friends, even when their religions and countries were different and widely separated. And why was this? Just because they wished and did their utmost to become so. How often do we not see strifes and enmities between people of the same race, religion and customs. Friendship, intercourse and sympathy are therefore not wholly dependent for their existence merely on the giver's and recipient's being of the same religion, race or country.

Want of cordiality towards the Indians.

Does not the Apostle Paul admonish us in these beautiful words? 'And the Lord make you to increase, and abound in love one toward another, and toward all men, even as we do toward you' 1st Epistle of Paul to the Thessalonians Ch. Ill verse 12. And does not Jesus admonish us in these?. . . 'Therefore all things whatsoever ye would that men should do to you, do ye even so to them, for this is the law and the Prophets' Matthew, VII 12.

These were meant to inculcate friendship and love to all men, and no one, no wise and thoughtful man will say that the admonition is wrong, that friendship and love to our fellow-men are not beneficial, that their results are nil, and that they do not blot out much that is wicked. As yet, truth compels me to state, Government has not cultivated the friendship of its people as was its duty to do. The Creator has instilled it into the heart of man and the instinct of animals that the strong should be kind to and care for the weak. The father loves his child before the child loves him. The man tries to win the woman, not the woman the man. If a man of low degree tries to win the esteem of one in high position, he is liable to be styled a flatterer and not a friend, It was, therefore, for Government to try and win the friendship of its subjects, not for the subjects to try and win that of the Government. If it had done so the results would have been great and the people would have rejoiced. Alas! That it has not done so. If Government says that what I say is untrue, that they tried to cultivate friendship and have only been repaid with enmity. I can only say, that if it had gone the right way to work, its subjects would most undoubtedly have been its friend and supporters; instead of, as in many instances, rising up in arms against it. Now friendship is a feeling which springs from the heart and which cannot be kindled by 'admonitions.' Men may meet on very friendly terms, but it does not therefore follow that they are friends in the real sense of the word, that they are friends at heart as well as in outward signs. This is a link, as it were, between hearts, a man instinctively feels that he likes a man or the contrary. Government has hitherto kept itself as isolated from the people of India as if it had been the fire and they the dry grass, as if it thought that were the two brought in contact, the latter would be burnt up. It and its people were like two different sorts of stone, one white and the other black, which stones too were being daily more and more widely separated. Now the relations between them ought to have been close like those between the streaks of white and black in the stone called Abri in which we see the former close alongside of the latter, the one blending with the other. Government was of course perfectly right in maintaining special friendly relation with its Christian subjects (the English) but it was at the same time incumbent upon it to show towards its native subjects that brotherly kindness which the Apostle Paul exhorts us to in these words, 'And to godliness brotherly kindness and to brotherly kindness charity.' II Peter 1.7. It must be borne in mind, that the blood of the Muhammadan conquerors and that of the people of the country was not the same; that their faith was not the same; their manners and customs not the same; that in their hearts the people did not like them; and that at first there was little or no amalgamation of the two. What then was the secret of their becoming friends! Let us glance at the former Indian dynasties. First came that of the Muhammadan

In ancient times as long as cordiality was not observed by the reigning powers, tranquility was not established.

conquerors. In the reign of the Turks and Pathans, there was no intercourse between the conquerors and the conquered until the Government of the former was made firm and easy. A feeling of cordiality was first established in the reign of the Mogul Emperor Akbar I, and continued till the reign of Shah Jehan. No doubt, owing to many defects in the system of Government the people were subjected to many evils, but these were lightened by the feelings just mentioned. This feeling unfortunately ceased during the reign of Alamger, A. D. 1779, when, owing to the rebellion of several Hindoos of note, such as Sewajee, the Mahratta etc. Alamger vowed vengeance against them all and sent orders to all his Lieutenants to treat them with rigour and harshness and to exempt none from paying tribute. The injury and disaffection which therefore ensued are well known. Now the English Government has been in existence upwards of a century, and up to the present hour has not secured the affections of the people.

Treating the Indians with contempt.

One great source of the stability of a Government is undoubtedly the treating of its subjects with honour and thus gaining their affections. Though a man's income be but small, treat him with honor and he is far more gratified than if he were presented with three or four times the amount than be treated with contempt. Contempt is an ineradicable wrong. Being treated contemptuously sinks deep into a man's heart, and although uninjured by the same as to his worldly goods, he still becomes an enemy. The wound rankles deep and cannot be healed, that given by a sword can be healed, but that inflicted by a contemptuous word can *not*. The results of kindness are different, an enemy even if treated courteously becomes a friend; friends by friendly intercourse, become greater friends, and strangers if created in a friendly manner are no longer strangers. By kindness we make the brute creature our willing slaves, how much more then would such treatment cement the bonds between a Government and its people? Now in the first years of the British rule in India, the people were heartily in favour of it. This good feeling the Government has now forfeited and the natives very generally say that they are treated with contempt. A native gentleman is in the eyes of any petty Official, as much lower than that Official as that same Official esteems himself lower than a Duke. The opinion of many of those Officials is that no native can be a gentleman.

The ill-temper and uncourtly address of local authorities towards the natives.
Now as Government is, throughout India, represented by its officials, it follows as a matter of course that the Natives will judge of the temper of Government towards them by what they see of these officials. However good the intention of Government with regard to its subjects may be, unless these same officials give practical proof thereof by kind treatment of the natives, the people will not believe in them. Theory and practice are not one and the same. In these days, or rather within the last few years the feeling of officials towards natives is not nearly so favorable as was formerly the case. In olden days natives were treated with honor and in a friendly manner by these officials and, consequently to use a native expession 'they carried their (the natives) hearts in their hands'. They sympathized with them in their joys and sorrows, and this too, notwithstanding their high position. They were consequently greatly liked, and the natives used to say 'How wonderful is this treatment from men in the highest position. who, though wielding the reins of empire are still without pride.'

Natives of rank were also treated in a highly honorable manner. They (the officials) really followed the precepts of St. Peter 'And to Godliness brotherly kindness to brotherly kindness, charity.' II Peter V.7., the reverse of which is unfortunately the case as regards the greater number of the officials of the present day. Has not their pride and arrogance caused them to esteem the Hindustanee as nothing in their eyes, and have not their ill-temper and want of solicitude for the natives, caused them to be looked upon with dread by the latter? Is it not well-known to Government that even natives of the highest rank never come into the presence of officials, but with an inward fear and trembling? Is it a secret that the 'Amlah' (native 'court officials') are often addressed harshly and abused by their superiors whilst reading out papers to them? These men, many of them of good birth, often inwardly exclaim 'Oh! that I could gain my living other-wise, cutting grass by the wayside were better than this.' I do not say that the behaviour of all English officials is like this. There are many who are well known for their kindness and friendly feeling toward the natives and these are in consequence much beloved by them, are, to use a native expression, as the sun and the moon to them, and are pointed out as types of the old race of officials.

These men truly follow the admonition of Christ Jesus who said to Simon called Peter and Andrew his brother when they were fishing 'Follow me and I will make you fishers of men.' They, by their good char-acter have drawn the people to them, as it were, in a net, they have not treated them with useless arrogance, without which some think that a high position in the eyes of the natives cannot be kept up. They have earned that blessing which Christ enunciated. 'Blessed are the poor in spirit, for theirs is the kingdom of heaven,' (Matt. V.3). They have treated the people with gentleness and leniency and have ruled the land according to the precept. 'Blessed are the meek for they shall inherit the earth.' Matt. V.5. They have also let their light shine before men, as Christ enjoined in Matthew, V.16. 'Let your light so shine before men that they may see your good works and glorify your Father which is in heaven.'

Few in number, wherever they are, they are held dear by the natives.

This treatment before alluded to was most offensive to all the people of India, but most especially so to the Muhammadans. The reasons for this

The ill treatment more repugnant to the feelings of the Muhammadans, and its cause are clear. For centuries the Muhammadan's position in India has been an honorable one. There is an element of shame in his disposition. He has no grasping desire for money, he esteems honor above all other things, and there are many proofs on record, which shew that the Muhammadan is not easily brought to do that, which, under the influence of temptations, other races in India will do without compunction. It may be that this is wrong but God having instilled it into him, his views and feelings cannot easily be changed. It may be unfortunate but, it is inculcated into them by their religion and is no fault of theirs. This ill treatment then it was which pained them grievously and which caused them heartily to wish for a change of Governors and to hear with joy of anything that was opposed to the present Government. It is much to be regretted that the Muhammadans did not know that Government was doing its utmost to further their interest, their education and to uphold their honour, This they did not know, as the intentions and wishes of Government were never made known by their various officials.

Another great reason for the dissatisfaction of the natives of India, and more especially of the Muhammadans, was the exclusion of natives from high appointments. A few short years ago Muhammadans filled the most honorable posts under their own Government and the desire and hope for such is still in them. Under the English Government they longed for the advancement of their honor in the eyes of the world, but there was no way open to them. In the early days of this Government, natives of rank were certainly singled out to fill high posts, but by degrees this fell into disuse. The assertion by Muhammadans, that the practice of holding examinations is a bad one, is a mistaken one. If they have not the qualifications to enable them to pass, they must not blame the system; undoubtedly the examination system goes far towards procuring an efficient staff of public servants, but many natives are appointed to high posts who, in the estimation of their countrymen are very small indeed. In the giving of certificates very little was thought of family and honor. Lord Bentinck did most for the advancement of the natives in this respect, but the high appointments

Exclusion of natives from promotion to high appointments. Lord Bentinck's system of employing natives in high grades of service an inadequate one.

which he bestowed upon a select few were utterly inadequate to the wants of the people. English officers of the highest rank have often admitted this of late years. Now is the passing an examination a sim qua non in England? Are the best English statesmen invariably those who have passed high examination? Are high diplomatic posts not often given to them on account of their birth and practical common sense and sometimes even without the latter qualification?

The not holding of Durbars by the Governor General of India and not conferring rank and honour due to merit according to the usage of former emperors.

The people of India have from time immemorial been always in the habit of attending the Durbars (levees) of their Sovereign and have always enjoyed seeing his pomp and state and influences. This feeling of gladness at the sight of the sovereign is a feeling instinctively felt by every one. Man feels the power of the ruler when thus brought face to face with him and acknowledge himself to be his subject. Now although the Governor General of India was certainly, whilst on tour, in the habit of holding durbars, still the few that he did hold were not sufficient for the wants of the country. Lords Auckland and Ellenborough held right regal durbars. This perhaps may not have been approved of by the Home Government, but it was a most excellent thing for India, although even their durbars were too few in number. May the Almighty always watch over and protect our most gracious sovereign Queen Victoria and Her representation in India, His Excellency the Viceroy and Governor General. Let us hope that the heartfelt wants of the natives of this country may be listened to and gradually satisfied.

QUESTIONS

1. Do you agree with Syed Ahmed Khan that if a government does not listen to the voices of the people it rules, it cannot be effective?
2. Why was it so important for Syed Ahmed Khan to write this book?
3. Do you think Syed Ahmed Khan's ideas about governance and society are progressive? Why or why not?
4. What ethical aspects of Christian teachings does Syed Ahmed Khan use to illustrate his arguments?

VOICES FROM THE TAIPING HEAVENLY KINGDOM

The Taiping Rebellion (1850–1864) represented a rejection not only of the ruling Qing Dynasty (Ch'ing; 1644–1911) who were of Manchu ethnicity, but also of many of the inequities and vices that had appeared in traditional Chinese society. The charismatic Taiping ("great peace") leader, Hong Xiuquan (Hung Hsiu-ch'uan; 1814–1864), grew up like many intelligent Chinese boys—seeking an official position through China's civil service examination system. After several failed attempts, Hong was overcome by illness, and in his delirium he claimed to have had a life-altering vision that incorporated his resentment of the Chinese system with ideas from a Protestant missionary tract. The vision, Hong later realized after a fourth and final failure to pass the exam, revealed that he was none other than the younger brother of Jesus Christ. Hong's mission was to overthrow China's Manchu overlords and establish a "Heavenly Kingdom of Great Peace" that would replace Confucianism with Hong's version of Christian egalitarianism. The Taipings rejected all aspects of Manchu domination and sought to eliminate Confucianism, opium and alcohol consumption, gender inequity, and the unequal distribution of land.

The failure of an initial Qing attempt to suppress the uprising stunned China's rulers and emboldened the rebels, who quickly marched north and seized the walled city of Nanjing (Nanking) in 1853. Nanjing became the headquarters of the rebellion until its defeat in 1864. Squabbles among the leadership and disillusionment among their followers weakened Taiping unity and military strength. By the time Qing armies, supported by several foreign powers, destroyed the last of the rebels and their supporters, an estimated twenty to thirty million people lay dead.

This selection includes two documents issued by the Taiping leadership. The first, written in 1852, is a lengthy ode by Hong Xiuquan that outlines the "six deadly sins" of Taiping society. The second is a proclamation issued in 1853 or 1854 during the Taiping occupation of Nanjing. It attempts to control what the Taiping leadership considered troubling behavior in the capital during a time of warfare.

THE TAIPING IMPERIAL DECLARATION

An Ode on the Origin of Virtue and the Saving of the World.[1]

The great origin of virtue is Heaven;
Let us reverently take Heaven's way to arouse the multitudes of the
    virtuous.
The way of Heaven is to punish the licentious and bless the good;
Repent while it is early; be the first.
The root and source of the true Way lies only in rectitude;
Successive generations have all observed this without distinction.
Enjoy heavenly bliss; free yourselves from worldly considerations;
Be not entangled by any of the common feelings.
Abandon at once every vicious view;
The true creating Spirit is God alone.
Without distinction between noble or lowly, all must reverently
    worship him;
God, the Heavenly Father, is shared by everyone.
That the world is one family has been passed down from of old,
From the time of P'an Ku[2] down to the Three Dynasties,[3]
Both princes and people as one body honored August Heaven.
During that time when the sovereigns honored God,
Nobles, scholars, and commoners all did the same.[4]
It might be compared, among men, to children serving their father;
For whether worthy or unworthy, all must follow the Domestic
    Rules.[5]

Heaven and man were of one mind, there were no two principles;
How could monarchs and sovereigns let their private views prevail?

192

Let God be worshipped;
Let all in this unite,
Whether west or north,
Whether south or east.
Every fibre and thread depends on God;
Every sip and morsel comes from the Heavenly Majesty.
It is your duty every morning to adore and every evening to worship
    him;
Reason demands that you should praise his goodness and sing his
    merits.
Should men set this aside, and worship another,
Or worship all other things, it would all be in vain.
. . .

Of all wrong things licentiousness is the chief;
When man becomes demon, Heaven is most enraged.
Debauch others and debauch oneself, and both are monstrous.
Why not sing of the footprints of the gentle deer, and celebrate a
    virtuous posterity.[6]
. . .

The second kind of wrong is disobedience to parents,
A great violation of the Heavenly Commandments; make haste to
    reform yourselves.
The lamb kneels to reach the teat, the crow returns the food to its
    dam;
When men are not equal to brutes, they disgrace their origin.
The dweller at Li-shan howled and wept, and Heaven was moved,[7]
The birds aided him in weeding, and the elephants in ploughing.
Though exalted as the Son of Heaven and rich in the possession of
    the four seas,
His filial virtues moved Heaven; how could they be viewed lightly![8]
. . .

The third kind of wrong is to kill;
To slay our fellow men is the worst of crimes.
Under heaven all are brothers;
The souls of all come alike from heaven.

193

God looks upon all men as his children;
For men to destroy one another is extremely lamentable,
Hence in former days there was no wanton killing.
Their virtue accorded with Heaven's will, and Heaven watched over
them.

. . .

The fourth kind of wrong is robbery and thievery;
Injustice and inhumanity are not proper.
Those who form gangs and are disorderly, Heaven will not protect;
When iniquities are excessive, calamity will surely follow.
A good man, meeting with wealth, does not take it illicitly.

. . .

The fifth kind of wrong is witchcraft;
By the evil arts of deceiving the multitude, Heaven's penalty is
incurred.
Death and life, calamity and sickness, all are determined by Heaven;
Why then deceive the people by the useless manufacture of charms?
Incantations to procure luck, vows to the demons, services to the
devils,
Fastings and processions, all are of no avail.
From of old, death and nature have been difficult to defend oneself
against;
How can anyone by intercession guard against harm?
From of old, wizards, witches, and necromancers
Have for numerous generations lived in poverty because Heaven will
not sustain them.
The devils' agents, having served the devils, are eventually possessed
by the devils;
The gates of hell are ever open to receive such heretic-followers.

. . .

The sixth kind of wrong is gambling;
He who uses the hidden blade to kill a man is evil at heart.
Beware! Beware! Beware!
For it is opposed to reason.
The seeking of wealth has its way, and its acquisition lies in fate.
Do not by deceit and fraud destroy the heart.

If fate provides for you, why need you gamble?

If fate does not, although you gamble, you will not obtain your wish.

In the end, poverty and riches are arranged by Heaven.

Follow your proper avocations, and you shall be at ease.

Confucius and Yen-tzu[9] were happy on water and thin gruel;

Knowing their fate they were content in poverty, and their spirits
    soared.[10]

Man's life in this world is like a dream at the third watch.[11]

Why ponder? Why worry? Why hope?

Small wealth comes from diligence and great wealth from fate.[12]

From of old, to be a man one must exert himself.

Oh you multitudes!

Do not say it does not matter;

There is nothing one might not do because of gambling.

Heroes, why do you sink and stray?

Unrighteous gain is like quenching one's thirst with poison;

Scholars, farmers, artisans, and merchants long forbear.[13]

Of one thousand who gamble, one thousand are mean;

I implore you to change your thoughts, and carefully deliberate.

There are others who drive on till they fall into a snare,

And cooking and smoking opium, they become mad.

In the present day so many brave men

Have wounded themselves with the opium gun.

With regard to the love of wine,[14] this is also a wrong.

Successful families ought to warn themselves against the family-
    destroying juice.

. . .

All the rest of the wrong things are too numerous to mention;

It is up to man himself to distinguish the obscure and indistinct;

If the small matters are not attended to, eventually this will prejudice
    your virtue.

Before the solid ice is formed, be careful in treading on the hoar
    frost.

Yü and Chi were diligent, and anxious to starve or drown.

Hence one became emperor, and the descendants of the other
    became rulers.

Wen of Chou and Confucius in their own persons were upright;

Hence their souls were permitted to advance and retreat in the
presence of God.[15]

True words,

Without affectation.

My soul has previously been allowed to ascend to heaven,

My words are true and real, without the slightest extravagance.

My parental feelings are strong, and I cannot forget;

Finding my words insufficient, I have thus spoken at length.

Those families which accumulate goodness will have a surplus of
blessings;

Those families which accumulate wickedness will have excessive
misfortune.

Those who obey Heaven will be preserved; those who disobey
Heaven perish.

So honor God and you will obtain glory and honor.

A PROCLAMATION EXHORTING ALL TO FOLLOW
THE CORRECT WAY

We, Wei [Chün] and Shih [Chen-hsiang],[16] royal kinsmen and military commanders of the Heavenly Court of the true Heavenly-ordained T'ai-p'ing
T'ien-kuo, issue this proclamation for the purpose of enlightening and
instructing officials, soldiers, the good people, and others, that each must
forgo evil practices and follow the correct Way. It must be known that to
forgo evil is to revere the correct; to forgo the old is to give birth to the
new. It is due to the heavenly favor generously bestowed by the Heavenly
Father and Heavenly Elder Brother that they personally sent to earth the
true Sovereign, the T'ien Wang, to reign over the country. They also sent
the Tung Wang and the various other Wangs to assist in carrying out the
dynastic principles: remove the evil, protect the upright, abolish violence,
and bring peace to the people; and they have already established their capital at T'ien-ching [Nanking]. People within the four seas have given their
allegiance, and people in all directions have turned to them. They [the
Wangs] have promoted the destiny of our still new country, and the peo-

ple have all yielded their hearts. They have abolished the already old and degenerate practices, and customs have all been changed from the old. The men's quarters have been strictly separated from the women's quater. The utmost justice and utmost righteousness prevail in their hearts. Our Heavenly Court deeply hates and thoroughly dislikes all under heaven that is not in accordance with the regulations and the commandments, and all that transgresses the ethical and righteous.

We, the royal kinsmen, respectfully, in accordance with the heavenly directives, have sent the troops to bring peace to the people, to abolish evil practices, and to forbid dissolute customs. It has been heard that in your locality there are those who are evil and lewd, and who deliberately violate the regulations and the Commandments. For this reason we earnestly advise and instruct so that you officials, soldiers, and good people all will know. For those who delude the people's hearts and corrupt the customs, there are also prohibitory regulations clearly listed below:

1. Men's quarters must necessarily be separated from women's quarters. Officials and soldiers sometimes send their dirty clothes to civilian women for washing, and sometimes hire civilian women to mend their clothes. With this type of intimate contact, love affairs between them cannot be prevented. We cannot do otherwise than forestall these minor infractions and prevent them from beginning in order to warn people against unvirtuous customs. From here on, if there are any officials or soldiers who hire civilian women to wash or sew clothes, without exception they shall be unsparingly decapitated. Any promiscuity between the men and the women will result in punishment for both.

2. Prostitution most necessarily must be prohibited. Men have their quarters and women theirs.[17] Men will engage in scholarship, farming, labor, and commerce; women will engage in needlework and cooking. Monogamy is a natural matter. If there are any who engage in evil practices, if officials or people privately stay with prostitutes, and if there are those who act as prostitutes against the regulations and the Commandments, they will be wiped out with their families, and the neighbors who seize and apprehend them will have rewards. Those who with intent assist them to escape will all be punished. Offenders with purpose and intent will be unsparingly decapitated.

3. The sale and the smoking of opium and "yellow" tobacco is forbid-

den. The smoking of opium is a harm given by the devil foreigners. When the smoking of opium becomes habitual the sickness becomes extreme, and the disease enters the vital regions. "Yellow" tobacco is harmful to the skin and body, does not satisfy hunger or thirst, and is also a depraved habit of the devils. If there are any who sell [opium or yellow tobacco], they shall be decapitated. If there are any who smoke these, they shall be decapitated. Those who fail to report [such activities] shall also be punished.

You, the officials, soldiers and people, must strictly forbid and end the various practices enumerated above and must not intentionally commit offense. Once discovered, offenders shall certainly be investigated and punished in accordance with the heavenly law. When we, the royal kinsmen, have spoken, the law follows and there will be no leniency. Fear this; heed this; do not disobey. Specially proclaimed.

Translated by M. Ivy and I. Wu

END NOTES

1. The later edition calls it a proclamation. The character *tao* is here rendered "virtue," following Medhurst's translation.
2. A legendary being, said to have assisted in the formation of the universe.
3. *From the time . . . Dynasties.* Later edition: "In high antiquity China was like the foreign nations."
4. *During the time . . . same.* Deleted from the later edition.
5. The *Nei-tze-pien,* one of the chapters of the *Li-chi.* Instead of *follow the Domestic Rules* the later edition reads "serve and nourish him faithfully."
6. Taken from the *Book of Odes;* see Legge, *The She-King,* p. 19.
7. An allusion to the great Shun of legendary antiquity.
8. *The dweller . . . lightly.* Deleted from the later edition.
9. A noted disciple of Confucius, who was content with simple living.
10. *Confucius . . . soared.* Deleted from the later edition.
11. *Man's life . . . watch.* Later edition: "If man lives in this world and respects Heaven's law."
12. *Small wealth . . . fate.* Later edition: "When worldly sentiments are completely discarded, then heavenly sentiments will be manifest."
13. *Scholars . . . forbear.* Later edition: "Obey and observe the Heavenly Commandments; long forbear."
14. *Love of wine.* Later edition: "drinking of wine."
15. *Yü . . . God.* Deleted in the later edition. Yü founded the Hsia dynasty; the descendants of Chi founded the Chou dynasty.
16. The *Shih-wen-ch'ao* editors contend that this Shih is Shih Feng-k'uei, who was also one of the commanders in this western campaign. However, Shih Chen-hsiang and Wei Chün were major commanders.
17. The terms used by the Taipings were *nan-hang* 男行 for men's quarters and *nü-hang* 女行 for women's quarters.

QUESTIONS

1. In what ways do the documents illustrate the blending of Christianity, Confucianism, and Chinese folk beliefs in Taiping ideology?
2. How did the Taiping leadership attempt to control undesirable behavior in the ranks? How do you think approach affected their followers?
3. Why do you think the Taipings were so adamant about sexual segregation?
4. Why do you think the Taiping belief system was considered such a threat to the Qing Dynasty rulers and traditional Chinese elites?

NATURAL SELECTION

Charles Darwin

Charles Darwin was born in Shrewsbury, England, in 1809, the son of noted physician Robert Waring Darwin and grandson of Erasmus Darwin, a doctor-poet who had been an early champion of the idea of evolutionary develop-ment. Darwin began medical studies at the University of Edinburgh in 1825, but his aptitude lay elsewhere, and he moved on to Christ's College, Cam-bridge, where he prepared to take holy orders. At Cambridge, he met the botanist John Stevens Henslow, who encouraged Darwin's scientific interests and helped him to obtain the position of naturalist on the HMS Beagle. *Darwin's five years aboard the ship, sailing around the coastline of South America, were a formative influence on his later career. He returned to England with numerous specimens and began arranging and studying them; this work would lead him to his theory of the origin of species. During this time, Darwin befriended a number of leading scientific specialists, including Charles Lyell, the author of the important* Principles of Geology. *In 1839, Darwin was elected a Fellow of the Royal Society and also married his cousin, Emma Wedgewood. Together, he and Emma settled in Down, where Darwin would spend the next forty years pursuing his scientific studies and fathering a large family.* The Origin of Species, *first published in book form in 1859, ran through numerous editions during Darwin's lifetime, sparked still-ongoing cultural and religious debate, and guaranteed Darwin's place as a scientific pioneer. Darwin died in 1882 and was buried in Westminster Abbey.*

First published in 1859, The Origin of Species *is counted among the most revolutionary of scientific works. The theory of natural selection championed*

Reprinted from *The Origin of Species*, 1859.

by Darwin in Origin *challenged many of his contemporaries' accepted beliefs, including Biblical literacy, Divine Providence, the fixity of species, and the primacy of humans in the natural order. Debate around the implications of Darwin's theory was, and continues to be, heated, but its importance in dictating the direction of much of modern science is uncontested. Despite this importance, many of the ideas put forth in* Origin *were neither new nor unique: eighteenth century and early nineteenth century thinkers such as Buffon, Darwin's own grandfather, Erasmus Darwin, Malthus, Paley, and Lamarck, as well as contemporaries such as Charles Lyell, Robert Chambers, and Alfred Wallace had previously suggested a number of Darwin's assertions. Darwin himself had presented many of his ideas about natural selection to the scientific community prior to publication of* Origin. *Darwin wrote* Origin *as a synthesis with the lay public in mind, though, and the work's readability contributed to its wide influence. In this passage, taken from Chapter Four, Darwin explained his theory of natural selection: how variations in organisms occurring over time, if useful, will increase an organism's chance of survival and tend to produce similar characteristics in its offspring.*

How will the struggle for existence, discussed too briefly in the last chapter, act in regard to variation? Can the principle of selection, which we have seen is so potent in the hands of man, apply in nature? I think we shall see that it can act most effectually. Let it be borne in mind in what an endless number of strange peculiarities our domestic productions, and, in a lesser degree, those under nature, vary; and how strong the hereditary tendency is. Under domestication, it may be truly said that the whole organization becomes in some degree plastic. Let it be borne in mind how infinitely complex and close-fitting are the mutual relations of all organic beings to each other and to their physical conditions of life. Can it, then, be thought improbable, seeing that variations useful to man have undoubtedly occurred, that other variations useful in some way to each being in the great and complex battle of life, should sometimes occur in the course of thousands of generations? If such do occur, can we doubt (remembering that many more individuals are born than can possibly survive) that individuals having any advantage, however slight, over others, would have the best chance of surviving and of procreating their kind? On the other hand, we may feel sure that any variation in the least degree injurious would be rigidly destroyed. This preservation of favorable variations and the rejection of injurious variations, I call Natural Selection. Variations neither useful nor injurious would not be affected by natural selection, and would be left a fluctuating element, as perhaps we see in the species called polymorphic.

We shall best understand the probable course of natural selection by taking the case of a country undergoing some physical change, for instance, of climate. The proportional numbers of its inhabitants would almost immediately undergo a change, and some species might become extinct. "We may conclude, from what we have seen of the intimate and complex manner in which the inhabitants of each country are bound together, that any change in the numerical proportions of some of the inhabitants, independently of the change of climate itself, would most seriously affect many of the others. If the country were open on its borders, new forms would certainly immigrate, and this also would seriously disturb the relations of some of the former inhabitants. Let it be remembered how powerful the influence of a single introduced tree or mammal has been shown to be. But in the case of an island, or of a country partly surrounded by barriers, into which new and better adapted forms could not freely enter, we should then have places in the economy of nature which would assuredly be better filled up, if some of the original inhabitants were in some manner modified; for, had the area been open to immigration, these same places would have been seized on by intruders. In such case, every slight modification, which in the course of ages chanced to arise, and which in any way favored the individuals of any of the species, by better adapting them to their altered conditions, would tend to be preserved; and natural selection would thus have free scope for the work of improvement.

We have reason to believe, as stated in the first chapter, that a change in the conditions of life, by specially acting on the reproductive system, causes or increases variability; and in the foregoing case the conditions of life are supposed to have undergone a change, and this would manifestly be favorable to natural selection, by giving a better chance of profitable variations occurring; and unless profitable variations do occur, natural selection can do nothing. Not that, as I believe, any extreme amount of variability is necessary; as man can certainly produce great results by adding up in any given direction mere individual differences, so could Nature, but far more easily, from having incomparably longer time at her disposal. Nor do I believe that any great physical change, as of climate, or any unusual degree of isolation to check immigration, is actually necessary to produce new and unoccupied places for natural selection to fill up by modifying and improving some of the varying inhabitants. For as all the inhabitants of each country are struggling together with nicely balanced forces, extremely slight modifications in the structure or habits of one inhabitant would often give it an advantage over others; and still further modifications of the same kind would often still further increase the advantage. No country can be named in which all the native inhabitants are now so perfectly adapted to each other and to the physical conditions under which they live, that none of them could anyhow be improved; for in all countries, the natives have been so far conquered by naturalized productions, that they have allowed foreigners to take firm possession of the land. And as foreigners have thus everywhere beaten some of the natives, we may safely conclude that the natives might have been modified with advantage, so as to have better resisted such intruders.

As man can produce and certainly has produced a great result by his methodical and unconscious means of selection, what may not nature effect? Man can act only on external and visible characters: nature cares nothing for appearances, except in so far as they may be useful to any being. She can act on every internal organ, on every shade of constitutional difference, on the whole machinery of life. Man selects only for his own good; Nature only for that of the being which she tends. Every selected character is fully exercised by her; and the being is placed under well-suited conditions of life. Man keeps the natives of many climates in the same country; he seldom exercises each selected character in some peculiar and fitting manner; he feeds a long and a short beaked pigeon on the same food; he does not exercise a long-backed or long-legged quadruped in any peculiar manner; he exposes sheep with long and short wool to the same climate. He does not allow the most vigorous males to struggle for the females. He does not rigidly destroy all inferior animals, but protects during each varying season, as far as lies in his power, all his productions. He often begins his selection by some half-monstrous form;

or at least by some modification prominent enough to catch his eye, or to be plainly useful to him. Under nature, the slightest difference of structure or constitution may well turn the nicely-balanced scale in the struggle for life, and so be preserved. How fleeting are the wishes and efforts of man! how short his time! and consequently how poor will his products be, compared with those accumulated by nature during whole geological periods. Can we wonder, then, that nature's productions should be far 'truer' in character than man's productions; that they should be infinitely better adapted to the most complex conditions of life, and should plainly bear the stamp of far higher workmanship?

It may be said that natural selection is daily and hourly scrutinizing, throughout the world, every variation, even the slightest; rejecting that which is bad, preserving and adding up all that is good; silently and insensibly working, whenever and wherever opportunity offers, at the improvement of each organic being in relation to its organic and inorganic conditions of life. We see nothing of these slow changes in progress, until the hand of time has marked the long lapses of ages, and then so imperfect is our view into long past geological ages, that we only see that the forms of life are now different from what they formerly were.

Although natural selection can act only through and for the good of each being, yet characters and structures, which we are apt to consider as of very trifling importance, may thus be acted on. When we see leaf-eating insects green, and bark-feeders mottled-grey; the alpine ptarmigan white in winter, the red-grouse the color of heather, and the black-grouse that of peaty earth, we must believe that these tints are of service to these birds and insects in preserving them from danger. Grouse, if not destroyed at some period of their lives, would increase in countless numbers; they are known to suffer largely from birds of prey; and hawks are guided by eyesight to their prey,—so much so, that on parts of the Continent persons are warned not to keep white pigeons, as being the most liable to destruction. Hence I can see no reason to doubt that natural selection might be most effective in giving the proper color to each kind of grouse, and in keeping that color, when once acquired, true and constant. Nor ought we to think that the occasional destruction of an animal of any particular color would produce little effect: we should remember how essential it is in a flock of white sheep to destroy every lamb with the faintest trace of black. In plants the down on the fruit and the color of the flesh are considered by botanists as characters of the most trifling importance: yet we hear from an excellent horticulturist, Downing, that in the United States smooth-skinned fruits suffer far more from a beetle, a curculio, than those with down; that purple plums suffer far more from a certain disease than yellow plums; whereas another disease attacks yellow-fleshed peaches far more than those with other colored flesh. If, with all the aids of art, these slight differences make a great difference in cultivating the several varieties, assuredly, in a state of nature, where the trees would have to struggle with other trees and with a host of enemies, such differences would effectually settle which variety, whether a smooth or downy, a yellow or purple fleshed fruit, should succeed.

In looking at many small points of difference between species, which, as far as our ignorance permits us to judge, seem to be quite unimportant, we must not forget that climate, food, &c., probably produce some slight and direct effect. It is, however, far more necessary to bear in mind that there are many unknown laws of correlation of growth, which, when one part of the organization is modified through variation, and the modifications are accumulated by natural selection for the good of the being, will cause other modifications, often of the most unexpected nature.

As we see that those variations which under domestication appear at any particular period of life, tend to reappear in the offspring at the same period;—for instance, in the seeds of the many varieties of our culinary and agricultural plants; in the caterpillar and cocoon stages of the varieties of the silkworm; in the eggs of poultry, and in the color of the down of their chickens; in the horns of our sheep and cattle when nearly adult;—so in a state of nature, natural selection will be enabled to act on and modify organic beings at any age, by the accumulation of profitable variations at that age, and by their inheritance at a corresponding age. If it profit a plant to have its seeds more and more widely disseminated by the wind, I can see no greater difficulty in this being effected through natural selection, than in the cotton-planter increasing and improving by selection the down in the pods on his cotton-trees. Natural selection may modify and adapt the larva of an insect to a score of contingencies, wholly different from those which concern the mature insect. These modifications will no doubt affect, through the laws of correlation, the structure of the adult; and probably in the case of those insects which live only for a few hours, and which never feed, a large part of their structure is merely the correlated result of successive changes in the structure of their larvae. So, conversely, modifications in the adult will probably often affect the structure of the larva; but in all cases natural selection will ensure that modifications consequent on other modifications at a different period of life, shall not be in the least degree injurious: for if they became so, they would cause the extinction of the species.

Natural selection will modify the structure of the young in relation to the parent, and of the parent in relation to the young. In social animals it will adapt the structure of each individual for the benefit of the community; if each in consequence profits by the selected change. What natural selection cannot do, is to modify the structure of one species, without giving it any advantage, for the good of another species; and though statements to this effect may be found in works of natural history, I cannot find one case which will bear investigation. A structure used only once in an animal's whole life, if of high importance to it, might be modified to any extent by natural selection; for instance, the great jaws possessed by certain insects, and used exclusively for opening the cocoon—or the hard tip to the beak of nestling birds, used for breaking the egg. It has been asserted, that of the best short-beaked tumbler-pigeons more perish in the egg than are able to get out of it; so that fanciers assist in the act of hatching. Now, if nature had to make the beak of a full-grown pigeon very short for the bird's own advantage, the process of modification would be very slow, and there would be simultaneously the most rigorous selection of the young birds within the egg, which had the most powerful and hardest beaks, for all with weak beaks would inevitably perish: or, more delicate and more easily broken shells might be selected, the thickness of the shell being known to vary like every other structure.

Illustrations of the action of Natural Selection. In order to make it clear how, as I believe, natural selection acts, I must beg permission to give one or two imaginary illustrations. Let us take the case of a wolf, which preys on various animals, securing some by craft, some by strength, and some by fleetness; and let us suppose that the fleetest prey, a deer for instance, had from any change in the country increased in numbers, or that other prey had decreased in numbers, during that season of the year when the wolf is hardest pressed for food. I can under such circumstances see no reason to doubt that the swiftest and slimmest wolves would have the best chance of surviving, and so be preserved or selected,—provided always that they retained strength to master their prey at this or at some other period of the year, when they might be compelled to prey on other animals. I can see no more reason to doubt this, than that man can improve the fleetness of his greyhounds by careful and methodical selection, or by that unconscious selection which results from each man trying to keep the best dogs without any thought of modifying the breed.

Even without any change in the proportional numbers of the animals on which our wolf preyed, a cub might be born with an innate tendency to pursue certain kinds of prey. Nor can this be thought very improbable; for we often observe great differences in the natural tendencies of our domestic animals; one cat, for instance, taking to catch rats, another mice; one cat, according to Mr St John, bringing home winged game, another hares or rabbits, and another hunting on marshy ground and almost nightly catching woodcocks or snipes. The tendency to catch rats rather than mice is known to be inherited. Now, if any slight innate change of habit or of structure benefited an individual wolf, it would have the best chance of surviving and of leaving offspring. Some of its young would probably inherit the same habits or structure, and by the repetition of this process, a new variety might be formed which would either supplant or coexist with the parent-form of wolf. Or, again, the wolves inhabiting a mountainous district, and those frequenting the lowlands, would naturally be forced to hunt different prey; and from the continued preservation of the individuals best fitted for the two sites, two varieties might slowly be formed. These varieties would cross and blend where they met; but to this subject of intercrossing we shall soon have to return. I may add, that, according to Mr Pierce, there are two varieties of the wolf inhabiting the Catskill Mountains in the United States, one with a light greyhound-like form, which pursues deer, and the other more bulky, with shorter legs, which more frequently attacks the shepherd's flocks.

Let us now take a more complex case. Certain plants excrete a sweet juice, apparently for the sake of eliminating something injurious from their sap: this is effected by glands at the base of the stipules in some

Leguminosae, and at the back of the leaf of the common laurel. This juice, though small in quantity, is greedily sought by insects. Let us now suppose a little sweet juice or nectar to be excreted by the inner bases of the petals of a flower. In this case insects in seeking the nectar would get dusted with pollen, and would certainly often transport the pollen from one flower to the stigma of another flower. The flowers of two distinct individuals of the same species would thus get crossed; and the act of crossing, we have good reason to believe (as will hereafter be more fully alluded to), would produce very vigorous seedlings, which consequently would have the best chance of flourishing and surviving. Some of these seedlings would probably inherit the nectar-excreting power. Those individual flowers which had the largest glands or nectaries, and which excreted most nectar, would be oftenest visited by insects, and would be oftenest crossed; and so in the long-run would gain the upper hand. Those flowers, also, which had their stamens and pistils placed, in relation to the size and habits of the particular insects which visited them, so as to favor in any degree the transportal of their pollen from flower to flower, would likewise be favored or selected. We might have taken the case of insects visiting flowers for the sake of collecting pollen instead of nectar; and as pollen is formed for the sole object of fertilization, its destruction appears a simple loss to the plant; yet if a little pollen were carried, at first occasionally and then habitually, by the pollen-devouring insects from flower to flower, and a cross thus effected, although nine-tenths of the pollen were destroyed, it might still be a great gain to the plant; and those individuals which produced more and more pollen, and had larger and larger anthers, would be selected.

When our plant, by this process of the continued preservation or natural selection of more and more attractive flowers, had been rendered highly attractive to insects, they would, unintentionally on their part, regularly carry pollen from flower to flower; and that they can most effectually do this, I could easily show by many striking instances. I will give only one—not as a very striking case, but as likewise illustrating one step in the separation of the sexes of plants, presently to be alluded to. Some holly-trees bear only male flowers, which have four stamens producing rather a small quantity of pollen, and a rudimentary pistil; other holly-trees bear only female flowers; these have a full-sized pistil, and four stamens with shriveled anthers, in which not a grain of pollen can be detected. Having found a female tree exactly sixty yards from a male tree, I put the stigmas of twenty flowers, taken from different branches, under the microscope, and on all, without exception, there were pollen-grains, and on some a profusion of pollen. As the wind had set for several days from the female to the male tree, the pollen could not thus have been carried. The weather had been cold and boisterous, and therefore not favorable to bees, nevertheless every female flower which I examined had been effectually fertilized by the bees, accidentally dusted with pollen, having flown from tree to tree in search of nectar. But to return to our imaginary case: as soon as the plant had been rendered so highly attractive to insects that pollen was regularly carried from flower to flower, another process might commence. No naturalist doubts the advantage of what has been called the 'physiological division of labor;' hence we may believe that it would be advantageous to a plant to produce stamens alone in one flower or on one whole plant, and pistils alone in another flower or on another plant. In plants under culture and placed under new conditions of life, sometimes the male organs and sometimes the female organs become more or less impotent; now if we suppose this to occur in ever so slight a degree under nature, then as pollen is already carried regularly from flower to flower, and as a more complete separation of the sexes of our plant would be advantageous on the principle of the division of labor, individuals with this tendency more and more increased, would be continually favored or selected, until at last a complete separation of the sexes would be effected.

Let us now turn to the nectar-feeding insects in our imaginary case: we may suppose the plant of which we have been slowly increasing the nectar by continued selection, to be a common plant; and that certain insects depended in main part on its nectar for food. I could give many facts, showing how anxious bees are to save time; for instance, their habit of cutting holes and sucking the nectar at the bases of certain flowers, which they can, with a very little more trouble, enter by the mouth. Bearing such facts in mind, I can see no reason to doubt that an accidental deviation in the size and form of the body, or in the curvature and length of the proboscis, &c., far too slight to be appreciated by us, might profit a bee or other insect, so that an individual so characterized would be able to obtain its food more quickly, and so have a better chance of living and leaving descendants. Its descendants would probably inherit a tendency to a similar slight deviation of structure. The tubes of the corollas of the common red and incarnate clovers (Trifolium pratense and incarnatum) do not on a hasty glance appear to differ in length; yet the hive-bee can easily suck the nectar out of the incarnate clover, but not out of the common red clover, which is visited by humble-bees alone; so that whole fields of the red clover offer in vain an abundant supply of precious nectar to the hive-bee. Thus it might be a great advantage to the hive-bee to have a slightly longer or differently constructed proboscis. On the other hand, I have found by experiment that the fertility of clover greatly depends on bees visiting and moving parts of the corolla, so as to push the pollen on to the stigmatic surface. Hence, again, if humble-bees were to become rare in any country, it might be a great advantage to the red clover to have a shorter or more deeply divided tube to its corolla, so that the hive-bee could visit its flowers. Thus I can understand how a flower and a bee might slowly become, either simultaneously or one after the other, modified and adapted in the most perfect manner to each other, by the continued preservation of individuals presenting mutual and slightly favorable deviations of structure.

I am well aware that this doctrine of natural selection, exemplified in the above imaginary instances, is open to the same objections which were at first urged against Sir Charles Lyell's noble views on 'the modern changes of the earth, as illustrative of geology;' but we now very seldom hear the action, for instance, of the coast-waves, called a trifling and insignificant cause, when applied to the excavation of gigantic valleys or to the formation of the longest lines of inland cliffs. Natural selection can act only by the preservation and accumulation of infinitesimally small inherited modifications, each profitable to the preserved being; and as modern geology has almost banished such views as the excavation of a great valley by a single diluvial wave, so will natural selection, if it be a true principle, banish the belief of the continued creation of new organic beings, or of any great and sudden modification in their structure.

Circumstances favourable to Natural Selection. This is an extremely intricate subject. A large amount of inheritable and diversified variability is favourable, but I believe mere individual differences suffice for the work. A large number of individuals, by giving a better chance for the appearance within any given period of profitable variations, will compensate for a lesser amount of variability in each individual, and is, I believe, an extremely important element of success. Though nature grants vast periods of time for the work of natural selection, she does not grant an indefinite period; for as all organic beings are striving, it may be said, to seize on each place in the economy of nature, if any one species does not become modified and improved in a corresponding degree with its competitors, it will soon be exterminated.

In man's methodical selection, a breeder selects for some definite object, and free intercrossing will wholly stop his work. But when many men, without intending to alter the breed, have a nearly common standard of perfection, and all try to get and breed from the best animals, much improvement and modification surely but slowly follow from this unconscious process of selection, notwithstanding a large amount of crossing with inferior animals. Thus it will be in nature; for within a confined area, with some place in its polity not so perfectly occupied as might be, natural selection will always tend to preserve all the individuals varying in the right direction, though in different degrees, so as better to fill up the unoccupied place. But if the area be large, its several districts will almost certainly present different conditions of life; and then if natural selection be modifying and improving a species in the several districts, there will be intercrossing with the other individuals of the same species on the confines of each. . . .

Intercrossing plays a very important part in nature in keeping the individuals of the same species, or of the same variety, true and uniform in character. It will obviously thus act far more efficiently with those animals "which unite for each birth; but . . . we have reason to believe that occasional intercrosses take place with all animals and with all plants. Even if these take place only at long intervals, I am convinced that the young thus produced will gain so much in vigor and fertility over the offspring from long-continued self-fertilization, that they will have a better chance of surviving and propagating their kind; and thus, in the long run, the influence of intercrosses, even at rare intervals, will be great. If there exist organic beings which never intercross, uniformity of character can be retained amongst them, as long as their conditions of life remain the same, only through the principle of inheritance, and through natural selection destroying any which depart from the proper type; but if their conditions of life change and they undergo modification, uniformity of character can be given to their modified offspring, solely by natural selection preserving the same favorable variations.

Isolation, also, is an important element in the process of natural selection. In a confined or isolated area, if not very large, the organic and inorganic conditions of life will generally be in a great degree uniform; so that natural selection will tend to modify all the individuals of a varying species throughout the area in the same manner in relation to the same conditions. Intercrosses, also, with the individuals of the same species, which otherwise would have inhabited the surrounding and differently circumstanced districts, will be prevented. But isolation probably acts more efficiently in checking the immigration of better adapted organisms, after any physical change, such as of climate or elevation of the land, &c., and thus new places in the natural economy of the country are left open for the old inhabitants to struggle for, and become adapted to, through modifications in their structure and constitution. Lastly, isolation, by checking immigration and consequently competition, will give time for any new variety to be slowly improved; and this may sometimes be of importance in the production of new species. If, however, an isolated area be very small, either from being surrounded by barriers, or from having very peculiar physical conditions, the total number of the individuals supported on it will necessarily be very small; and fewness of individuals will greatly retard the production of new species through natural selection, by decreasing the chance of the appearance of favorable variations.

If we turn to nature to test the truth of these remarks, and look at any small isolated area, such as an oceanic island, although the total number of the species inhabiting it, will be found to be small, as we shall see in our chapter on geographical distribution; yet of these species a very large proportion are endemic,—that is, have been produced there, and nowhere else. Hence an oceanic island at first sight seems to have been highly favorable for the production of new species. But we may thus greatly deceive ourselves, for to ascertain whether a small isolated area, or a large open area like a continent, has been most favorable for the production of new organic forms, we ought to make the comparison within equal times; and this we are incapable of doing.

Although I do not doubt that isolation is of considerable importance in the production of new species, on the whole I am inclined to believe that largeness of area is of more importance, more especially in the production of species, which will prove capable of enduring for a long period, and of spreading widely. Throughout a great and open area, not only will there be a better chance of favorable variations arising from the large number of individuals of the same species there supported, but the conditions of life are infinitely complex from the large number of already existing species; and if some of these many species become modified and improved, others will have to be improved in a corresponding degree or they will be exterminated. Each new form, also, as soon as it has been much improved, will be able to spread over the open and continuous area, and will thus come into competition with many others. Hence more new places will be formed, and the competition to fill them will be more severe, on a large than on a small and isolated area. Moreover, great areas, though now continuous, owing to oscillations of level, will often have recently existed in a broken condition, so that the good effects of isolation will generally, to a certain extent, have concurred. Finally, I conclude that, although small isolated areas probably have been in some respects highly favorable for the production of new species, yet that the course of modification will generally have been more rapid on large areas; and what is more important, that the new forms produced on large areas; which already have been victorious over many competitors, will be those that will spread most widely, will give rise to most new varieties and species, and will thus play an important part in the changing history of the organic world.

To sum up the circumstances favorable and unfavorable to natural selection, as far as the extreme intricacy of the subject permits. I conclude, looking to the future, that for terrestrial productions a large continental area, which will probably undergo many oscillations of level, and which consequently will exist for long periods in a broken condition, will be the most favorable for the production of many new forms of life, likely to endure long and to spread widely. For the area will first have existed as a continent, and the inhabitants, at this period numerous in individuals and kinds, will have been subjected to very severe competition. When converted by subsidence into large separate islands, there will still exist many individuals of the same species on each island: intercrossing on the confines of the range of each species will thus be checked: after physical changes of any kind, immigration will be prevented, so that new places in the polity of each island will have to be filled up by modifications of the old inhabitants; and time will be allowed for the varieties in each to become well modified and perfected. When, by renewed elevation, the islands shall be re-converted into a continental area, there will again be severe competition: the most favored or improved varieties will be enabled to spread: there will be much extinction of the less improved forms, and the relative proportional numbers of the various inhabitants of the renewed continent will again be changed; and again there will be a fair field for natural selection to improve still further the inhabitants, and thus produce new species.

That natural selection will always act with extreme slowness, I fully admit. Its action depends on there being places in the polity of nature, which can be better occupied by some of the inhabitants of the country undergoing modification of some kind. The existence of such places will often depend on physical changes, which are generally very slow, and on the immigration of better adapted forms having been checked. But the action of natural selection will probably still oftener depend on some of the inhabitants becoming slowly modified; the mutual relations of many of the other inhabitants being thus disturbed. Nothing can be effected, unless favorable variations occur, and variation itself is apparently always a very slow process. The process will often be greatly retarded by free intercrossing. Many will exclaim that these several causes are amply sufficient wholly to stop the action of natural selection. I do not believe so. On the other hand, I do believe that natural selection will always act very slowly, often only at long intervals of time, and generally on only a very few of the inhabitants of the same region at the same time. I further believe, that this very slow, intermittent action of natural selection accords perfectly well with what geology tells us of the rate and manner at which the inhabitants of this world have changed.

Slow though the process of selection may be, if feeble man can do much by his powers of artificial selection, I can see no limit to the amount of change, to the beauty and infinite complexity of the coadaptations between all organic beings, one with another and with their physical conditions of life, which may be effected in the long course of time by nature's power of selection.

Extinction. This subject will be more fully discussed in our chapter on Geology; but it must be here alluded to from being intimately connected with natural selection. Natural selection acts solely through the preservation of variations in some way advantageous, which consequently endure. But as from the high geometrical powers of increase of all organic beings, each area is already fully stocked with inhabitants, it follows that as each selected and favored form increases in number, so will the less favored forms decrease and become rare. Rarity, as geology tells us, is the precursor to extinction. We can, also, see that any form represented by few individuals will, during fluctuations in the seasons or in the number of its enemies, run a good chance of utter extinction. But we may go further than this; for as new forms are continually and slowly being produced, unless we believe that the number of specific forms goes on perpetually and almost indefinitely increasing, numbers inevitably must become extinct. That the number of specific forms has not indefinitely increased, geology shows us plainly; and indeed we can see reason why they should not have thus increased, for the number of places in the polity of nature is not indefinitely great,—not that we have any means of knowing that any one region has as yet got its maximum of species. Probably no region is as yet fully stocked, for at the Cape of Good Hope, where more species of plants are crowded together than in any other quarter of the world, some foreign plants have become naturalized, without causing, as far as we know, the extinction of any natives.

Furthermore, the species which are most numerous in individuals will have the best chance of producing within any given period favorable variations. We have evidence of this, in the facts given in the second chapter, showing that it is the common species which afford the greatest number of recorded varieties, or incipient species. Hence, rare species will be less quickly modified or improved within any given period, and they will consequently be beaten in the race for life by the modified descendants of the commoner species.

From these several considerations I think it inevitably follows, that as new species in the course of time are formed through natural selection, others will become rarer and rarer, and finally extinct. The forms which stand in closest competition with those undergoing modification and improvement, will naturally suffer most. And we have seen in the chapter on the Struggle for Existence that it is the most closely-allied forms,—varieties of the same species, and species of the same genus or of related genera,—which, from having nearly the same structure, constitution, and habits, generally come into the severest competition with each other. Consequently, each new variety or species, during the progress of its formation, will generally press hardest on its nearest kindred, and tend to exterminate them. We see the same process of extermination amongst our domesticated productions, through the selection of improved forms by man. Many curious instances could be given showing how quickly new breeds of cattle, sheep, and other animals, and varieties of flowers, take the place of older and inferior kinds. In Yorkshire, it is historically known that the ancient black cattle were displaced by the long-horns, and that these 'were swept away by the short-horns' (I quote the words of an agricultural writer) 'as if by some murderous pestilence.'

Divergence of Character. The principle, which I have designated by this term, is of high importance on my theory, and explains, as I believe, several important facts. In the first place, varieties, even strongly-marked ones, though having somewhat of the character of species—as is shown by the hopeless doubts in many cases how to rank them—yet certainly differ from each other far less than do good and distinct species. Nevertheless, according to my view, varieties are species in the process of formation, or are, as I have called them, incipient species. How, then, does the lesser difference between varieties become augmented into the greater difference between species? That this does habitually happen, we must infer from most of the innumerable species throughout nature presenting well-marked differences; whereas varieties, the supposed prototypes and parents of future well-marked species, present slight and ill-defined differences. Mere chance, as we may call it, might cause one variety to differ in some character from its parents, and the offspring of this variety again to differ from its parent in the very same character and in a greater degree; but this alone would never account for so habitual and large an amount of difference as that between varieties of the same species and species of the same genus.

As has always been my practice, let us seek light on this head from our domestic productions. We shall here find something analogous. A fancier is struck by a pigeon having a slightly shorter beak; another fancier is struck by a pigeon having a rather longer beak; and on the acknowledged principle that 'fanciers do not and will not admire a medium standard, but like extremes,' they both go on (as has actually occurred with tumbler-pigeons) choosing and breeding from birds with longer and longer beaks, or with shorter and shorter beaks. Again, we may suppose that at an early period one man preferred swifter horses; another stronger and more bulky horses. The early differences would be very slight; in the course of time, from the continued selection of swifter horses by some breeders, and of stronger ones by others, the differences would become greater, and would be noted as forming two sub-breeds; finally, after the lapse of centuries, the sub-breeds would become converted into two well-established and distinct breeds. As the differences slowly become greater, the inferior animals with intermediate characters, being neither very swift nor very strong, will have been neglected, and will have tended to disappear. Here, then, we see in man's productions the action of what may be called the principle of divergence, causing differences, at first barely appreciable, steadily to increase, and the breeds to diverge in character both from each other and from their common parent.

But how, it may be asked, can any analogous principle apply in nature? I believe it can and does apply most efficiently, from the simple circumstance that the more diversified the descendants from any one species become in structure, constitution, and habits, by so much will they be better enabled to seize on many and widely diversified places in the polity of nature, and so be enabled to increase in numbers.

We can clearly see this in the case of animals with simple habits. Take the case of a carnivorous quadruped, of which the number that can be supported in any country has long ago arrived at its full average. If its natural powers of increase be allowed to act, it can succeed in increasing (the country not undergoing any change in its conditions) only by its varying descendants seizing on places at present occupied by other animals: some of them, for instance, being enabled to feed on new kinds of prey, either dead or alive; some inhabiting new stations, climbing trees, frequenting water, and some perhaps becoming less carnivorous. The more diversified in habits and structure the descendants of our carnivorous animal became,

217

the more places they would be enabled to occupy. What applies to one animal will apply throughout all time to all animals— that is, if they vary— for otherwise natural selection can do nothing. So it will be with plants. It has been experimentally proved, that if a plot of ground be sown with one species of grass, and a similar plot be sown with several distinct genera of grasses, a greater number of plants and a greater weight of dry herbage can thus be raised. The same has been found to hold good when first one variety and then several mixed varieties of wheat have been sown on equal spaces of ground. Hence, if any one species of grass were to go on varying, and those varieties were continually selected which differed from each other in at all the same manner as distinct species and genera of grasses differ from each other, a greater number of individual plants of this species of grass, including its modified descendants, would succeed in living on the same piece of ground. And we well know that each species and each variety of grass is annually sowing almost countless seeds; and thus, as it may be said, is striving its utmost to increase its numbers. Consequently, I cannot doubt that in the course of many thousands of generations, the most distinct varieties of any one species of grass would always have the best chance of succeeding and of increasing in numbers, and thus of supplanting the less distinct varieties; and varieties, when rendered very distinct from each other, take the rank of species.

The truth of the principle, that the greatest amount of life can be supported by great diversification of structure, is seen under many natural circumstances. In an extremely small area, especially if freely open to immigration, and where the contest between individual and individual must be severe, we always find great diversity in its inhabitants. For instance, I found that a piece of turf, three feet by four in size, which had been exposed for many years to exactly the same conditions, supported twenty species of plants, and these belonged to eighteen genera and to eight orders, which shows how much these plants differed from each other. So it is with the plants and insects on small and uniform islets; and so in small ponds of fresh water. Farmers find that they can raise most food by a rotation of plants belonging to the most different orders: nature follows what may be called a simultaneous rotation. Most of the animals and plants which live close round any small piece of ground, could live on it (supposing it not to be in any way peculiar in its nature), and may be said to be striving to the utmost to live there; but, it is seen, that where they come into the closest competition with each other, the advantages of diversification of structure, with the accompanying differences of habit and constitution, determine that the inhabitants, which thus jostle each other most closely, shall, as a general rule, belong to what we call different genera and orders.

The same principle is seen in the naturalization of plants through man's agency in foreign lands. It might have been expected that the plants which have succeeded in becoming naturalized in any land would generally have been closely allied to the indigenes; for these are commonly looked at as specially created and adapted for their own country. It might, also, perhaps have been expected that naturalized plants would have belonged to a few groups more especially adapted to certain stations in their new homes. But the case is very different; and Alph. De Candolle has well remarked in his great and admirable work, that floras gain by naturalization, proportionally with the number of the native genera and species, far more in new genera than in new species. To give a single instance: in the last edition of Dr Asa Cray's 'Manual of the Flora of the Northern United States,' 260 naturalized plants are enumerated, and these belong to 162 genera. We thus see that these naturalized plants are of a highly diversified nature. They differ, moreover, to a large extent from the indigenes, for out of the 162 genera, no less than 100 genera are not there indigenous, and thus a large proportional addition is made to the genera of these States.

By considering the nature of the plants or animals which have struggled successfully with the indigenes of any country, and have there become naturalized, we can gain some crude idea in what manner some of the natives would have had to be modified, in order to have gained an advantage over the other natives; and we may, I think, at least safely infer that diversification of structure, amounting to new generic differences, would have been profitable to them.

The advantage of diversification in the inhabitants of the same region is, in fact, the same as that of the physiological division of labor in the organs of the same individual body—a subject so well elucidated by Milne Edwards. No physiologist doubts that a stomach by being adapted to digest vegetable matter alone, or flesh alone, draws most nutriment from these substances. So in the general economy of any land, the more widely and perfectly the animals and plants are diversified for different habits of life, so will a greater number of individuals be capable of there supporting themselves. A set of animals, with their organization but little diversified, could hardly compete with a set more perfectly diversified in structure. It may be doubted, for instance, whether the Australian marsupials, which are divided into groups differing but little from each other, and feebly representing, as Mr Waterhouse and others have remarked, our carnivorous, ruminant, and rodent mammals, could successfully compete with these well-pronounced orders. In the Australian mammals, we see the process of diversification in an early and incomplete stage of development.

After the foregoing discussion, which ought to have been much amplified, we may, I think, assume that the modified descendants of any one species will succeed by so much the better as they become more diversified in structure, and are thus enabled to encroach on places occupied by other beings.

But during the process of modification, . . . another of our principles, namely that of extinction, will have played an important part. As in each fully stocked country natural selection necessarily acts by the selected form having some advantage in the struggle for life over other forms, there will be a constant tendency in the improved descendants of any one species to supplant and exterminate in each stage of descent their predecessors and their original parent. For it should be remembered that the competition will generally be most severe between those forms which are most nearly related to each other in habits, constitution, and structure. Hence all the intermediate forms between the earlier and later states, that is between the less and more improved state of a species, as well as the original parent-species itself, will generally tend to become extinct. So it probably will be with many whole collateral lines of descent, which will be conquered by later and improved lines of descent. If, however, the modified offspring of a species get into some distinct country, or become quickly adapted to some quite new station, in which child and parent do not come into competition, both may continue to exist.

We have seen that in each country it is the species of the larger genera which oftenest present varieties or incipient species. This, indeed, might have been expected; for as natural selection acts through one form having some advantage over other forms in the struggle for existence, it will chiefly act on those which already have some advantage; and the largeness of any group shows that its species have inherited from a common ancestor some advantage in common. Hence, the struggle for the production of new and modified descendants, will mainly lie between the larger groups, which are all trying to increase in number. One large group will slowly conquer another large group, reduce its numbers, and thus lessen its chance of further variation and improvement. Within the same large group, the later and more highly perfected sub-groups, from branching out and seizing on many new places in the polity of Nature, will constantly tend to supplant and destroy the earlier and less improved sub-groups. Small and broken groups and sub-groups will finally tend to disappear. Looking to the future, we can predict that the groups of organic beings which are now large and triumphant, and which are least broken up, that is, which as yet have suffered least extinction, will for a long period continue to increase. But which groups will ultimately prevail, no man can predict; for we well know that many groups, formerly most extensively developed, have now become extinct. Looking still more remotely to the future, we may predict that, owing to the continued and steady increase of the larger groups, a multitude of smaller groups will become utterly extinct, and leave no modified descendants; and consequently that of the species living at any one period, extremely few will transmit descendants to a remote futurity. I shall have to return to this subject in the chapter on Classification, but I may add that on this view of extremely few of the more ancient species having transmitted descendants, and on the view of all the descendants of the same species making a class, we can understand how it is that there exist but very few classes in each main division of the animal and vegetable kingdoms. Although extremely few of the most ancient species may now have living and modified descendants, yet at the most remote geological period, the earth may have been as well peopled with many species of many genera, families, orders, and classes, as at the present day.

Summary of Chapter. If during the long course of ages and under varying conditions of life, organic beings vary at all in the several parts of their organization, and I think this cannot be disputed; if there be, owing to the high geometrical powers of increase of each species, at some age, season, or year, a severe struggle for life, and this certainly cannot be disputed; then, considering the infinite complexity of the relations of all organic beings to each other and to their conditions of existence, causing an infinite diversity in structure, constitution, and habits, to be advantageous to them, I think it would be a most extraordinary fact if no variation ever had occurred useful to each being's own welfare, in the same way as so many variations have occurred useful to man. But if variations useful to any organic being do occur, assuredly individuals thus characterized will have the best chance of being preserved in the struggle for life; and from the strong principle of inheritance they will tend to produce offspring similarly characterized. This principle of preservation, I have called, for the sake of brevity, Natural Selection. Natural selection, on the principle of qualities being inherited at corresponding ages, can modify the egg, seed, or young, as easily as the adult. Amongst many animals, sexual selection will give its aid to ordinary selection, by assuring to the most vigorous and best adapted males the greatest number of offspring. Sexual selection will also give characters useful to the males alone, in their struggles with other males.

Whether natural selection has really thus acted in nature, in modifying and adapting the various forms of life to their several conditions and stations, must be judged of by the general tenor and balance of evidence given in the following chapters. But we already see how it entails extinction; and how largely extinction has acted in the world's history, geology plainly declares. Natural selection, also, leads to divergence of character; for more living beings can be supported on the same area the more they diverge in structure, habits, and constitution, of which we see proof by looking at the inhabitants of any small spot or at naturalized productions. Therefore during the modification of the descendants of any one species, and during the incessant struggle of all species to increase in numbers, the more diversified these descendants become, the better will be their chance of succeeding in the battle of life. Thus the small differences distinguishing varieties of the same species, will steadily tend to increase till they come to equal the greater differences between species of the same genus, or even of distinct genera.

We have seen that it is the common, the widely-diffused, and widely-ranging species, belonging to the larger genera, which vary most, and these will tend to transmit to their modified offspring that superiority which now makes them dominant in their own countries. Natural selection, as has just been remarked, leads to divergence of character and to much extinction of the less improved and intermediate forms of life. On these principles, I believe, the nature of the affinities of all organic beings may be explained. It is a truly wonderful fact—the wonder of which we are apt to overlook from familiarity—that all animals and all plants throughout all time and space should be related to each other in group subordinate to group, in the manner which we everywhere behold—namely, varieties of the same species most closely related together, species of the same genus less closely and unequally related together, forming sections and sub-genera, species of distinct genera much less closely related, and genera related in different degrees, forming subfamilies, families, orders, sub-classes, and classes. The several subordinate groups in any class cannot be ranked in a single file, but seem rather to be clustered round points, and these round other points, and so on in almost endless cycles. On the view that each species has been independently created, I can see no explanation of this great fact in the classification of all organic beings; but, to the best of my judgment, it is explained through inheritance and the complex action of natural selection, entailing extinction and divergence of character, as we have seen illustrated in the diagram.

The affinities of all the beings of the same class have sometimes been represented by a great tree. I believe this simile largely speaks the truth. The green and budding twigs may represent existing species; and those produced during each former year may represent the long succession of extinct species. At each period of growth all the growing twigs have tried to branch out on all sides, and to overtop and kill the surrounding twigs and branches, in the same manner as species and groups of species have tried to overmaster other species in the great battle for life. The limbs divided into great branches, and these into lesser and lesser branches, were themselves once, when the tree was small, budding twigs; and this connexion of the former and present buds by ramifying branches may well represent the classification of all extinct and living species in groups subordinate to groups. Of the many twigs which flourished when the tree was a mere bush, only two or three, now grown into great branches, yet survive and bear all the other branches; so with the species which lived during long-past geological periods, very few now have living and modified descendants. From the first growth of the tree, many a limb and branch has decayed and dropped off; and these lost branches of various sizes may represent those whole orders, families, and genera which have now no living representatives, and which are known to us only from having been found in a fossil state. As we here and there see a thin straggling branch springing from a fork low down in a tree, and which by some chance has been favored and is still alive on its summit, so we occasionally see an animal like the Ornithorhynchus or Lepidosiren, which in some small degree connects by its affinities two large branches of life, and which has apparently been saved from fatal competition by having inhabited a protected station. As buds give rise by growth to fresh buds, and these, if vigorous, branch out and overtop on all sides many a feebler branch, so by generation I believe it has been with the great Tree of Life, which fills with its dead and broken branches the crust of the earth, and covers the surface with its ever branching and beautiful ramifications.

QUESTIONS

1. How does Darwin use the example of nectar-excreting plants and the insects that are attracted to them to illustrate the operation of natural selection? What different aspects of Darwin's theory does this demonstrate?
2. What are intercrosses and why does Darwin think they are beneficial to a species?
3. Why does Darwin suggest that large areas will more readily contribute to the development of vigorous species than small or isolated ones?
4. How does species extinction occur?

THE INTEREST IN SEA POWER, PRESENT AND FUTURE

Alfred Thayer Mahan

Rear Admiral Alfred Thayer Mahan (1840–1914) was an officer in the United States Navy and a leading turn-of-the-century theorist on matters relating to American naval power and American foreign policy. As commandant of the Naval War College, Mahan taught future President Theodore Roosevelt and almost certainly influenced Roosevelt's thinking.

Mahan focused almost exclusively on sea power, which made him eccentric in a nation obsessed with westward expansion. In his lectures and books, Mahan emphasized that historically, nations that controlled the sea lanes were able to dominate other nations economically and militarily. Mahan thought that the United States should also follow this course, developing its naval power rather than being concerned with control of North American land. In this selection from The Interest in Sea Power, Present and Future, *a collection of essays written in 1897 and appearing between 1890 and 1895 in periodicals such as the* Atlantic Monthly *and* Harper's, *Mahan argued that the United States must be dominant in the Caribbean and in South America. He further asserted that the United States had a "special interest" in the Western Hemisphere that it must protect through sea power. He also justified American control of the Panama Canal ("the Isthmus"). His arguments presaged the standard American defense of the Spanish-American War (1898).*

It is essential to our own good, it is yet more essential as part of our duty to the commonwealth of peoples to which we racially belong, that we look with clear, dispassionate, but resolute eyes upon the fact that civilizations on different planes of material prosperity and progress, with different spiritual ideals, and with very different political capacities, are fast closing together. It is a condition not unprecedented in the history of the world. When it befell a great united empire, enervated by long years of unwarlike habits among its chief citizens, it entailed ruin, but ruin deferred through centuries, thanks to the provision made beforehand by a great general and statesman. The Saracenic and Turkish invasions, on the contrary, after generations of advance, were first checked, and then rolled back; for they fell upon peoples, disunited indeed by internal discords and strife, like the nations of Europe to-day, but still nations of warriors, ready by training and habit to strike for their rights, and, if need were, to die for them. In the providence of God, along with the immense increase of prosperity, of physical and mental luxury, brought by this century, there has grown up also that counterpoise stigmatized as "militarism," which has converted Europe into a great camp of soldiers prepared for war. The ill-timed cry for disarmament, heedless of the menacing possibilities of the future, breaks idly against a great fact, which finds its sufficient justification in present conditions, but which is, above all, an unconscious preparation for something as yet noted but by few.

On the side of the land, these great armies, and the blind outward impulse of the European peoples, are the assurance that generations must elapse ere the barriers can be overcome behind which rests the citadel of Christian civilization. On the side of the sea there is no state charged with weightier responsibilities than the United States. In the Caribbean, the sensitive resentment by our people of any supposed fresh encroachment by another state of the European family has been manifested too plainly and too recently to admit of dispute. Such an attitude of itself demands of us to be ready to support it by organized force, exactly as the mutual jealousy of states within the European Continent imposes upon them the maintenance of their great armies—destined, we believe, in the future, to fulfil a nobler mission. Where we thus exclude others, we accept for ourselves the responsibility for that which is due to the general family of our civilization; and the Caribbean Sea, with its isthmus, is the nexus where will meet the chords binding the East to the West, the Atlantic to the Pacific.

The Isthmus, with all that depends upon it,—its canal and its approaches on either hand,—will link the eastern side of the American continent to the western as no network of land communications ever can. In it the United States has asserted a special interest. In the present she can maintain her claim, and in the future perform her duty, only by the creation of that sea power upon which predominance in the Caribbean must ever depend. In short, as the internal jealousies of Europe, and the purely democratic institution of the levée en masse—the general enforcement of military training—have prepared the way for great national armies, whose mission seems yet obscure, so the gradual broadening and tightening hold upon the sentiment of American democracy of that conviction loosely characterized as the Monroe doctrine finds its logical and inevitable outcome in a great sea power, the correlative, in connection with that of Great Britain, of those armies which continue to flourish under the most popular institutions, despite the wails of economists and the lamentations of those who wish peace without paying the one price which alone has ever insured peace,—readiness for war.

Thus it was, while readiness for war lasted, that the Teuton was held back until he became civilized, humanized, after the standard of that age; till the root of the matter was in him, sure to bear fruit in due season. He was held back by organized armed force—by armies. Will it be said that that was in a past barbaric age? Barbarism, however, is not in more or less material prosperity, or even political development, but in the inner man, in the spiritual ideal; and the material, which comes first and has in itself no salt of life to save from corruption, must be controlled by other material forces, until the spiritual can find room and time to germinate. We need not fear but that which appeals to the senses in our civilization will be appropriated, even though it be necessary to destroy us, if disarmed, in order to obtain it. Our own civilization less its spiritual element is barbarism; and barbarism will be the civilization of those who assimilate its material progress without imbibing the indwelling spirit.

Let us worship peace, indeed, as the goal at which humanity must hope to arrive; but let us not fancy that peace is to be had as a boy wrenches an unripe fruit from a tree. Nor will peace be reached by ignoring the conditions that confront us, or by exaggerating the charms of quiet, of prosperity, of ease, and by contrasting these exclusively with the alarms and horrors of war. Merely utilitarian arguments have never convinced nor converted mankind, and they never will; for mankind knows that there is something better. Its homage will never be commanded by peace, presented as the tutelary deity of the stock-market.

Nothing is more ominous for the future of our race than that tendency, vociferous at present, which refuses to recognize in the profession of arms, in war, that something which inspired Wordsworth's "Happy Warrior," which soothed the dying hours of Henry Lawrence, who framed the ideals of his career on the poet's conception, and so nobly illustrated it in his self-sacrifice; that something which has made the soldier to all ages the type of heroism and of self-denial. When the religion of Christ, of Him who was led as a lamb to the slaughter, seeks to raise before its followers the image of self-control, and of resistance to evil, it is the soldier whom it presents. He Himself, if by office King of Peace, is, first of all, in the essence of His Being, King of Righteousness, without which true peace cannot be.

Conflict is the condition of all life, material and spiritual; and it is to the soldier's experience that the spiritual life goes for its most vivid metaphors and its loftiest inspirations. Whatever else the twentieth century may bring us, it will not, from anything now current in the thought of the nineteenth, receive a nobler ideal.

QUESTIONS

1. What areas of the world does Mahan believe the United States should control?
2. How does Mahan connect his proposed policies to the Monroe Doctrine (1823)?
3. Why do you think Mahan thought that gaining and maintaining American sea power was so important?
4. How do you think Mahan's arguments might have affected Americans discussing the extension of American power abroad around the turn of the twentieth century?

DOCUMENT

AN ISLAMIC RESPONSE TO MODERNITY

Jamāl al-Dīn al-Afghānī

*Jamāl al-Dīn al-Afghānī ʾwas one of the most seminal—and most mysterious—
of the nineteenth-century Muslim reformers who grappled, both intellectually
and politically, with the European cultural, military, and intellectual dominance
of their era. Although Jamāl al-Dīn claimed to be an Afghan-born Sunni Muslim,
he was apparently originally a Shi'ite Muslim from Iran. He was educated, apparently, in Afghanistan and India, in became involved in politics in both of those
countries, both of which he also found it prudent to quit in some haste, eventually making his way around 1870 to Istanbul, at that time the capital city of the
Sunni Ottoman Empire. In 1871 al-Afghānī went to Cairo, where he was active
in nationalist circles until he was expelled by the British in 1879. He then returned
to India, where he composed his most famous work (in Persian), excerpted here,
"A Refutation of the Materialists."*

*Al-Afghānī then spent several years in Europe, including London, Paris, and
Russia, finally spending his declining years in Istanbul as an honored guest and
advisor of the Ottoman Sultan 'Abd al-Hamid II, who more or less officially
adopted al-Afghānī's pan-Islamic ideology. Al-Afghānī's greatest impact, however, was felt in his posthumous legacy, which provided the foundation for the
ensuing generations of Islamic revivalist movements, ranging from the Muslim
Brotherhood to al-Qa'ida.*

Reprinted from *An Islamic Response to Imperialism,* translated by Nikki R. Keddie, by
permission of Dr. Nikki Keddie. Copyright © 1968 by Dr. Nikki Keddie.

THE TRUTH ABOUT THE NEICHERI[1] SECT

Since it is known that religion is unquestionably the source of man's welfare, therefore, if it is placed on firm foundations and sound bases, that religion will naturally become the complete source of total happiness and perfect tranquillity. Above all it will be the cause of material and moral progress. It will elevate the banner of civilization among its followers. It will cause those who are religious to attain all intellectual and spiritual perfections and to achieve good fortune in this world and the next.

If we think deeply about religions we will find no religion resting on such firm and sure foundations as the religion of Islam.

For, the rise of nations on the ranks of perfection; the climbing of peoples on the steps of knowledge; the ascent of groups on the stairs of virtue; the awareness of the nations of humanity of the details of truth; and their acquisition of true and complete happiness in this world and the hereafter— all these depend on several things:

[First] That the slate of the minds of tribes and nations be clear of the muddiness of superstition, and the rust of vain and groundless beliefs. For superstitious belief is a dirty curtain that intervenes between the holder of such a belief and truth and reality. It prevents the discovery of the reality of a matter. When someone accepts a superstition his reason comes to a stop and he refrains from intellectual movement. Then he will take up many similar beliefs, and will accept all superstitions and fancies. This will cause him to fall far short of true perfection, and the truths of existent beings will be hidden from him. It will even cause him to spend all his life in fantasies, loneliness, fear, terror, and dread. He will fall into shuddering from the movements of birds and the stirrings of beasts. He will be upset by the blowing of winds, the sound of thunder, and the gleam of lightning. He will be kept from most of the occasions of his happiness through belief in evil omens, and he will submit to every trick, ruse, and impostor. What misfortune, ill luck, or bad life could be worse than such a life?

The first pillar of the Islamic religion is that by the luster of unity [tauhīd—the absolute unity of God] it purifies and cleans off the rust of superstition, the turbidity of fantasies, and the contamination of imaginings. Its first teaching is that man should not consider another man or an inanimate object, high or low, to be the Creator, the Possessor, the Omnipotent, the Giver, the Preventer, the Strengthener, the Debaser, the Healer, and the Destroyer. Nor should he believe that the First Cause has appeared, or will appear, in human guise to improve or worsen things. Nor that Pure Being in order [to secure] some benefits bore, in human guise, pains and illnesses; nor other such superstitions, any one of which alone suffices to blind reason. Most existing religions are not free of these fancies and superstitions. Look at the Christian, Brahman, and Zoroastrian religions.

[Second] Their souls must be characterized by the greatest nobility. This means that every member of that community considers himself worthy and suited for any human rank and stage, except for the rank of prophecy, which is a divine rank. He does not imagine in himself deficiencies, decadence, and lack of ability. When the souls of men are endowed with this quality, each one competes with others in the wide arena of virtues, and enters into contest and competition; and they spare nothing to attain greatness and honor, and to acquire a high rank in the world.

If some men believe that their nature and character has less nobility than others, and that their rank is lower than others, naturally there will be defects in their zeal, languor in their movements, and weakness in their perception. They will remain deprived of many perfections, of high degree and worldly happiness, and will remain within the boundaries of a narrow arena.

The Islamic religion opens the doors of nobility before souls; strengthens the right of each soul to every excellence and perfection; and removes the distinction of nobility of race and occupation, basing distinctions among human beings only on intellectual and spiritual perfection.

Few religions can be found with this advantage. Look how the Brahman religion divides men into four classes—first the Brahmans, second the Kshatriyas, third the Vaishyas, and fourth the Shudras—and reserves the highest degree of natural nobility to the Brahmans and the next to the Kshatriyas, while the fourth class is considered the lowest of all in all human distinctions. This may be considered one of the main causes for the lack of proper progress among the followers of this religion in the sciences, knowledge, and the arts, despite the fact that they are the most ancient of peoples.

The Christian religion, according to the Gospel, affirms nobility for the race of the sons of Israel, and refers to other races in contemptuous terms. The followers of that religion, however, refused this rule and denied race distinctions, but they gave so much honor to the class of priests that it became a cause for lowering others. For the priests were given control over the acceptance of belief and the forgiveness of sins. They said that other men, even if they had reached the highest degree of perfection, did not have the power to present their own sins before the divine threshold and seek forgiveness. This has to be achieved through the mediation of priests.

Similarly they said that the acceptance of faith in the eyes of God Almighty depends on the acceptance of a priest. They took this rule, which debases people, from the Gospel, since in it was written: "Whatever you unbind on earth will be unbound in heaven, and whatever you bind on earth will be bound in heaven."[2] As long as this debasing belief was firm and well established among the Christian community in European lands no progress was achieved among that community.

Luther, the leader of the Protestants, who rejected this rule, in opposition to the Gospels, was following the example of the Muslims.

[The third foundation of human virtues] is that the members of each community must found their beliefs, which are the first things written on the slates of their minds, on certain proofs and firm evidence. In their beliefs they must shun submission to conjectures and not be content with mere imitation (taqlīd) of their ancestors. For if man believes in things without proof or reason, makes a practice of following unproven opinions, and is satisfied to imitate and follow his ancestors, his mind inevitably desists from intellectual movement, and little by little stupidity and imbecility overcome him—until his mind becomes completely idle and he becomes unable to perceive his own good and evil; and adversity and misfortune overtake him from all sides.

It is no wonder that Guizot, the French minister who wrote the history of civilisation,* that is, civilization, of the European peoples,[3] said as follows: One of the greatest causes for European civilization was that a group appeared, saying: "Although our religion is the Christian religion, we are seeking the proofs of the fundamentals of our beliefs." The corpus of priests did not give permission, and they said that religion was founded on imitation. When the group became strong their ideas spread; minds emerged from their state of stupidity and dullness into movement and progress; and men made efforts to achieve the attributes of civilization.

The Islamic religion is the only religion that censures belief without proof and the following of conjectures; reproves blind submission; seeks to show proof of things to its followers; everywhere addresses itself to reason; considers all happiness the result of wisdom and clearsightedness; attributes perdition to stupidity and lack of insight; and sets up proofs for each fundamental belief in such a way that it will be useful to all people. It even, when it mentions most of its rules, states their purposes and benefits. (Refer to the Holy Koran.)

There is no other religion having this excellence. I believe that the non-Muslims will also acknowledge these distinctions. It is no secret that the foundation of the Christian religion is the worship of the Trinity. All Christians confess that it is not possible for reason to understand it, which means that one must abandon reason in order to comprehend it.

As to the principles of the Brahman religion, it is clear to everyone that most of them are contrary to plain reason, whether the followers of that religion acknowledge it or not.

Fourth, there must be in each community a group of people who are constantly occupied with teaching the others, who do not shirk from adorning their intellects with true knowledge, and who do not fail to teach the ways of felicity. And there must be another group that always strives to straighten and rectify souls; to explain virtuous qualities and describe their benefits; and explain wicked manners and elucidate their harm and injuries. They should not neglect to enjoin the good and forbid the evil.[4] For naturally all man's knowledge is acquired, and if man does not have a teacher he will not derive advantage or benefit from his reason. And he will live in this world like the animals and will leave this world barred from the happiness of both this world and the next.

Thus a teacher is indispensable. And since the lust and desires of man have no limit or measure, if there is no straightener and adjuster it will inevitably result in transgressions and oppression, and the possessor of those desires will deprive others of tranquillity and safety, and even burn himself on the fire of his passions. Man will then go to the abode of misfortune in the greatest wretchedness. Thus an enjoiner of the good, a forbidder of evil, and a rectifier of morals are indispensable.

The greatest duties and obligations of the Islamic religion are these two matters. (Refer to the noble Koran.)

In other religions there has not been such concern for these two matters, and since there are many pillars of the Islamic religion, and to explain

233

the benefits of each one for civilization and to describe how each of them is the source of perfect felicity would cause me to go beyond the subject of my discourse, I have considered it incumbent on me to write a separate treatise on this matter; in that treatise I will explain why the virtuous city for which philosophers have died hoping will only be achieved by man with the Islamic religion.[5]

If someone says: If the Islamic religion is as you say, then why are the Muslims in such a sad condition? I will answer: When they were [truly] Muslims, they were what they were and the world bears witness to their excellence. As for the present, I will content myself with this holy text:

"Verily, God does not change the state of a people until they change themselves inwardly."[6]

This is a summary of what I wished to explain about the evils and corruption of the *neicheri* path for civilization and the social order, and the benefits of religions and of Islam.

Completed by the writer Jamāl ad-Dīn Husainī.

END NOTES

1. Materialism; the belief that there is no metaphysical reality, only a physical one.
2. Matt. 16:19. As Afghānī implies, this passage is part of one that has been taken as legitimizing the Catholic church, though this is unclear without the full passage. Christ says to Peter: "And I say also unto thee, that thou art Peter, and upon this rock I will build my church; and the gates of hell shall not prevail against it. And I will give thee the keys of the kingdom of heaven: and whatsoever thou shalt bind on earth shall be bound in heaven; and whatsoever thou shalt loose on earth shall be loosed in heaven."
3. The reference is to Guizot's *History of Civilization in Europe*, which assigns to the Reformation a key role in the progress of freedom of thought and of civilization. This book had recently been translated into Arabic.
4. A Koranic phrase found, with some variation, in several different passages in the Koran.
5. This is the third approving reference to the "virtuous city," the others being referenced prior to this section. The phrase is part of the title of a popular work of political philosophy by al-Fārābī, and was used also by later philosophers.
6. Koran 13:11. Since Afghānī first used it, this has become a favorite passage for modernists exhorting the Muslims to self-improvement. According to a statement by Professor H. A. R. Gibb in the autumn of 1963, however, the verb used for "change," *ghayyara*, had, at that time, the sense of "to change for the worse." This is certainly its sense in this Koranic passage, which reads (in 'Abdallāh Yūsuf 'Alī's translation): "Verily never will God change the condition of a people until they change it themselves. But when God willeth a people's punishment, there can be no turning it back, nor will they find,

besides Him, any to protect." In Afghānī's brief citation here it is unclear whether he is thinking of the Muslims' past decline, their future improvement, or, most likely, both.

QUESTIONS

1. What is al-Afghānī's view of "naturalists" or materialists?
2. What does al-Aghānī state about religion generally, and the Islamic religion in particular?
3. To what is al-Afghānī referring when he states that "Luther . . . was following the example of the Muslims"?
4. How does al-Afghānī explain the disparity between what he holds to be the evident superiority of Islam and the "sad condition" of Muslims and Muslim societies?

WHAT IS TRUE CIVILIZATION?

Mohandas K. Gandhi

Mohandas K. Gandhi (1869–1948) was born in a modest Gujarati family in the middle of the nineteenth century and sent at age twenty to study law in England. There he discovered vegetarianism, and the work of critics of the industrial revolution such as John Ruskin, Thomas Carlyle, and Leo Tolstoy.

Hind Swaraj is one of his most important works, a book in which he proposed a plan for how India would gain independence from the British. He wrote it in 1909 on a ten-day trip from England to South Africa, where he had been living for almost two decades and had waged campaigns of civil disobedience on behalf of Indians in Natal against the government in South Africa. Hind Swaraj formed the basis of his political philosophy of self-reliance and self-control, becoming the foundation for his national campaigns of nonviolent protest. There were two nationwide campaigns for which Gandhi was best known. The non-cooperation movement (1920–1922) asked Indians to withhold their labor and participation from all colonial enterprises, while participating in nonviolent actions against the government. The civil disobedience movement, which followed a decade later (1930–1932), asked Indians to withdraw from working for the colonial government as lawyers, clerks, teachers, doctors and so on; it also called on Indians to live on handmade, locally produced goods, such as homespun fabrics and homemade salt. The widescale popularity of these protest movements was based on some of the ideas that Gandhi expressed in Hind Swaraj.

Reprinted by permission from *Hind Swaraj and Other Writings*, edited by Anthony J. Parel. Copyright © 1997 by Cambridge University Press.

In a dialogue with an imaginary interlocutor, Gandhi explains how Indians would achieve self-government. Swaraj *or self-rule was defined by Gandhi as a twofold process: first, the demand for an independent government and second, the need to govern and improve oneself. For Gandhi, moral self-improvement, pious reflection, and autonomy from a desire for foreign goods and technologies was necessary if India was to move beyond its colonized status and become modern. As the selection shows, Gandhi was skeptical of the claims that Britain was "civilized" and questioned whether industrialization had brought progress to Indians.*

THE CONDITION OF ENGLAND

READER: Then from your statement I deduce that the Government of England is not desirable and not worth copying by us.

EDITOR: Your deduction is justified. The condition of England at present is pitiable. I pray to God that India may never be in that plight. That which you consider to be the Mother of Parliaments is like a sterile woman and a prostitute.[1] Both these are harsh terms, but exactly fit the case. That Parliament has not yet of its own accord done a single good thing, hence I have compared it to a sterile woman. The natural condition of that Parliament is such that, without outside pressure, it can do nothing. It is like a prostitute because it is under the control of ministers who change from time to time. Today it is under Mr Asquith, tomorrow it may be under Mr Balfour.

READER: You have said this sarcastically. The term 'sterile woman' is not applicable. The Parliament, being elected by the people, must work under public pressure. This is its quality.

EDITOR: You are mistaken. Let us examine it a little more closely. The best men are supposed to be elected by the people. The members serve without pay[2] and, therefore, it must be assumed, only for the public weal. The electors are considered to be educated, and, therefore, we should assume that they would not generally make mistakes in their choice. Such a Parliament should not need the spur of petitions or any other pressure. Its work should be so smooth that its effect would be more apparent day by day. But, as a matter of fact, it is generally acknowledged that the members are hypocritical and selfish. Each thinks of his own little interest. It is fear that is the guiding motive. What is done today may be undone tomorrow. It is not possible to recall a single instance in which finality can be predicated for its work. When the greatest questions are debated, its members have been seen to stretch themselves and to doze.[3] Sometimes the members talk away until the listeners are disgusted. Carlyle has called it the 'talking-shop of the world'.[4] Members vote for their party without a thought. Their so-called discipline binds them to it. If any member, by way of exception, gives an independent vote, he is considered a renegade. If the money and the time wasted by the Parliament were entrusted to a few good men, the English nation would be occupying today a much higher platform. The Parliament is simply a costly toy of the nation. These views are by no means peculiar to me. Some great English thinkers have expressed them. One of the members of that Parliament recently said that a true Christian[5] could not become a member of it. Another said that it was a baby. And, if it has remained a baby after an existence of seven hundred years, when will it outgrow its babyhood?

READER: You have set me thinking; you do not expect me to accept at once all you say. You give me entirely novel views. I shall have to digest them. Will you now explain the epithet 'prostitute'?

EDITOR: That you cannot accept my views at once is only right. If you will read the literature on this subject, you will have some idea of it. The Parliament is without a real master. Under the Prime Minister, its movement is not steady, but it is buffeted about like a prostitute. The Prime Minister is more concerned about his power[6] than about the welfare of the Parliament. His energy is concentrated upon securing the success of his party.[7] His care is not always that the Parliament shall do right. Prime Ministers are known to have made the Parliament do things merely for party advantage. All this is worth thinking over.

READER: Then you are really attacking the very men whom we have hitherto considered to be patriotic and honest?

EDITOR: Yes, that is true; I can have nothing against Prime Ministers, but what I have seen leads me to think that they cannot be considered really patriotic. If they are to be considered honest because they do not take what is generally known as bribery, let them be so considered, but they are open to subtler influences. In order to gain their ends, they certainly bribe people with honours. I do not hesitate to say that they have neither real honesty nor a living conscience.

READER: As you express these views about the Parliament, I would like to hear you on the English people, so that I may have your view of their Government.

EDITOR: To the English voters their newspaper is their Bible. They take their cue from their newspapers, which latter are often dishonest. The same fact is differently interpreted by different newspapers, according to the party in whose interests they are edited.[8] One newspaper would consider a great Englishman to be a paragon of honesty, another would consider him dishonest. What must be the condition of the people whose newspapers are of this type?

READER: You shall describe it.

EDITOR: These people change their views frequently. It is said that they change them every seven years. These views swing like the pendulum of a clock and are never steadfast. The people would follow a powerful orator or a man who gives them parties, receptions, etc. As are the people, so is their Parliament. They have certainly one quality very strongly developed. They will never allow their country to be lost. If any person were to cast an evil eye on it, they would pluck out his eyes. But that does not mean that the nation possesses every other virtue or that it should be imitated. If India copies England, it is my firm conviction that she will be ruined.

READER: To what do you ascribe this state of England?

EDITOR: It is not due to any peculiar fault of the English people, but the condition is due to modern civilisation.[9] It is a civilisation only in name. Under it the nations of Europe are becoming degraded and ruined day by day.

CIVILISATION

READER: Now you will have to explain what you mean by civilisation.[10]

EDITOR: It is not a question of what I mean. Several English writers refuse to call that civilisation which passes under that name. Many books have been written upon that subject. Societies[11] have been formed to cure the nation of the evils of civilisation. A great English writer[12] has written a work called 'Civilization: its Cause and Cure.' Therein he has called it a disease.

READER: Why do we not know this generally?

239

EDITOR: The answer is very simple. We rarely find people arguing against themselves. Those who are intoxicated by modern civilisation are not likely to write against it. Their care will be to find out facts and arguments in support of it, and this they do unconsciously, believing it to be true. A man, whilst he is dreaming, believes in his dream; he is undeceived only when he is awakened from his sleep. A man labouring under the bane of civilisation is like a dreaming man. What we usually read are the works of defenders of modern civilisation, which undoubtedly claims among its votaries very brilliant and even some very good men. Their writings hypnotise us. And so, one by one, we are drawn into the vortex.

READER: This seems to be very plausible. Now will you tell me something of what you have read and thought of this civilisation?

EDITOR: Let us first consider what state of things is described by the word 'civilisation'.[13] Its true test lies in the fact that people living in it make bodily welfare the object of life. We will take some examples. The people of Europe today live in better built houses than they did a hundred years ago. This is considered an emblem of civilisation, and this is also a matter to promote bodily happiness. Formerly, they wore skins, and used as their weapons spears. Now, they wear long trousers, and, for embellishing their bodies, they wear a variety of clothing, and, instead of spears, they carry with them revolvers containing five or more chambers. If people of a certain country, who have hitherto not been in the habit of wearing much clothing, boots, etc., adopt European clothing, they are supposed to have become civilised out of savagery. Formerly, in Europe, people ploughed their lands mainly by manual labour. Now, one man can plough a vast tract by means of steam-engines, and can thus amass great wealth. This is called a sign of civilisation. Formerly, the fewest men wrote books that were most valuable. Now, anybody writes and prints anything he likes and poisons people's mind. Formerly, men travelled in wagons; now they fly through the air in trains at the rate of four hundred and more miles per day. This is considered the height of civilisation. It has been stated that, as men progress, they shall be able to travel in airships and reach any part of the world in a few hours. Men will not need the use of their hands and feet. They will press a button and they will have their clothing by their side. They will press another button and they will have their newspaper. A third, and a motorcar will be in waiting for them.

240

They will have a variety of delicately dished-up food. Everything will be done by machinery. Formerly, when people wanted to fight with one another, they measured between them their bodily strength; now it is possible to take away thousands of lives by one man working behind a gun from a hill. This is civilisation. Formerly, men worked in the open air only so much as they liked. Now, thousands of workmen meet together and for the sake of maintenance work in factories or mines. Their condition is worse than that of beasts. They are obliged to work, at the risk of their lives, at most dangerous occupations, for the sake of millionaires. Formerly, men were made slaves under physical compulsion, now[14] they are enslaved by temptation of money and of the luxuries that money can buy. There are now diseases of which people never dreamt before, and an army of doctors is engaged in finding out their cures, and so hospitals have increased. This is a test of civilisation. Formerly, special messengers were required and much expense was incurred in order to send letters; today, anyone can abuse his fellow by means of a letter for one penny. True, at the same cost, one can send one's thanks also. Formerly, people had two or three meals consisting of homemade bread and vegetables; now, they require something to eat every two hours, so that they have hardly leisure for anything else. What more need I say? All this you can ascertain from several authoritative books. These are all true tests of civilisation. And, if anyone speaks to the contrary, know that he is ignorant. This civilisation takes note neither of morality nor of religion.[15] Its votaries calmly state that their business is not to teach religion. Some even consider it to be a superstitious growth. Others put on the cloak of religion, and prate about morality. But, after twenty years' experience, I have come to the conclusion that immorality is often taught in the name of morality. Even a child can understand that in all I have described above there can be no inducement to morality. Civilisation seeks to increase bodily comforts, and it fails miserably even in doing so.

This civilisation is irreligion,[16] and it has taken such a hold on the people in Europe that those who are in it appear to be half mad. They lack real physical strength or courage. They keep up their energy by intoxication. They can hardly be happy in solitude. Women, who should be the queens of households, wander in the streets, or they slave away in factories. For the sake of a pittance, half a million women in England alone are labouring under trying circumstances in factories or similar institutions. This awful fact is one of the causes of the daily growing suffragette movement.[17]

This civilisation is such that one has only to be patient and it will be self-destroyed. According to the teaching of Mahomed this would be considered a Satanic civilisation. Hinduism calls it the Black Age.[18] I cannot give you an adequate conception of it. It is eating into the vitals of the English nation.[19] It must be shunned.[20] Parliaments are really emblems of slavery. If you will sufficiently think over this, you will entertain the same opinion, and cease to blame the English. They rather deserve our sympathy. They are a shrewd nation and I, therefore, believe that they will cast off the evil. They are enterprising and industrious, and their mode of thought is not inherently immoral. Neither are they bad at heart. I, therefore, respect them. Civilisation is not an incurable disease,[21] but it should never be forgotten that the English people are at present afflicted by it.

WHAT IS TRUE CIVILISATION?

READER: You have denounced railways, lawyers and doctors. I can see that you will discard all machinery.[22] What, then, is civilisation?

EDITOR: The answer to that question is not difficult. I believe that the civilisation India has evolved is not to be beaten in the world. Nothing can equal the seeds sown by our ancestors. Rome went, Greece shared the same fate, the might of the Pharaohs was broken, Japan has become westernised, of China nothing can be said, but India is still, somehow or other, sound at the foundation.[23] The people of Europe learn their lessons from the writings of the men of Greece or Rome, which exist no longer in their former glory. In trying to learn from them, the Europeans imagine that they will avoid the mistakes of Greece and Rome. Such is their pitiable condition. In the midst of all this, India remains immovable, and that is her glory. It is a charge against India that her people are so uncivilised, ignorant and stolid, that it is not possible to induce them to adopt any changes. It is a charge really against our merit. What we have tested and found true on the anvil of experience, we dare not change. Many thrust their advice upon India, and she remains steady. This is her beauty; it is the sheet-anchor of our hope.

Civilisation is that mode of conduct which points out to man the path of duty. Performance of duty and observance of morality are convertible terms. To observe morality is to attain mastery over our mind and our passions. So doing, we know ourselves.[24] The Gujarati equivalent for civilisation means 'good conduct'.[25]

If this definition be correct, then India, as so many writers[26] have shown, has nothing to learn from anybody else,[27] and this is as it should be. We notice that mind is a restless bird; the more it gets the more it wants, and still remains unsatisfied. The more we indulge our passions, the more unbridled they become. Our ancestors, therefore, set a limit to our indulgences. They saw that happiness was largely a mental condition.[28] A man is not necessarily happy because he is rich, or unhappy because he is poor. The rich are often seen to be unhappy, the poor to be happy. Millions will always remain poor. Observing all this, our ancestors dissuaded us from luxuries and pleasures. We have managed with the same kind of plough as it existed thousands of years ago. We have retained the same kind of cottages that we had in former times, and our indigenous education remains the same as before. We have had no system of life-corroding competition.[29] Each followed his own occupation or trade,[30] and charged a regulation wage. It was not that we did not know how to invent machinery, but our forefathers knew that, if we set our hearts after such things, we would become slaves and lose our moral fibre. They therefore, after due deliberation, decided that we should only do what we could with our hands and feet. They saw that our real happiness and health consisted in a proper use of our hands[31] and feet. They further reasoned that large cities were a snare and a useless encumbrance,[32] and that people would not be happy in them, that there would be gangs of thieves and robbers, prostitution and vice flourishing in them, and that poor men would be robbed by rich men. They were, therefore, satisfied with small villages. They saw that kings and their swords were inferior to the sword of ethics, and they, therefore, held the sovereigns of the earth to be inferior to the Rishis and the Fakirs.[33] A nation with a constitution like this is fitter to teach others than to learn from others. This nation had courts, lawyers and doctors, but they were all within bounds.[34] Everybody knew that these professions were not particularly superior; moreover, these vakils and vaids[35] did not rob people; they were considered people's dependants, not their masters.

Justice was tolerably fair. The ordinary rule was to avoid courts. There were no touts to lure people into them. This evil, too, was noticeable only in and around capitals. The common people lived independently, and followed their agricultural occupation. They enjoyed true Home Rule.

And where this cursed modern civilisation has not reached, India remains as it was before. The inhabitants of that part of India will very properly laugh at your new-fangled notions. The English do not rule over them, nor will you ever rule over them. Those in whose name we speak we do not know, nor do they know us. I would certainly advise you and those like you who love the motherland to go into the interior that has yet not been polluted by the railways, and to live there for six months;[36] you might then be patriotic and speak of Home Rule.

Now you see what I consider to be real civilisation. Those who want to change conditions such as I have described are enemies of the country and are sinners.

READER: It would be all right if India were exactly as you have described it, but it is also India where there are hundreds of child widows, where two-year-old babies are married, where twelve-year-old girls are mothers and housewives, where women practise polyandry, where the practice of Niyog[37] obtains, where, in the name of religion, girls dedicate themselves to prostitution, and where, in the name of religion, sheep and goats are killed.[38] Do you consider these also symbols of the civilisation that you have described?[39]

EDITOR: You make a mistake. The defects that you have shown are defects. Nobody mistakes them for ancient civilisation. They remain in spite of it. Attempts have always been made, and will be made, to remove them. We may utilise the new spirit that is born in us[40] for purging ourselves of these evils. But what I have described to you as emblems of modern civilisation are accepted as such by its votaries. The Indian civilisation as described by me has been so described by its votaries. In no part of the world, and under no civilisation, have all men attained perfection. The tendency of Indian civilisation is to elevate the moral being, that of the Western civilisation is to propagate immorality. The latter is godless, the former is based on a belief in God. So understanding and so believing, it behoves every lover of India to cling to the old Indian civilisation even as a child clings to its mother's breast.

END NOTES

1. 'a sterile woman and a prostitute': Gandhi was criticised by one of his English friends (Mrs Annie Beasant?) for using the metaphor of 'prostitute'; and he regretted using it (*CW* 15: 330); this was the only word he was prepared to drop from the book. The word 'prostitute' occurs again in ch. v, and the word 'prostitution' in chs. xi and xiii. Erikson (1969, 219) exaggerates the point when he writes that the word 'prostitution' is 'a word used rather often' in *HS*.

   The criticism of parliament in this chapter and elsewhere may not be interpreted to mean that Gandhi was against the institution of parliament. For example, in 1920 he said that what he wanted for India was 'a parliament chosen by the people with the fullest power over the finance, the police, the military, the navy, the courts and the educational institutions' (*CW* 19: 80). In 1921 he advised the readers of *HS* that his corporate activity was devoted to 'the attainment of parliamentary swaraj in accordance with the wishes of the people of India' (*CW* 19: 277–8).

2. Remuneration for British MPs was introduced only in 1911.

3. 'doze': given as 'dose' in original text.

4. 'the talking-shop of the world': the Gujarati text does not mention Carlyle, referring instead to 'one of their great writers'. The source of this remark is Carlyle (1907, 319) where he is discussing the inability of the Rump Parliament to give a clear answer to Cromwell: 'For three years, Cromwell says, this question had been sounded in the ears of the Parliament. They would make no answer; nothing but talk, talk. Perhaps it lies in the nature of parliamentary bodies; perhaps no Parliament could in such case make any answer but even that of talk, talk.' Professor C. N. Patel of Ahmedabad drew my attention to this passage.

5. 'a true Christian': the Gujarati text has *dharmisht*, 'an ethical person'.

6. 'power': *satta*.

7. 'party': i.e., political party, *paksh*.

8. The Gujarati text adds: 'One party magnifies its own importance while the other party minimises it.'

9. The distinction between 'British people' whom Gandhi admired, and 'modern' British civilisation, which Gandhi criticised, is crucial to his argument, which is that modern civilisation has corrupted a basically good people. The root of this corruption he traces back to the de-Christianisation of modern Britain.

10. The Gujarati text adds: 'According to you, [modern] civilisation [*sudharo*] is not civilisation, but barbarism [*kudharo*].' The *sudharo*/*kudharo* dichotomy adds colour to the Gujarati text.

11. In 1906 Gandhi made contacts with officials of the Union of Ethical Societies in London. It had then fourteen member societies in London, and nine elsewhere in England. Henry Polak and his wife Millie Graham were members of the South Place Ethical Society. Miss Florence Winterbottom, who helped Gandhi with his lobbying in London, was the Secretary of the Union of Ethical Societies (Hunt 1986, 8–10). On his 1909 visit to London Gandhi gave a lecture to the Union of Ethical Societies at the Emerson Club (*CW* 9: 473–4, 475–6). On the same visit he also visited an ex-Tolstoyan Colony at Whiteway, near Stroud (ibid., 369). Gandhi was also familiar with the activities of 'New Crusade Society', a society based on the social teachings of John Ruskin, propagating the values of country life, agriculture, handicrafts, homespun clothes, and opposing the 'increasing dependence on machinery' and 'competitive mechanical production'. The moving spirit behind this society was Godfrey Blount, author of *A New*

Crusade: An Appeal (1903). This book is listed in the Appendix to *HS*. A brief summary of its activities was also published in *Indian Opinion* (1905).

12. Edward Carpenter.

13. 'Civilisation': what is meant here is the civilisation produced by the industrial revolution. 'Let it be remembered that Western civilisation is only a hundred years old, or to be more precise fifty. Within this short span the Western people appear to have been reduced to a state of cultural anarchy. We pray that India may never be reduced to the same state as Europe' (*CW* 8: 374).

14. Tolstoy's *The Slavery of Our Times,* and Taylor's *White Slaves of England* (both listed in the Appendix to *HS*) speak of the 'slavery' created by the new industrial civilisation.

15. 'neither of morality nor of religion': morality = *niti;* religion = *dharma.*

16. 'irreligion': *adharma,* contrary to dharma.

17. During his 1906 and 1909 visits to London Gandhi established direct contact with the British suffragette movement. *Indian Opinion* carried reports on the arrests of Miss Cobden and Emmeline Pankhurst; while he was very sympathetic to their cause he disapproved of their violent tactics—the attack on the residence of Asquith, disruption of meetings addressed by Balfour and Winston Churchill, harassment of prison officials, hunger strike in jail, destruction of prison property, etc. (*CW* 9: 303, 324–5).

18. 'the Black Age': *kali juga.* According to Hindu mythology the cycle of time is divided into *kalpa, mahayuga* and *yuga.* The four yugas—*krita, treta, dvapara,* and *kali*—constitute one *mahayuga* (supposedly 4,320,000 years); and 1,000 mahajugas constitute one *kalpa.* At the end of each *kalpa* the cycle starts again. Humankind at present lives in the *kali yuga,* the worst segment in the entire cycle of time. It is supposed to have started in 3102 BC and is supposed to last a total of 432,000 years. During the *kali yuga* the sway of dharma is the weakest, compared to the other three yugas, and humans are normally led by violence and egoism (Zimmer 1963, 13–19).

19. The Gujarati text adds: 'This civilisation is destructive, and it is itself bound to perish.'

20. The Gujarati text adds: 'That is why the British Parliament and other parliaments are ineffective against this civilisation.'

21. 'Civilisation is not an incurable disease': the Gujarati text reads, 'For them [the British] this civilisation is not an incurable disease.' The metaphor of disease occurs again in chs. VII and IX.

22. 'machinery': ch. XIX deals with this topic. By introducing it here Gandhi alerts the reader to the tension that exists between 'true civilisation' and a civilisation based on machinery.

23. 'India is still, somehow or other, sound at the foundation': this is the bedrock of Gandhi's defence of Indian civilisation in *HS*. That foundation is that *artha* and *kama* should be pursued within the framework of dharma. In modern civilisation *artha* and *kama,* according to Gandhi, assert their autonomy from dharma.

24. In this definition of true civilisation, central to the argument of the book, Gandhi connects the notions of self-knowledge, duty (*farajj*), morality (*niti*), mastery over the mind (*man*) and the senses (*indriyo*).

25. In 1911, in response to a question as to whether it would not have been more accurate to write 'The Gujarati equivalent for civilisation is good conduct (*sudharo*)', Gandhi wrote the following reply:

> If 'is' were to be used, the meaning would change. 'Is' is implied in 'equivalent' . . . the Gujarati word generally used for 'civilisation' means 'a good way of life'. That is what I had meant to say. The sentence 'The Gujarati equivalent

for civilisation is *sudharo*' is quite correct. But it is not what I intended to say. Were we to say, "The Gujarati equivalent for civilisation is "good conduct"', according to the rules of grammar, 'good conduct' would have to be taken as a Gujarati phrase . . . Please let me know whether it was for this reason or for any other reasons that you concluded that 'means' was the right word. (*CW* 11: 153)

26. 'as so many writers': in the Gujarati text this reads: 'as so many British writers'. See *HS*, Appendix II.

27. 'India . . . has nothing to learn from anybody else': an obvious hyperbole, to be corrected by his other statements. Thus in 1911 he recommended that Chhaganlal Gandhi, his right-hand man at Phoenix Settlement, should go to London and 'imbibe' its particular atmosphere: 'My own idea was that you should live in London for a year and gather whatever experience and knowledge you could . . . if you imbibe the particular kind of atmosphere that obtains there, the voyage to England will have, to my mind, fulfilled its purpose' (*CW* 10: 401–2). In 1929 he wrote: 'The "Western civilisation" which passes for civilisation is disgusting to me. I have given a rough picture of it in *Hind Swaraj*. Time has brought no change in it. It is not my purpose even to imply that everything Western is bad. I have learnt a lot from the West' (*CW* 40: 300). And in 1931 he wrote:

European civilisation is no doubt suited for the Europeans but it will mean ruin for India, if we endeavour to copy it. This is not to say that we may not adopt and assimilate whatever may be good and capable of assimilation by us as it does not also mean that even the Europeans will not have to part with whatever evil might have crept into it. The incessant search for comforts and their multiplication is such an evil, and I make bold to say that the Europeans themselves will have to remodel their outlook, if they are not to perish under the weight of the comforts to which they are becoming slaves. It may be that my reading is wrong, but I know that for India to run after the Golden Fleece is to court certain death. Let us engrave on our hearts the motto of a Western philosopher, 'plain living and high thinking'. (*CW* 46: 55–6)

As late as 1936, Gandhi thought of London as being 'our Mecca or Kashi [Benares]'. In a letter of recommendation for Kamalnayan Bajaj written to H. S. L. Polak, he stated the following: 'However much we may fight Great Britain, London is increasingly becoming our Mecca or Kashi. Kamalnayan is no exception. I have advised him to take up a course in the London School of Economics. Perhaps you will put him in touch with Professor Laski who may not mind guiding young Bajaj. Muriel [Lester] has undertaken to mother him' (*CW* 63: 122).

28. The psychology of the mind adumbrated here is basic to Gandhi's moral theory and is derived from *The Bhagavad Gita*. Swaraj, or self-control, means control over the *mind*. On the *Gita's* teachings on the relationship of the mind to the body and the senses, and on how one may attain control over the mind, see Zaehner 1973, 423–5.

29. 'life-corroding competition': following Ruskin, Gandhi wants to *moderate* competition by introducing 'social affections' into economic relations.

30. Here Gandhi defends the 'idea' of *varna* and rejects the 'historical' institutions of caste. This quasi-'platonic' approach to *varna* has not convinced critics such as B. R. Ambedkar and the more recent Dalit elite.

31. Manual labour, extolled here, is not a valued activity according to the norms of traditional Indian civilisation. Gandhi came to appreciate it from his reading of Ruskin, Tolstoy and Bondaref. Promotion of manual labour became an integral part of the Gandhian revolution.

32. Gandhi saw in modern Indian cities a real threat to civilised living (*CW* 9: 476); 'Bombay, Calcutta, and the other chief cities of India are the real plague spots' (ibid., 479); 'To me the rise of the cities like Calcutta and Bombay is a matter for sorrow rather than congratulations' (ibid., 509). He idealised and romanticised the Indian village and hoped to reinstate it in a Gandhian India.

33. 'Rishis and Fakirs': *rishis* are sages according to Hindu culture; *fakirs*, according to Muslim culture, are religious mendicants of great moral authority.

34. 'within bounds': the bounds of dharma. This passage throws light on the real point of his earlier criticism of lawyers and doctors: modernity has 'freed' these professions from the restraints required by traditional morality.

35. 'vakils and vaids': lawyers and doctors, respectively, of pre-modern Indian culture.

36. ' . . . go into the interior . . . for six months': Gandhi believed that home rule would mean something only if it improved the lot of the villagers. This is a belief that the modern Indian elite has not understood or accepted. Writing to Henry Polak from Wardha in 1936 he stated: 'I am trying to become a villager. The place where I am writing this has a population of about 600—no roads, no post-office, no shop' (*CW* 63: 122).

37. 'Niyog': a custom permitting a man to have sexual intercourse with his brother's childless widow, or with the wife of an impotent kinsman, in order to raise children, without committing the sin of incest. Children born out of such unions were regarded as the issue of the woman's husband. Originally intended to provide legitimate heirs for childless relatives, in course of time the custom became corrupted, and became part of the 'privileges' of brahmins. While in some regions brahmins claimed the right to provide the issue upon a childless widow, in others they offered their 'services' even when the woman had other children and the husband was alive. Over the centuries, Niyoga remained a great affront to the dignity of Indian women.

38. Gandhi gives a gruesome account of his 1902 visit to the Kali temple in Calcutta: 'On the way I saw a stream of sheep going to be sacrificed to Kali . . . We were greeted by rivers of blood. I could not bear to stand there. I was exasperated and restless. I have never forgotten that sight' (*CW* 39: 190).

39. The social evils enumerated in this paragraph constitute the subject matter of Gandhi's critique of Indian civilisation in *HS*.

40. 'the new spirit that is born in us': a very important point. Gandhi does recognise the positive contributions made by colonialism. It made Indians self-critical and creative.

SUN YATSEN'S THREE PRINCIPLES OF THE PEOPLE

Sun Yatsen

Sun Yatsen (Sun Zhongshan, 1866–1925) is not only heralded as the father of Chinese revolution, but is among a tiny number of political activists who are revered in both the People's Republic of China and on Taiwan, in the Republic of China. Sun was born to a peasant family in China, but spent much of his early life abroad studying medicine and becoming involved in political organization to overthrow the Qing Dynasty (1644–1911). While in Tokyo in 1905, he founded the Revolutionary Alliance (Tongmenghui), and after the Revolution of 1911 toppled the Qing, Sun briefly became the provisional president of China. The Revolutionary Alliance became the Nationalist Party (Guomindang or Kuomintang) and garnered considerable popular support until the new president, Yuan Shikai (Yuan Shih-k'ai, 1859–1916) had one of the Nationalist leaders killed and Sun fled to Japan. During the ensuing warlord era (1916–1927), Sun Yatsen prepared the Nationalist Party and its army in southern China to unify the nation, and even entered into an alliance with the fledgling Chinese Communist Party in 1923. When Sun died of cancer in 1925, Chiang Kaishek (1887–1975) became the new Nationalist Party leader, and he was deeply suspicious of the Communists.

Sun wished to unify China under Nationalist Party leadership, and he had to galvanize support for his plan. The Three Principles constituted the core of Sun's philosophy. The third principle, translated here as "socialism," is also translated as "the people's livelihood," a less politically charged term that makes it far more acceptable in Taiwan.

"SAN-MIN-CHU" (THE THREE PRINCIPLES)*

COMRADES,

To-day, at the opening of our Executive session, the question involuntarily arises before me: what does our organisation represent? This in brief is its history, and the principles which guide it.

Our Party was formed after the overthrow of the Tsing (Manchu) dynasty and the establishment of a republican form of Government. It has to play a tremendous part in the future of our country. From the time this Party was dissolved, China has been constantly in a state of disorder. It is, of course, natural that the reason for the disturbances and sufferings of the Chinese people was the dissolution of our Party. For many years we have fought, and are still fighting, against the traitors to the people who live to this day in the northern provinces of China, where the influence of our Party is very small: nevertheless, sooner or later the northerners will join us. In the south of China, in the sphere of influence of the Party, there is only the single province of Kwantung.

Our Party is revolutionary. In the second year after the establishment of the republican order, many of its members went abroad, where they worked energetically for the development of the revolutionary movement in China. Hence the name of the Party. . . .

. . . The principles of President Lincoln completely coincide with mine. He said: "A government of the people, elected by the people and for the people." These principles have served as the maximum of achievement for Europeans as well as Americans. Words which have the same sense can be found in China: I have translated them: "nationalism, democracy and Socialism." Of course, there can be other interpretations. The wealth and power of the United States are a striking example of the results of great men's teachings in that country. I am glad to observe that my prin-

---

* A speech by Sun-Yat-Sen, delivered on March 6th, 1921, at a meeting of the Executive Committee of the Kuomintang at Canton.

ciples, too, are shared by the greatest political minds abroad and are not in contradiction to all the world's democratic schools of thought.

I now wish to speak of nationalism.

(I) Nationalism

What meaning do we impart to the word "nationalism"? With the establishment of the Manchu dynasty in China, the people remained under an incredible yoke for over two hundred years. Now that dynasty has been overthrown, and the people, it would seem, ought to enjoy complete freedom. But does the Chinese people enjoy all the blessings of liberty? No. Then what is the reason? Why, that our Party has as yet far from fulfilled its appointed tasks, and has carried out only the negative part of its work, without doing anything of its positive work.

Since the end of the great European War, the world position has sharply changed: the eyes of the whole world are now turned to the Far East, particularly to China. Strictly speaking, amongst all the nations of the Far East only Siam and Japan are completely independent. China, vast territorially and exceeding dozens of times in population the independent countries, is yet in effect only semi-independent. What is the reason?

After the overthrow of the monarchy and the establishment of the republican system in the territory populated by the five nationalities (Chinese, Manchus, Mongols, Tartars and Tibetans), a vast number of reactionary and religious elements appeared. And here lies the root of the evil. Numerically, these nationalities stand as follows: there are several million Tibetans, less than a million Mongols, about ten million Tartars, and the most insignificant number of Manchus. Politically their distribution is as follows: Manchuria is in the sphere of Japanese influence, Mongolia, according to recent reports, is under the influence of Russia, and Tibet is the booty of Great Britain. These races have not sufficient strength for self-defence, but they might unite with the Chinese to form a single State.

There are 400 million Chinese: if they cannot organise a single nation, a united State, this is their disgrace, and moreover a proof that we have not given complete effect even to the first principle, and that we must fight for a long while yet to carry out our tasks to the full. We shall establish an united Chinese Republic in order that all the peoples—Manchus, Mongols, Tibetans, Tartars and Chinese—should constitute a single powerful nation. . . .

The name "Republic of Five Nationalities" exists only because there exists a certain racial distinction which distorts the meaning of a single Republic. We must facilitate the dying out of all names of individual peoples inhabiting China, i.e. Manchus, Tibetans, etc. In this respect we must follow the example of the United States of America, i.e. satisfy the demands and requirements of all races and unite them in a single cultural and political whole, to constitute a single nation with such a name, for example, as "Chunhua" (China—in the widest application of the name). Organise the nation, the State. . . .

But let us imagine that the work of uniting all the tribes who inhabit China has been completed, and one nation, "Chunhua," has been formed. Still the object has not been achieved. There are still many peoples suffering from unjust treatment: the Chinese people must assume the mission of setting free these people from their yoke, in the sense of direct aid for them or uniting them under the banner of a single Chinese nation. This would give them the opportunity to enjoy the feeling of equality of man and man, and of a just international attitude, i.e. that which was expressed in the declaration of the American President Wilson by the words "self-determination of nations." Up to the moment of reaching this political stage, our work cannot be considered as finished. Everyone who wishes to join China must be considered Chinese. This is the meaning of nationalism—but "positive" nationalism, and to this we must give special attention.

(2) Democracy

I have already said that in Switzerland democracy has reached its highest point of development: but at the same time the system of representation prevailing there does not constitute real democracy, and only the direct right of the citizen fully answers to the requirements of democracy. Although revolutions took place at various times in France, America and England, and resulted in the establishment of the existing representative system, nevertheless that system does not mean direct and equal rights for all citizens, such as we are fighting for to-day. The most essential of such rights are: the franchise for all citizens: the right of recall (the officials elected by the people can be dismissed by them at will): the right of referendum (if the legislative body passes a law contrary to the wishes of the citizens, the latter may reject the law): the right of initiative (the citizens may propose draft laws to be carried and adopted by the legislative body).

These four fundamental clauses constitute the basis of what I call "direct electoral rights."

(3) Socialism

The theory of Socialism has become known in China comparatively recently. Its chief advocates usually limit their knowledge of this tendency to a few empty words, without having any definite programme. By long study I have formed a concrete view of this question. The essence of Socialism amounts to solving the problem of land and capital. . . .

. . . The first task of my plan is to bring about the proportional distribution of the land. During my stay at Nanking (as Provisional President), I tried to carry out this proposal, but my desire was not fulfilled, as I was not understood. Social questions arise from the inequality between rich and poor. What do we understand by inequality? In ancient times, although there was a distinction between rich and poor, it was not so sharp as to-day. Today the rich own all the land, while the poor have not even a little plot. The reason for this inequality is the difference in productive power. For example, in ancient times timber-cutters used axes, knives, etc., for their work, whereas to-day industry is greatly developed, machines have replaced human labour, and the result is that a much greater quantity of products is secured at the expense of much less human energy. . . .

. . . First we shall speak of the socialisation of land. The land systems of Europe and America are very different. In England up to this day the feudal system of land-holding has survived, whereas in the United States all the land is private property. But my social theory advocates the proportionalisation of the land, as a means of providing against future evils.

. . . The old Chinese land system partially conforms to the principle of proportionalisation of land. In the event of this principle being applied, the two following conditions must be observed: taxation according to the value of the land, and compensation according to declared value. . . .

QUESTIONS

1. What are the Three Principles of the People, as articulated by Sun Yatsen, and how does he define each?
2. Why does Sun believe that these principles must be the core of his party's approach to governance?
3. At what social and/or ethnic groups do you think Sun Yatsen is aiming his message? What groups might be opposed to Sun's approach? Use evidence from the speech to defend your argument.
4. Why do you think Sun Yatsen frequently uses Western nations as examples in this speech? In particular, why do you think he mentions the United States so often?

THE FOURTEEN POINTS*

Woodrow Wilson

Born just before the American Civil War and dying just after World War I, Woodrow Wilson (1856–1924), was a noted historian, a scholar of government systems, a governor of New Jersey, and a president of Princeton University before being elected President of the United States in 1913. The United States' involvement in World War I marked his second term in office (1917–1921). Although Wilson had initially attempted to avoid involvement in what he saw as a European war, he eventually came to see the war as a threat to humanity and to civilization. Wilson also devised a postwar plan, enunciated in his famous "Fourteen Points" speech given before Congress in 1918.

The Fourteen Points, intended to facilitate the reconstruction of Europe after the war, contained suggestions that were both general (freedom of the seas, for example, or the right to self-determination) and specific (Belgian sovereignty). The Points also made explicit recommendations regarding the boundaries of newly created countries—countries that were crafted around recently recognized ethnic and national boundaries. Above all, Wilson's Fourteen Points were idealistic, expressing a vision for peace that appealed to a world torn by a long and destructive war. The last and most important Point, the formation of a "general association of nations" led to the founding of the League of Nations, a body intended to prevent further wars. Although the Points guided the Versailles Treaty that ended World War I, the United States

---

* Woodrow Wilson, *The Fourteen Points*, 65 Congress, 2 Session, *House Document No. 765*, Serial No. 7443 (Washington, 1918), 3–7.

Congress never ratified the treaty or joined the League, rendering many of Wilson's points ineffectual. The concept of a League of Nations, however, survived and helped inspire the founding of the United Nations after World War II.

There is no confusion of counsel among the adversaries of the Central Powers, no uncertainty of principle, no vagueness of detail. The only secrecy of counsel, the only lack of fearless frankness, the only failure to make definite statement of the objects of the war, lies with Germany and her allies. The issues of life and death hang upon these definitions. No statesman who has the least conception of his responsibility ought for a moment to permit himself to continue this tragical and appalling outpouring of blood and treasure unless he is sure beyond a peradventure that the objects of the vital sacrifice are part and parcel of the very life of society and that the people for whom he speaks think them right and imperative as he does. . . .

It will be our wish and purpose that the processes of peace, when they are begun, shall be absolutely open and that they shall involve and permit henceforth no secret understandings of any kind. The day of conquest and aggrandizement is gone by; so is also the day of secret covenants entered into in the interest of particular governments and likely at some unlooked-for moment to upset the peace of the world. . . . This happy fact . . . makes it possible for every nation whose purposes are consistent with justice and the peace of the world to avow now or at any other time the objects it has in view. . . .

We demand in this war . . . nothing peculiar to ourselves. It is that the world be made fit and safe to live in; and particularly that it be made safe for every peace-loving nation which, like our own, wishes to live its own life, determine its own institutions, be assured of justice and fair dealing by the other peoples of the world as against force and selfish aggression. All the peoples of the world are in effect partners in this interest, and for our own part we see very clearly that unless justice be done to others it will not be done to us. The program of the world's peace, therefore, is our program; and that program, the only possible program, as we see it, is this:

I. Open covenants of peace, openly arrived at, after which there shall be no private international understandings of any kind but diplomacy shall proceed always frankly and in the public view.

II. Absolute freedom of navigation upon the seas, outside territorial waters, alike in peace and in war, except as the seas may be closed in whole or in part by international action for the enforcement of international covenants.

III. The removal, so far as possible, of all economic barriers and the establishment of an equality of trade conditions among all the nations consenting to the peace and associating themselves for its maintenance.

IV. Adequate guarantees given and taken that national armaments will be reduced to the lowest point consistent with domestic safety.

V. A free, open-minded, and absolutely impartial adjustment of all colonial claims, based upon a strict observance of the principle that in determining all such questions of sovereignty the interests of the populations concerned must have equal weight with the equitable claims of the government whose title is to be determined.

VI. The evacuation of all Russian territory and such a settlement of all questions affecting Russia as will secure the best and freest cooperation of the other nations of the world in obtaining for her an unhampered and unembarrassed opportunity for the independent determination of her own political development and national policy and assure her of a sincere welcome into the society of free nations under institutions of her own choosing; and, more than a welcome, assistance also of every kind that she may need and may herself desire. . . .

VII. Belgium, the whole world will agree, must be evacuated and restored, without any attempt to limit the sovereignty which she enjoys in common with all other free nations. No other single act will serve as this will serve to restore confidence among the nations in the laws which they have themselves set and determined for the government of their relations with one another. Without this healing act the whole structure and validity of international law is forever impaired.

VIII. All French territory should be freed and the invaded portions restored, and the wrong done to France by Prussia in 1871 in the matter of Alsace-Lorraine, which has unsettled the peace of the world for nearly fifty years, should be righted, in order that peace may once more be made secure in the interest of all.

IX. A readjustment of the frontiers of Italy should be effected along clearly recognizable lines of nationality.

X. The peoples of Austria-Hungary, whose place among the nations we wish to see safeguarded and assured, should be accorded the freest opportunity of autonomous development.

XI. Rumania, Serbia, and Montenegro should be evacuated; occupied territories restored; Serbia accorded free and secure access to the sea; and the relations of the several Balkan states to one another determined by friendly counsel along historically established lines of allegiance and nationality; and international guarantees of the political and economic independence and territorial integrity of the several Balkan states should be entered into.

XII. The Turkish portions of the present Ottoman Empire should be assured a secure sovereignty, but the other nationalities which are now under Turkish rule should be assured an undoubted security of life and an absolutely unmolested opportunity of autonomous development, and the Dardanelles should be permanently opened as a free passage to the ships and commerce of all nations under international guarantees.

XIII. An independent Polish state should be erected which should include the territories inhabited by indisputably Polish populations, which should be assured a free and secure access to the sea, and whose political and economic independence and territorial integrity should be guaranteed by international covenant.

XIV. A general association of nations must be formed under specific covenants for the purpose of affording mutual guarantees of political independence and territorial integrity to great and small states alike.

In regard to these essential rectifications of wrong and assertions of right we feel ourselves to be intimate partners of all the governments and peoples associated together against the Imperialists. We cannot be separated in interest or divided in purpose. We stand together until the end.

For such arrangements and covenants we are willing to fight and to continue to fight until they are achieved; but only because we wish the right to prevail and desire a just and stable peace such as can be secured only by removing chief provocations to war, which this program does remove. We have no jealousy of German greatness, and there is nothing in this program that impairs it. We grudge her no achievement or distinction of learning or of pacific enterprise such as have made her record very bright and very enviable. We do not wish to injure her or to block in any way her legitimate influence or power. We do not wish to fight her either with arms or with hostile arrangements of trade if she is willing to associate herself with us and the other peace-loving nations of the world in covenants of justice and law and fair dealings. We wish her only to accept a place of equality among the peoples of the world—the new world in which we now live—instead of a place of mastery.

Neither do we presume to suggest to her any alteration or modification of her institutions. But it is necessary, we must frankly say, and necessary as a preliminary to any intelligent dealings with her on our part, that we should know whom her spokesmen speak for when they speak to us, whether for the Reichstag majority or for the military party and the men whose creed is imperial domination.

QUESTIONS

1. Which countries' borders were directly affected by the Fourteen Points?
2. What do the Fourteen Points say about trade and commerce between nations?
3. Do you think the Fourteen Points are idealistic?
4. Which provisions do you find appealing about the Fourteen Points? Which provisions do you find unappealing? Why?

DOCUMENT

MAO ON PEASANT MOVEMENTS

Mao Zedong

No man has had a more profound impact on the Chinese people in the twentieth century than Mao Zedong (1893–1976), a founder of the Chinese Communist Party (CCP) and later, its most commanding leader and ideologue. Mao was born to a relatively well-off farming family in Shaoshan, Hunan, where he received a traditional Confucian education until he left the village as a teenager to pursue further education in the provincial capital of Changsha and then the national capital of Beijing. It was in Beijing that Mao found himself immersed in the vibrant and radical intellectual movement that would later generate the Chinese Communist Party.

Despite his voracious appetite for books and periodicals on history, politics, philosophy, and economics, Mao remained deeply ambivalent about the role of intellectuals in creating a new and revolutionary Chinese society. His own country roots and the disdain with which some intellectual activists treated him cemented Mao's conviction that knowledge acquired from books had to be tested by experience. As a young Communist Party activist in the 1920s, Mao became inspired by the potential of China's enormous farming population, particularly the poorest peasants. As many of his comrades worked to organize labor in urban centers such as Shanghai, Mao was drawn to the countryside. On a trip to his home province of Hunan in 1927, Mao witnessed a peasant uprising that inspired the often passionate report excerpted here.

This selection contains two of the most frequently cited passages of Mao's voluminous works—his stirring description of the whirlwind that is peasant anger and his more chilling warning that "a revolution is not a dinner party." Mao also refers here to Dr. Sun Yatsen, founder of the Kuomintang (Guomindang) or Nationalist Party. Mao admired Sun's revolutionary ideals, but detested Sun's successor, Chiang Kaishek, who mistrusted communists and turned on them violently in spring 1927 despite having entered into a Kuomintang-CCP alliance several years earlier. Chiang and the Kuomintang became Mao's arch enemies.

REPORT ON AN INVESTIGATION OF THE PEASANT MOVEMENT IN HUNAN *MARCH 1927*

The Importance of the Peasant Problem

During my recent visit to Hunan I made a first-hand investigation of conditions in the five counties of Hsiangtan, Hsianghsiang, Hengshan, Liling and Changsha. In the thirty-two days from January 4 to February 5, I called together fact-finding conferences in villages and county towns, which were attended by experienced peasants and by comrades working in the peasant movement, and I listened attentively to their reports and collected a great deal of material. Many of the hows and whys of the peasant movement were the exact opposite of what the gentry in Hankow and Changsha are saying. I saw and heard of many strange things of which I had hitherto been unaware. I believe the same is true of many other places, too. All talk directed against the peasant movement must be speedily set right. All the wrong measures taken by the revolutionary authorities concerning the peasant movement must be speedily changed. Only thus can the future of the revolution be benefited. For the present upsurge of the peasant movement is a colossal event. In a very short time, in China's central, southern and northern provinces, several hundred million peasants will rise like a mighty storm, like a hurricane, a force so swift and violent that no power, however great, will be able to hold it back. They will smash all the trammels that bind them and rush forward along the road to liberation. They will sweep all the imperialists, warlords, corrupt officials, local tyrants and evil gentry into their graves. Every revolutionary party and every revolutionary comrade will be put to the test, to be accepted or rejected as they decide. There are three alternatives. To march at their head and lead them? To trail behind them, gesticulating and criticizing? Or to stand in their way and oppose them? Every Chinese is free to choose, but events will force you to make the choice quickly.

"It's Terrible!" or "It's Fine!"

The peasants' revolt disturbed the gentry's sweet dreams. When the news from the countryside reached the cities, it caused immediate uproar among the gentry. Soon after my arrival in Changsha, I met all sorts of people and picked up a good deal of gossip. From the middle social strata upwards to the Kuomintang right-wingers, there was not a single person who did not sum up the whole business in the phrase, "It's terrible!" Under the impact of the views of the "It's terrible!" school then flooding the city, even quite revolutionary-minded people became down-hearted as they pictured the events in the countryside in their mind's eye; and they were unable to deny the word "terrible". Even quite progressive people said, "Though terrible, it is inevitable in a revolution." In short, nobody could altogether deny the word "terrible". But, as already mentioned, the fact is that the great peasant masses have risen to fulfil their historic mission and that the forces of rural democracy have risen to overthrow the forces of rural feudalism. The patriarchal-feudal class of local tyrants, evil gentry and lawless landlords has formed the basis of autocratic government for thousands of years and is the cornerstone of imperialism, warlordism and corrupt officialdom. To overthrow these feudal forces is the real objective of the national revolution. In a few months the peasants have accomplished what Dr. Sun Yat-sen wanted, but failed, to accomplish in the forty years he devoted to the national revolution. This is a marvellous feat never before achieved, not just in forty, but in thousands of years. It's fine. It is not "terrible" at all. It is anything but "terrible". "It's terrible!" is obviously a theory for combating the rise of the peasants in the interests of the landlords; it is obviously a theory of the landlord class for preserving the old order of feudalism and obstructing the establishment of the new order of democracy, it is obviously a counter-revolutionary theory. No revolutionary comrade should echo this nonsense. If your revolutionary viewpoint is firmly established and if you have been to the villages and looked around, you will undoubtedly feel thrilled as never before. Countless thousands of the enslaved—the peasants—are striking down the enemies who battened on their flesh. What the peasants are doing is absolutely right; what they are doing is fine! "It's fine!" is the theory of the peasants and of all other revolutionaries. Every revolutionary comrade should know that the national revolution requires a great change in the countryside. The Revolution of 1911 did not bring about this change, hence its failure. This change is now taking place, and it is an important factor for the completion of the revolution. Every revolutionary comrade must support it, or he will be taking the stand of counter-revolution.

The Question of "Going Too Far"

Then there is another section of people who say, "Yes, peasant associations are necessary, but they are going rather too far." This is the opinion of the middle-of-the-roaders. But what is the actual situation? True, the peasants are in a sense "unruly" in the countryside. Supreme in authority, the peasant association allows the landlord no say and sweeps away his prestige. This amounts to striking the landlord down to the dust and keeping him there. The peasants threaten, "We will put you in the other register!" They fine the local tyrants and evil gentry, they demand contributions from them, and they smash their sedan-chairs. People swarm into the houses of local tyrants and evil gentry who are against the peasant association, slaughter their pigs and consume their grain. They even loll for a minute or two on the ivory-inlaid beds belonging to the young ladies in the households of the local tyrants and evil gentry. At the slightest provocation they make arrests, crown the arrested with tall paper-hats, and parade them through the villages, saying, "You dirty landlords, now you know who we are!" Doing whatever they like and turning everything upside down, they have created a kind of terror in the countryside. This is what some people call "going too far", or "exceeding the proper limits in righting a wrong", or "really too much". Such talk may seem plausible, but in fact it is wrong. First, the local tyrants, evil gentry and lawless landlords have themselves driven the peasants to this. For ages they have used their power to tyrannize over the peasants and trample them underfoot; that is why the peasants have reacted so strongly. The most violent revolts and the most serious disorders have invariably occurred in places where the local tyrants, evil gentry and lawless landlords perpetrated the worst outrages. The peasants are clear-sighted. Who is bad and who is not, who is the worst and who is not quite so vicious, who deserves severe punishment and who deserves to be let off lightly—the peasants keep clear accounts, and very seldom has the punishment exceeded the crime. Secondly, a revolution is not a dinner party, or writing an essay, or painting a picture, or doing embroidery; it cannot be so refined, so leisurely and gentle, so temperate, kind, courteous, restrained and magnanimous. A revolution is an insurrection, an act of violence by which one class overthrows another. A rural revolution is a revolution by which the peasantry overthrows the power of the feudal landlord class. Without using the greatest force, the peasants cannot possibly overthrow the deep-rooted authority of the landlords which has lasted for thousands of years. The rural areas need a mighty revolutionary upsurge, for it alone can rouse the people in their millions to become a powerful force.

QUESTIONS

1. What role does Mao think revolutionaries should play in the peasant movement? Why?
2. Why does Mao scorn those who characterize the peasant movement as "terrible" and who also worry that the peasants, in their zeal to get rid of their oppressors, will "go too far"?
3. Why do you think that Mao had such faith in the judgment of the peasant masses, most of whom were impoverished and illiterate?
4. Based on this selection, can you make any predictions about Mao's leadership style and/or his political agenda in the future?

CONTINENTAL GOVERNMENT FOR AFRICA

Kwame Nkrumah

Kwame Nkrumah was born in the British colony of the Gold Coast (now Ghana) in 1909. As a young man he traveled to the United States and to Great Britain to pursue his education, and during this time he came in contact with the ideas of early Pan-Africanist Marcus Garvey. In 1945, Nkrumah and George Padmore organized the fifth Pan-Africanist Conference in Manchester, England. After the conference, Nkrumah became increasingly involved in anti-imperial politics and in agitation for African political freedom. He arrived back in the Gold Coast in 1947 and within two years had established a new political party, the Convention People's Party (CPP). Nkrumah was involved in protests and civil disobedience against the British colonial government. He was imprisoned for this, but his actions also helped to convince the British that their hold on the Gold Coast was untenable. In 1951, Nkrumah was released from jail and asked by the British governor to work in cooperation to bring the Gold Coast to independence. He agreed, and when the former colony became the independent state of Ghana in 1957, he was its first president. As head of state, he emphasized the importance of the Organization for African Unity (OAU) and worked to disentangle African economies from colonial ties. At the same time, he became more totalitarian in his policies, and he was ultimately overthrown by a military coup in 1966.

Africa Must Unite constitutes a kind of manifesto of Pan-Africanism. It was published in 1963, at a time when the wave of decolonization had just swept across the continent and optimism ran high. In "Continental Government for

Africa," Nkrumah seeks to learn from the examples set by colonial powers while at the same time extricating Africa from what he sees as the artificial boundaries laid down by colonial occupation.

We have seen, in the example of the United States, how the dynamic elements within society understood the need for unity and fought their bitter civil war to maintain the political union that was threatened by the reactionary forces. We have also seen, in the example of the Soviet Union, how the forging of continental unity along with the retention of national sovereignty by the federal states, has achieved a dynamism that has lifted a most backward society into a most powerful unit within a remarkably short space of time. From the examples before us, in Europe and the United States of America, it is therefore patent that we in Africa have the resources, present and potential, for creating the kind of society that we are anxious to build. It is calculated that by the end of this century the population of Africa will probably exceed five hundred millions.

Our continent gives us the second largest land stretch in the world. The natural wealth of Africa is estimated to be greater than that of almost any other continent in the world. To draw the most from our existing and potential means for the achievement of abundance and a fine social order, we need to unify our efforts, our resources, our skills and intentions.

Europe, by way of contrast, must be a lesson to us all. Too busy hugging its exclusive nationalisms, it has descended, after centuries of wars interspersed with intervals of uneasy peace, into a state of confusion, simply because it failed to build a sound basis of political association and understanding. Only now, under the necessities of economic stringency and the threat of the new German industrial and military rehabilitation, is Europe trying—unsuccessfully—to find a *modus operandi* for containing the threat. It is deceptively hoped that the European Community will perform this miracle. It has taken two world wars and the break-up of empires to press home the lesson, still only partly digested, that strength lies in unity.

While we in Africa, for whom the goal of unity is paramount, are striving to concert our efforts in this direction, the neo-colonialists are straining every nerve to upset them by encouraging the formation of communities based on the languages of their former colonizers. We cannot allow ourselves to be so disorganized and divided. The fact that I speak English does not make me an Englishman. Similarly, the fact that some of us speak French or Portuguese does not make us Frenchmen or Portuguese. We are Africans first and last, and as Africans our best interests can only be served by uniting within an African Community. Neither the Commonwealth nor a Franco-African Community can be a substitute.

To us, Africa with its islands is just one Africa. We reject the idea of any kind of partition. From Tangier or Cairo in the North to Capetown in the South, from Cape Guardafui in the East to Cape Verde Islands in the West, Africa is one and indivisible.

I know that when we speak of political union, our critics are quick to observe an attempt to impose leadership and to abrogate sovereignty. But we have seen from the many examples of union put forward, that equality of the states is jealously guarded in every single constitution and that sovereignty is maintained. There are differences in the powers allotted to the central government and those retained by the states, as well as in the functions of the executive, legislature and judiciary. All of them have a common trade and economic policy. All of them are secular, in order that religion might not be dragged across the many problems involved in maintaining unity and securing the greatest possible development.

We in Africa who are pressing now for unity are deeply conscious of the validity of our purpose. We need the strength of our combined numbers and resources to protect ourselves from the very positive dangers of returning colonialism in disguised forms. We need it to combat the entrenched forces dividing our continent and still holding back millions of our brothers. We need it to secure total African liberation. We need it to carry forward our construction of a socio-economic system that will support the great mass of our steadily rising population at levels of life which will compare with those in the most advanced countries.

But we cannot mobilize our present and potential resources without concerted effort. If we developed our potentialities in men and natural resources in separate isolated groups, our energies would soon be dissipated in the struggle to outbid one another. Economic friction among us would certainly lead to bitter political rivalry, such as for many years hampered the pace of growth and development in Europe.

At present most of the independent African States are moving in directions which expose us to the dangers of imperialism and neo-colonialism. We therefore need a common political basis for the integration of our policies in economic planning, defence, foreign and diplomatic relations. That basis for political action need not infringe the essential sovereignty of the separate African States. These States would continue to exercise independent authority, except in the fields defined and reserved for common action in the interests of the security and orderly development of the whole continent.

In my view, therefore, a united Africa—that is, the political and economic unification of the African Continent—should seek three objectives:

Firstly, we should have an over-all economic planning on a continental basis. This would increase the industrial and economic power of Africa. So long as we remain balkanized, regionally or territorially, we shall be at the mercy of colonialism and imperialism. The lesson of the South American Republics *vis-à-vis* the strength and solidarity of the United States of America is there for all to see.

The resources of Africa can be used to the best advantage and the maximum benefit to all only if they are set within an overall framework of a continentally planned development. An overall economic plan, covering an Africa united on a continental basis, would increase our total industrial and economic power. We should therefore be thinking seriously now of ways and means of building up a Common Market of a United Africa and not allow ourselves to be lured by the dubious advantages of association with the so-called European Common Market. We in Africa have looked outward too long for the development of our economy and transportation. Let us begin to look inwards into the African Continent for all aspects of its development. Our communications were devised under colonial rule to stretch outwards towards Europe and elsewhere, instead of developing internally between our cities and states. Political unity should give us the power and will to change all this. We in Africa have untold agricultural, mineral and water-power resources. These almost fabulous resources can be fully exploited and utilized in the interest of Africa and the African people, only if we develop them within a Union Government of African States. Such a Government will need to maintain a common currency, a monetary zone and a central bank of issue. The advantages of these financial and monetary arrangements would be inestimable, since monetary transactions between our several States would be facilitated and the pace of financial activity generally quickened. A central bank of issue is an inescapable necessity, in view of the need to re-orientate the economy of Africa and place it beyond the reach of foreign control.

Secondly, we should aim at the establishment of a unified military and defence strategy. I do not see much virtue or wisdom in our separate efforts to build up or maintain vast military forces for self-defence which, in any case, would be ineffective in any major attack upon our separate States. If we examine this problem realistically, we should be able to ask ourselves this pertinent question: which single State in Africa today can protect its sovereignty against an imperialist aggressor? In this connection, it should be mentioned that anti-*apartheid* leaders have alleged that South Africa is building a great military force with all the latest weapons of destruction, in order to crush nationalism in Africa. Nor is this all. There are grave indications that certain settler governments in Africa have already been caught in the dangerous arms race and are now arming themselves to the teeth. Their military activities constitute a serious threat not only to the security of Africa, but also to the peace of the world. If these reports are true, only the unity of Africa can prevent South Africa and these other governments from achieving their diabolical aims.

If we do not unite and combine our military resources for common defence, the individual States, out of a sense of insecurity, may be drawn into making defence pacts with foreign powers which may endanger the security of us all.

There is also the expenditure aspect of this problem. The maintenance of large military forces imposes a heavy financial burden on even the most wealthy States. For young African States, who are in great need of capital for internal development, it is ridiculous—indeed suicidal—for each State separately and individually to assume such a heavy burden of self-defence, when the weight of this burden could be easily lightened by sharing it among themselves. Some attempt has already been made by the Casablanca Powers and the Afro-Malagasy Union in the matter of common defence, but how much better and stronger it would be if, instead of two such ventures, there was one over-all (land, sea and air) Defence Command for Africa.

The third objective which we should have in Africa stems from the first two which I have just described. If we in Africa set up a unified economic

269

planning organization and a unified military and defence strategy, it will be necessary for us to adopt a unified foreign policy and diplomacy to give political direction to our joint efforts for the protection and economic development of our continent. Moreover, there are some sixty odd States in Africa, about thirty-two of which are at present independent. The burden of separate diplomatic representation by each State on the Continent of Africa alone would be crushing, not to mention representation outside Africa. The desirability of a common foreign policy which will enable us to speak with one voice in the councils of the world, is so obvious, vital and imperative that comment is hardly necessary.

I am confident that it should be possible to devise a constitutional structure applicable to our special conditions in Africa and not necessarily framed in terms of the existing constitutions of Europe, America or elsewhere, which will enable us to secure the objectives I have defined and yet preserve to some extent the sovereignty of each State within a Union of African States.

We might erect for the time being a constitutional form that could start with those states willing to create a nucleus, and leave the door open for the attachment of others as they desire to join or reach the freedom which would allow them to do so. The form could be made amenable to adjustment and amendment at any time the consensus of opinion is for it. It may be that concrete expression can be given to our present ideas within a continental parliament that would provide a lower and an upper house, the one to permit the discussion of the many problems facing Africa by a representation based on population; the other, ensuring the equality of the associated States, regardless of size and population, by a similar, limited representation from each of them, to formulate a common policy in all matters affecting the security, defence and development of Africa. It might, through a committee selected for the purpose, examine likely solutions to the problems of union and draft a more conclusive form of constitution that will be acceptable to all the independent States.

The survival of free Africa, the extending independence of this continent, and the development towards that bright future on which our hopes and endeavours are pinned, depend upon political unity.

Under a major political union of Africa there could emerge a United Africa, great and powerful, in which the territorial boundaries which are the relics of colonialism will become obsolete and superfluous, working for the complete and total mobilization of the economic planning organization under a unified political direction. The forces that unite us are far greater than the difficulties that divide us at present, and our goal must be the establishment of Africa's dignity, progress and prosperity.

Proof is therefore positive that the continental union of Africa is an inescapable desideratum if we are determined to move forward to a realization of our hopes and plans for creating a modern society which will give our peoples the opportunity to enjoy a full and satisfying life. The forces that unite us are intrinsic and greater than the superimposed influences that keep us apart. These are the forces that we must enlist and cement for the sake of the trusting millions who look to us, their leaders, to take them out of the poverty, ignorance and disorder left by colonialism into an ordered unity in which freedom and amity can flourish amidst plenty.

Here is a challenge which destiny has thrown out to the leaders of Africa. It is for us to grasp what is a golden opportunity to prove that the genius of the African people can surmount the separatist tendencies in sovereign nationhood by coming together speedily, for the sake of Africa's greater glory and infinite well-being, into a Union of African States.

QUESTIONS

1. What lessons does Nkrumah suggest can be learned from the European experience?

2. What factors lead Nkrumah to believe that no "single state in Africa today can protect its sovereignty against an imperialist aggressor"?

3. To what extent and in what ways does Nkrumah's plan for a United Africa mirror the United States? In what ways is it different?

4. How does Nkrumah's experience of traveling outside of Africa seem to have an impact on his understanding of African identity?

THE CUBAN REVOLUTION OF 1959

Fidel Castro

The Cuban Revolution, which overthrew dictator Fulgencio Batista (1940–1944 and 1952–1959) in 1959, is currently still in power after nearly half a century. The current Cuban regime is by far the longest lasting in the Americas. And Fidel Castro is the head of state with the second longest tenure (next to Emperor Pedro II of Brazil, 1831–1889) in the history of Latin America since independence. From the beginning Castro and his revolution have been the center of historical controversy. The revolution has gone through a number of stages, ranging from the somewhat chaotic 1960s through the economically depressed 1990s. The overall record of the revolution is mixed. Among its most notable successes were universal literacy, excellent health care and training, equalization of wealth, and some advances in gender and racial equality. The most notable failures were the continued reliance on sugar exports and on a single market for that crop (the Soviet Union). Cuba also relied on the Soviet Union as a principal source of industrial products. Severe shortages of basic consumer commodities forced periodic rationing. Meanwhile, despite some advances in women's status, there was a conspicuous lack of women in the highest echelons of the government.

As a very young man in 1953 Castro and his followers unsuccessfully raided a military base and after barely avoiding being executed, he served a few years in prison. While in prison he clandestinely wrote a revolutionary

tract that became an underground best-seller in Cuba and vaulted him into the
forefront of the opposition to the dictatorship.

·················

In the brief of this cause there must be recorded the five revolutionary laws
that would have been proclaimed immediately after the capture of the
Moncada barracks and would have been broadcast to the nation by radio.
It is possible that Colonel Chaviano may deliberately have destroyed these
documents, but even if he has done so, I conserve them in my memory.

The First Revolutionary Law would have returned power to the people
and proclaimed the Constitution of 1940 the supreme Law of the land, until
such time as the people should decide to modify or change it. And, in order
to effect its implementation and punish those who had violated it—there
being no organization for holding elections to accomplish this—the revolutionary movement, as the momentous incarnation of this sovereignty, the
only source of legitimate power, would have assumed all the faculties inherent to it, except that of modifying the Constitution itself: In other words it
would have assumed the legislative, executive and judicial powers.

This approach could not be more crystal clear nor more free of vacil-
lation and sterile charlatanry. A government acclaimed by the mass of
rebel people would be vested with every power, everything necessary in
order to proceed with the effective implementation of the popular will and
true justice. From that moment, the Judicial Power, which since March
10th has placed itself *against* the Constitution and *outside* the Constitution, would cease to exist and we would proceed to its immediate and
total reform before it would again assume the power granted to it by the
Supreme Law of the Republic. Without our first taking those previous
measures, a return to legality by putting the custody of the courts back into
the hands that have crippled the system so dishonorably would constitute
a fraud, a deceit, and one more betrayal.

The Second Revolutionary Law would have granted property, not
mortgageable and not transferable, to all planters, sub-planters, lessees,
partners and squatters who hold parcels of five or less "caballerias" of
land, and the state would indemnify the former owners on the basis of the
rental which they would have received for these parcels over a period of
ten years.

273

The Third Revolutionary Law would have granted workers and employees the right to share 30% of the profits of all the large industrial, mercantile and mining enterprises, including the sugar mills. The strictly agricultural enterprises would be exempt in consideration of other agrarian laws which would have been implemented.

The Fourth Revolutionary Law would have granted all planters the right to share 55% of the sugar production and a minimum quota of forty thousand "arrobas" for all small planters who have been established for three or more years.

The Fifth Revolutionary Law would have ordered the confiscation of all holdings and ill-gotten gains of those who had committed frauds during previous regimes, as well as the holdings and ill-gotten gains of all their legatees and heirs. To implement this, special courts with full powers would gain access to all records of all corporations registered or operating in this country [in order] to investigate concealed funds of illegal origin, and to request that foreign governments extradite persons and attach holdings [rightfully belonging to the Cuban people]. Half of the property recovered would be used to subsidize retirement funds for workers and the other half would be used for hospitals, asylums and charitable organizations.

Furthermore, it was to be declared that the Cuban policy in the Americas would be one of close solidarity with the democratic people of this continent, and that those politically persecuted by bloody tyrants oppressing our sister nations would find generous asylum, brotherhood, and bread in the land of Marti. Not the persecution, hunger and treason that they find today. Cuba should be the bulwark of liberty and not a shameful link in the chain of despotism.

These laws would have been proclaimed immediately, as soon as the upheaval were ended and prior to a detailed and far-reaching study, they would have been followed by another series of laws and fundamental measures, such as, the Agrarian Reform, Integral Reform of Education, nationalization of the Utilities Trust and the Telephone Trust, refund to the people of the illegal excessive rates this company has charged, and payment to the Treasury of all taxes brazenly evaded in the past.

All these laws and others would be inspired in the exact fulfillment of two essential articles of our Constitution. One of these orders the outlawing of feudal estates by indicating the maximum area of land any person or entity can possess for each type of agricultural enterprise, by adopting measures which would tend to revert the land to the Cubans. The other categorically orders the State to use all means at its disposal to provide employment to all those who lack it and to insure a decent livelihood to each manual laborer or intellectual.

None of these articles may be called unconstitutional. The first popularly elected government would have to respect these laws, not only because of moral obligation to the nation, but because when people achieve something they have yearned for throughout generations, no force in the world is capable of taking it away again.

The problems concerning land, the problem of industrialization, the problem of housing, the problem of unemployment, the problem of education and the problem of the health of the people; these are the six problems we would take immediate steps to resolve, along with the restoration of public liberties and political democracy.

Perhaps this exposition appears cold and theoretical if one does not know the shocking and tragic conditions of the country with regard to these six problems, to say nothing of the most humiliating political oppression.

85% of the small farmers in Cuba pay rent and live under the constant threat of being dispossessed from the land that they cultivate. More than half the best cultivated land belongs to foreigners. In *Oriente,* the largest province, the lands of the United Fruit Company and West Indian Company join the north coast to the southern one. There are two hundred thousand peasant families who do not have a single acre of land to cultivate to provide food for their starving children. On the other hand, nearly three hundred thousand "caballerias" of productive land owned by powerful interests remains uncultivated.

Cuba is above all an agricultural state. Its population is largely rural. The city depends on these rural areas. The rural people won the Independence. The greatness and prosperity of our country depends on a healthy and vigorous rural population that loves the land and knows how to cultivate it, within the framework of a state that protects and guides them. Considering all this, how can the present state of affairs be tolerated any longer?

With the exception of a few food, lumber and textile industries, Cuba continues to be a producer of raw materials. We export sugar to import candy, we export hides to import shoes, we export iron to import plows. Everybody agrees that the need to industrialize the country is urgent, that we need steel industries, paper and chemical industries; that we must improve cattle and grain products, the technique and the processing in our food industry, in order to balance the ruinous competition of the Europeans in cheese products, condensed milk, liquors and oil, and that of the Americans in canned goods; that we need merchant ships; that tourism should be an enormous source of revenue. But the capitalists insist that the workers remain under a . . . yoke; the State folds its arms and industrialization can wait . . .

Just as serious or even worse is the housing problem. There are two hundred thousand huts and hovels in Cuba; four hundred thousand families in the country and in the cities live cramped into barracks and tenements without even the minimum sanitary requirements; two million two hundred thousand of our urban population pay rents which absorb between one fifth and one third of their income; and two million eight hundred thousand of our rural and suburban population lack electricity. If the State proposes lowering rents, landlords threaten to freeze all construction; if the State does not interfere construction goes on so long as the landlords get high rents, otherwise, they would not lay a single brick even though the rest of the population should have to live exposed to the elements. The utilities monopoly is no better: they extend lines as far as it is profitable and beyond that point, they don't care if the people have to live in darkness for the rest of their lives. The State folds its arms and the people have neither homes nor electricity.

Our educational system is perfectly compatible with the rest of our national situation. Where the *guajiro* is not the owner of his land, what need is there for agricultural schools? Where there are no industries what need is there for technical or industrial schools? Everything falls within the same absurd logic: there is neither one thing nor the other. In any small European country there are more than 200 technical and industrial arts schools; in Cuba, there are only six such schools, and the boys graduate without having anywhere to use their skills. The little rural schools are attended by only half the school-age children—barefoot, half-naked and undernourished—and frequently the teacher must buy necessary materials from his own salary. Is this the way to make a nation great?

Only death can liberate one from so much misery. In this, however,— early death—the state is most helpful. 90% of rural children are consumed by parasites which filter through their bare feet from the earth. Society is moved to compassion upon hearing of the kidnapping or murder of one child, but they are criminally indifferent to the mass murder of so many thousands of children who die every year from lack of facilities, agonizing with pain. Their innocent eyes—death already shining in them—seem to look into infinity as if entreating forgiveness for human selfishness, as if asking God to stay his wrath. When the head of a family works only four months a year, with what can he purchase clothing and medicine for his children? They will grow up with rickets, with not a single good tooth in their mouths by the time they reach thirty; they will have heard ten million speeches and will finally die of misery and deception. Public hospitals, which are always full, accept only patients recommended by some powerful politician who, in turn, demands the electoral votes of the unfortunate one and his family so that Cuba may continue forever the same or worse.

With this background, is it not understandable that from May to December over a million persons lost their jobs, and that Cuba, with a population of five and a half million, has a greater percentage of unemployed than France or Italy with a population of forty million each?

When you judge a defendant for robbery, Your Honors, do you ask him how long he has been unemployed? Do you ask him how many children he has, which days of the week he ate and which he didn't, do you concern yourselves with his environment at all? You send him to jail without further thought. But those who burn warehouses and stores to collect insurance do not go to jail, even though a few human beings should have happened to [be cremated with the property insured]. The insured have money to hire lawyers and bribe judges. You jail the poor wretch who steals because he is hungry; but none of the hundreds who steal from the Government has ever spent a night in jail; you dine with them at the end of the year in some elegant place and they enjoy your respect.

In Cuba when a bureaucrat becomes a millionaire overnight and enters the fraternity of the rich, he could very well be greeted with the words of that opulent Balzac character, Taillefer, who, in his toast to the young heir to an enormous fortune, said: "Gentlemen, let us drink to the power of gold! Mr. Valentine, a millionaire six time over has just ascended the throne. He is king, can do everything, is above everything—like all the rich. Henceforward, equality before the law, before the Constitution, will be a myth for him; for he will not be subject to laws, the laws will be subject to him. There are no courts or sentences for millionaires."

The future of the country and the solution of its problems cannot continue to depend on the selfish interests of a dozen financiers, nor on the cold calculations of profits that ten or twelve magnates draw up in their air-conditioned offices. The country cannot continue begging on its knees for miracles from a few golden calves, similar to the Biblical one destroyed by the fury of a prophet. Golden calves cannot perform miracles of any kind. The problems of the Republic can be solved only if we dedicate ourselves to fight for that Republic with the same energy, honesty and patriotism our liberators had when they created it.

QUESTIONS

1. What were the five revolutionary laws Castro proposed in *History Will Absolve Me*?
2. What is his program's first economic priority?
3. What are Castro's views on land reform?
4. What were the most radical aspects of Castro's program? Do you regard them as particularly radical?

THE GREAT LEAP FORWARD

Yin Tse-ming

The Great Leap Forward, a mass campaign designed to allow China to "leap" over the capitalist stage of Marxist economic development and land in a socialist economy, was the culmination of social, economic, and political changes already implemented by Mao Zedong (Mao Tse-tung; 1893–1976). He and the Chinese Communist Party had already rid the countryside of the landlord class in the early 1950s, silenced dissent among intellectuals with the Anti-Rightist Campaign in the mid-1950s, and moved to push peasants into collectives and communes just prior to the launching of the Great Leap. Now it was time to show the world that the People's Republic of China would follow its own path, relying primarily on the strength and ideological fervor of the masses.

Although the Great Leap encouraged increased agricultural and industrial output, this selection deals with strategies for the latter. Mao's goal was to surpass Great Britain's steel production in less than fifteen years—an audacious aim, given China's undeveloped industrial sector at that time—and he set about doing so by putting the masses to work. All across China, people took anything metal that they owned or could find and melted it down in so-called "backyard steel furnaces." As they fed the fires of tens of thousands of these furnaces, the Party fanned the flames of popular devotion to the Party and its charismatic chairman. However, despite the massive efforts of the Chinese people, the intentional rejection of foreign aid and technology ultimately resulted in the production of large amounts of poor quality metal. Coupled with the disastrous effects of the push to increase agricultural pro-

duction, the Great Leap Forward resulted in a nationwide famine that claimed an estimated twenty million lives.

THE STRENGTH OF THE MASSES IS LIMITLESS*

Iron smelting and steel making in the Shaoyang Special Administrative Region, Hunan Province, are rapidly developing on a mass scale. In a short period in the autumn of 1958, 12,378 local blast furnaces were built in this area. Of these, 4816 went into immediate operation, with a daily output of more than 2400 tons. The highest daily output has reached the 2438 ton mark, which is an average of half a ton a day for each local furnace in operation. In the first ten days of September, 1958, daily output of iron more than trebled (the daily output on September 1 was 595 tons). Now this region has already produced 50,000 tons of iron. Not only is there a "bumper harvest" in many places but the Chinhua Iron Works in Shaotung County, "king" of local blast furnaces, has produced the remarkable record of almost three tons (5836 catties) a day.

At present, people in many districts are working with increasing enthusiasm to produce iron and steel, and as more and more effective measures are taken, it is anticipated that there will be even greater achievement in steel and iron production in the near future.

The main reason for this remarkable progress in iron and steel production in such a short time in Shaoyang region is the fact that this region has fully carried out the Communist Party's directive to let the whole party and all the people work in iron and steel production, in keeping with the party's general line of socialist construction.

Iron and steel production is not simply a technical job; it is also a political task that has an important bearing on all other activities. Therefore, the first condition for the rapid development of production is for the party secretaries to take the lead and have the entire party membership mobilized. The party committees of Shaoyang region are all clearly convinced

---

*Excerpted from a pamphlet, *Six Hundred Million Build Industry,* prepared by the editors of Foreign Language Press, Peking, 1958.

of the importance of the guiding principle of making steel production the first task, in order to hasten the progress of industry and agriculture and they gave iron and steel production priority. The first secretaries of different party committees all took personal charge, leading more than ten thousand government functionaries and nearly one million workers in this battle for iron and steel. Many government functionaries organized experimental units in the factories and workshops and they all took part in actual production. By joining the movement first the leaders not only set an example for the masses and hastened its progress, but they also learned much and became experienced workers. By the beginning of September, 1958, government functionaries in this region had set up a total of 2352 experimental blast furnaces and 500 experimental coal pits. In Lienyuan County 15 members of the county party committee and 29 township party secretaries have already mastered the technique of smelting iron.

In Lunghui County, deputy secretary of the county party committee, Hsieh Kuo, set up experimental furnaces at Shihmen, but failed to produce iron in 22 successive attempts. He persisted, studying and trying again and again and finally he produced iron in all the five local furnaces. In Shaotung County, the head of Niumasze Township, Chao Lin-fu, stayed by the furnace, sleeping and eating on the spot. After 21 experiments he finally increased the daily output of each furnace from 300 to 2250 catties. Leaders of co-ops, peasants, men and women of all ages, workers, government officials, and soldiers are all trying their skill with experimental furnaces. Many peasants want to be capable of running agricultural co-ops and factories, capable of farming as well as smelting iron.

When they first began to work in iron and steel production, many people wanted to have big "foreign" blast furnaces. They were not interested in these small native furnaces. They thought it necessary to wait for elaborate equipment. Actually that line of thinking would result in producing less, slower, more expensively, and not so well; and it would not lead to production on a mass basis. Under the timely guidance of the Central Committee and the provincial committee of the Communist Party, that policy was firmly rejected and the policy of putting iron and steel production on a mass basis, of mobilizing all the party members, and letting politics take the lead was carried out. From the beginning, Shaoyang region initiated a gigantic propaganda campaign. All the people were encouraged to voice their opinions in a general debate on such subjects as the following: Why must iron and steel production be developed? How can it be done? What is the relationship between the production of iron and steel and agriculture? Through voicing different opinions and public debates the masses achieved a clearer understanding and became convinced; thus their enthusiasm was aroused. Within a few days more than half a million written pledges were sent to the party in support of the campaign. The people felt elated and stimulated; millions of hearts had only one wish—to fight hard to achieve and surpass the goal of producing 300,000 tons of iron in 1958.

The strength of the masses is tremendous. All the problems of funds, raw materials, equipment, fuel, and geological survey of resources, which seemed hard to solve in the past, disappeared before the resourcefulness of the people. In honor of the anniversary of the Communist Party (July 1), 67,000 people in Hsinhua County worked for three days and nights on end and built 1025 blast furnaces. Many people hearing the news came from as far as 100 *li* away to join in the work, carrying timber and bamboo and their food and clothes. In Szetu Township, 53 couples came to put their names down offering to help in industrial production. Within a few days this county collected a fund of more than 1.6 million yuan. There was a 50-year-old woman who voluntarily contributed more than 200 *yuan,* her savings of many years, for the local industry. The people contributed 1280 pigs, more than 700,000 catties of vegetables, and 180,000 pairs of straw sandals for the people who were taking part in this industrial construction project. To solve the housing problem, the people of Tienping Township, in one morning, spontaneously vacated more than 500 rooms. The contributions from the masses became a mighty torrent, and the blast furnaces were set up very quickly. The people composed a song describing this event:

The Communist Party is really wonderful.

In three days more than a thousand furnaces were built.

The masses' strength is really tremendous.

The American imperialists will run off, tails between legs.

The Chinese people will now surpass Britain.

The East wind will always prevail over the West wind.

282

QUESTIONS

1. According to this document, how did the Chinese people respond to the Great Leap Forward? What were its major successes?
2. Can you find in this piece any indication of problems implementing this campaign? If so, what were they and how were those problems overcome?
3. What do you think the author of this piece meant when he said that the production of iron and steel was both a technical and political task?
4. Why do you think Mao favored the use of mass campaigns like the Great Leap Forward as a means of implementing his policies?

ISLAMIC GOVERNMENT

Ayatollah Ruhollah Khomeini

Few people have had as deep an influence on the modern Islamic world as Ayatollah Ruhollah Khomeini. Ruhollah Musavi Khomeini, a descendant of the Prophet Muhammad, was born in the town of Khomein in 1900. He was exiled from Iran in 1964 for his criticisms of the government of Shah Mohammed Reza Pahlavi, and moved first to Turkey, then to the Shiite holy cities in Iraq, and finally to France, where the French government supposedly offered to arrange a "lethal accident"—an offer that the Shah, no doubt to his everlasting regret, declined. After mass demonstrations in 1978 and 1979, the Shah fled from Iran and Khomeini returned and was declared "Supreme Leader" for life, a position that he indeed held until his death in 1989. Over nine million grief-stricken mourners attended his funeral.

This selection is from Khomeini's most influential work, usually called Islamic Government *but perhaps better translated as "The Rulership of the Juriconsults." In this book, Khomeini revolutionized Shiite theology and political philosophy, which has traditionally held that there can be no real Islamic government until the Hidden Imam returns from his Occultation. Khomeini, on the contrary, maintained that the religious clerics, headed by one Supreme Leader, the most respected religious authority of the age, could act as deputies for the Hidden Imam. The practical implications of this theory were that it established the obligation of Shiite Muslims to institute an Islamic government, in which all laws would be based on Islam and monitored by a council of clerics under*

Reprinted from *Islam and Revolution*, translated by Hamid Algar. Copyright © 1981 by Hamid Algar.

the Supreme Leader (since Khomeini's death, Ayatollah 'Ali Khamane'i). The Islamic Republic of Iran was modeled on this blueprint.

PROGRAM FOR THE ESTABLISHMENT OF AN ISLAMIC GOVERNMENT

It is our duty to work toward the establishment of an Islamic government. The first activity we must undertake in this respect is the propagation of our cause; that is how we must begin.

It has always been that way, all over the world: a group of people came together, deliberated, made decisions, and then began to propagate their aims. Gradually the number of like-minded people would increase, until finally they became powerful enough to influence a great state or even to confront and overthrow it, as was the case with the downfall of Muhammad 'Ali Mirza and the supplanting of his absolute monarchy with constitutional government.[1] Such movements began with no troops or armed power at their disposal; they always had to resort to propagating the aims of their movement first. The thievery and tyranny practiced by the regime would be condemned and the people awakened and made to understand that the thievery inflicted on them was wrong. Gradually the scope of this activity would be expanded until it came to embrace all groups of society, and the people, awakened and active, would attain their goal.

You have neither a country nor an army now, but propagating activity is possible for you, because the enemy has been unable to deprive you of all the requisite means.

You must teach the people matters relating to worship, of course, but more important are the political, economic, and legal aspects of Islam. These are, or should be, the focus of our concern. It is our duty to begin exerting ourselves now in order to establish a truly Islamic government. We must propagate our cause to the people, instruct them in it, and convince them of its validity. We must generate a wave of intellectual awakening, to emerge as a current throughout society, and gradually, to take shape as an organized Islamic movement made up of the awakened, committed, and religious masses who will rise up and establish an Islamic government.

Propagation and instruction, then, are our two fundamental and most important activities. It is the duty of the *fuqaha* to promulgate religion and instruct the people in the creed, ordinances, and institutions of Islam, in order to pave the way in society for the implementation of Islamic law and the establishment of Islamic institutions. In one of the traditions we have cited, you will have noticed that the successors of the Most Noble Messenger (upon whom be peace and blessings) are described as "teaching the people"—that is, instructing them in religion.

This duty is particularly important under the present circumstances, for the imperialists, the oppressive and treacherous rulers, the Jews, Christians, and materialists are all attempting to distort the truths of Islam and lead the Muslims astray. Our responsibilities of propagation and instruction are greater than ever before. We see today that the Jews (may God curse them) have meddled with the text of the Qur'an and have made certain changes in the Qur'ans they have had printed in the occupied territories.[2] It is our duty to prevent this treacherous interference with the text of the Qur'an. We must protest and make the people aware that the Jews and their foreign backers are opposed to the very foundations of Islam and wish to establish Jewish domination throughout the world. Since they are a cunning and resourceful group of people, I fear that—God forbid!—they may one day achieve their goal, and that the apathy shown by some of us may allow a Jew to rule over us one day. May God never let us see such a day!

At the same time, a number of orientalists serving as propaganda agents for the imperialist institution are also active in endeavors to distort and misrepresent the truths of Islam. The agents of imperialism are busy in every corner of the Islamic world drawing our youth away from us with their evil propaganda. They are not converting them into Jews and Christians; they are corrupting them, making them irreligious and indifferent, which is sufficient for their purposes. In our own city of Tehran now there are centers of evil propaganda run by the churches, the Zionists, and the Baha'is in order to lead our people astray and make them abandon the ordinances and teachings of Islam. Do we not have a duty to destroy these centers that are damaging to Islam? Is it enough for us simply to possess Najaf? (Actually, we do not even have Najaf!)[3] Should we be content to sit lamenting in Qum, or should we come to life and be active?

You, the younger generation in the religious institution, must come fully to life and keep the cause of God alive. Develop and refine your thinking, and lay aside your concern with the minutiae and subtleties of the religious sciences, because that kind of concentration on petty detail has kept many of us from performing our more important duties. Come to the aid of Islam; save Islam! They are destroying Islam! Invoking the laws of Islam and the name of the Most Noble Messenger (upon whom be peace and blessings), they are destroying Islam! Agents—both foreigners sent by the imperialists and natives employed by them—have spread out into every village and region of Iran and are leading our children and young people astray, who might otherwise be of service to Islam one day. Help save our young people from this danger!

It is your duty to disseminate among the people the religious knowledge you have acquired and to acquaint them with the subjects you have learned. The scholar or the *faqih* is accorded praise and glorified in the traditions because he is the one who makes the ordinances, doctrines, and institutions of Islam known to the people and instructs them in the Sunna of the Most Noble Messenger (upon whom be peace and blessings). You now must devote your energies to the tasks of propagation and instruction in order to present Islam more fully to the people.

It is our duty to dispel the doubts about Islam that have been created; until we have erased these doubts from people's minds, we will not be able to accomplish anything. We must impress upon ourselves and upon the next generation—and even the generation after that—the necessity for dispelling these doubts about Islam that have arisen in the minds of many people, even the educated among us, as the result of centuries of false propaganda. You must acquaint the people with the world-view, social institutions, and form of government proposed by Islam, so that they may come to know what Islam is and what its laws are.

It is the duty of the teaching institution today in Qum, Mash-had, and elsewhere to propagate Islam, to expound this faith and school of thought. In addition to Islam, you must make yourselves known to the people of the world and also authentic models of Islamic leadership and government. You must address yourselves to the university people in particular, the educated class. The students have had their eyes opened. I assure you that if you present Islam and Islamic government to the universities accurately, the students will welcome it and accept it. The students are opposed to tyranny; they are opposed to the puppet regimes imperialism imposes;

they are opposed to thievery and the plundering of public wealth; they are opposed to this consumption of what is forbidden and this deceitful propaganda. But no student could be opposed to Islam, whose form of government and teachings are beneficial to society. The students are looking to Najaf, appealing for help. Should we sit idle, waiting for them to enjoin the good upon us and call us to our duties?[4] Our young people studying in Europe are enjoining the good upon us; they say to us: "We have organized Islamic associations; now help us!"[5]

It is our duty to bring all these matters to the attention of the people. We must explain what the form of government is in Islam and how rule was conducted in the earliest days of Islamic history. We must tell them how the center of command and the seat of the judiciary under it were both located in part of the mosque, at a time when the Islamic state embraced the farthest reaches of Iran, Egypt, the Hijaz, and the Yemen. Unfortunately, when government passed into the hands of the next generations, it was converted into a monarchy, or even worse than a monarchy.

The people must be instructed in these matters and helped to mature, intellectually and politically. We must tell them what kind of government we want, what kinds of people would assume responsibility for affairs in the government we propose, and what policies and programs they would follow. . . .

. . . The first Muslims, on the other hand, used to accomplish important business on the occasion of the *hajj* or at their Friday gatherings. The Friday sermon was more than a *sura* from the Qur'an and a prayer followed by a few brief words. Entire armies used to be mobilized by the Friday sermon and proceed directly from the mosque to the battlefield—and a man who sets out from the mosque to go into battle will fear only God, not poverty or hardship, and his army will be victorious and triumphant. When you look at the Friday sermons given in that age and the sermons of the Commander of the Faithful (upon whom be peace), you see that their purpose was to set people in motion, to arouse them to fight and sacrifice themselves for Islam, to resolve the sufferings of the people of this world.

If the Muslims before us had gathered every Friday and reminded themselves of their common problems, and solved them or resolved to solve them, we would not be in the position we find ourselves in today. Today we must start organizing these assemblies in earnest and make use of them for the sake of propagation and instruction. The ideological and political movement of Islam will thus develop and advance toward its climax. . . .

If you present Islam accurately and acquaint people with its world-view, doctrines, principles, ordinances, and social system, they will welcome it ardently (God knows, many people want it). I have witnessed that myself. A single word was enough once to cause a wave of enthusiasm among the people, because then, like now, they were all dissatisfied and unhappy with the state of affairs. They are living now in the shadow of the bayonet, and repression will let them say nothing. They want someone to stand up fearlessly and speak out. So, courageous sons of Islam, stand up! Address the people bravely; tell the truth about our situation to the masses in simple language; arouse them to enthusiastic activity, and turn the people in the street and the bazaar, our simple-hearted workers and peasants, and our alert students into dedicated *mujahids*. The entire population will become *mujahids*. All segments of society are ready to struggle for the sake of freedom, independence, and the happiness of the nation, and their struggle needs religion. Give the people Islam, then, for Islam is the school of *jihad*, the religion of struggle; let them amend their characters and beliefs in accordance with Islam and transform themselves into a powerful force, so that they may overthrow the tyrannical regime imperialism has imposed on us and set up an Islamic government.

Only those *fuqaha* who make the people acquainted with the beliefs and institutions of Islam, and who defend and protect them, are truly "citadels of Islam." They must deliver rousing, impassioned speeches and lead the people in order to fulfill this function. Only then, if they live to be, say, 120, will the people feel that Islam has suffered a misfortune with their passing and that a gap has appeared in the Muslim community, or as the tradition puts it, "A crack will appear in the fortress of Islam." Will some irremediable deficiency occur in Islamic society now if one of us dies after spending his life at home reading books? What loss could our death mean? But when Islam lost Imam Husayn (upon whom be peace), then indeed the loss was irreparable. . . .

END NOTES

1. On June 23, 1908, Muhammad 'Ali Shah carried out with Russian aid a military coup against the first Iranian Majlis. He was overthrown and constitutional rule restored on July 16, 1909, as a result of popular resistance, largely directed by the most important religious scholars of the day in Najaf. See Browne, *The Persian Revolution of 1905–1909*, chs. 7-10.

2. Soon after the Six-Day War, it was reported that copies of the Qur'an were circulating in the territories seized by the Zionists, as well as in African countries, from which all verses critical of the Jews had been excised. [This was, of course, merely another anti-Semitic conspiracy the theory; Arabic Qur'ans printed in Israel or in territory under Israeli control are identical to all other Qur'ans]

3. Najaf is the main center of learning in the Shi'i world. The lament here that "we do not even have Najaf" refers to the restrictions and pressure placed on the Shi'i scholars of Najaf by the Baathist regime of Baghdad. The Baathist persecution of Najaf reached a highpoint in May 1969—ten months before these lectures were given—when a number of *ulama* were arrested and tortured and religious endowments were confiscated. See anon., *Hayat-e-Hakeem*, in Eng. (Karachi, 1973), pp. 73–84.

4. Insofar as the "enjoining of the good" is the particular duty of the religious scholars, it would be shaming for them to need a reminder from students.

5. Throughout his exile in Najaf, Imam Khomeini gave special attention to the Islamic associations of Iranian students in Europe and the United States, sending them guidance and encouragement. For an example of his messages to the Iranian Muslim students in North America, see pp. 209–211.

QUESTION

1. What does Khomeini state to be the "two fundamental and most important activities" of religious clerics?

2. Whom does Khomeini name as the enemies? What does he claim these enemies are trying do?

3. What does Khomeini mean by the last paragraph? To what is he exhorting his audience?

4. At one point in this excerpt, Khomeini gives a short disquisition on the government of the Islamic state at the height of its power. What can you infer from his statement?

WHAT AL-QA'EDA WANTS FROM AMERICA

Usama bin Ladin

Usama bin Muhammad bin 'Awad bin Ladin was born in Riyadh, Saudi Arabia in 1957, the seventeenth son of one of Saudi Arabia's wealthiest businessmen, who had many wives and concubines. He earned a degree in civil engineering from King 'Abd al-'Aziz University in Jeddah in 1979. Bin Ladin has four wives and at least twenty-four children, several of whom are active in his movement.

After receiving an inheritance from his father, Bin Ladin devoted his money and connections to assisting the Muslim jihad fighters in Afghanistan against the Soviet occupation. By 1988 he had founded al-Qa'eda and, after the Soviet withdrawal from Afghanistan in 1989, Bin Ladin was hailed as an Islamic hero in his home country. Relations with the Saudi government soured after the 1990 Iraqi invasion of Kuwait, however, because the Saudi government rejected Bin Ladin's offer to defend the country using al-Qa'eda forces and instead used non-Muslim America. In the early 1990s Bin Ladin embarked on a series of terrorist attacks against both the Saudis and the United States, culminating in the 1996 "Declaration of Jihad Against the Americans Occupying the Land of the Two Holy Places [Mecca and Medina]," for its ongoing military presence on the soil of Arabia (according to Islam, no religion other than Islam is permitted to exist in the Arabian Peninsula; this is why non-Muslims are by law not allowed to be citizens or permanent residents of

Reprinted from *Guardian Unlimited: Observer Worldview Extra*, November 24, 2002. Excerpted from *What Does Al-Qaeda Want?: Unedited Communiqués*, by permission of North Atlantic Books.

Saudi Arabia). The most notorious event in bin Ladin's career to date, however, was doubtless the destruction of the World Trade Center in New York and the partial destruction of the Pentagon in Washington on September 11, 2001. The following passages are excerpted from the "Letter to America," which was first posted in Arabic on a Saudi Arabian Web site in 2002. This translation was printed in the Guardian *newspaper in England on Sunday, November 24, 2002. Bin Ladin states that this letter was written to clarify al-Qa'eda's grievances against, and demands of the United States.*

(Question 2.) What are we calling you to, and what do we want from you?

1) The first thing that we are calling you to is Islam.

(a) The religion of the Unification of God; of freedom from associating partners with Him, and rejection of this; of complete love of Him, the Exalted; of complete submission to His Laws; and of the discarding of all the opinions, orders, theories, and religions which contradict the religion He sent down to His Prophet Muhammad (peace be upon him). Islam is the religion of all the prophets, and makes no distinction between them—peace be upon them all.

It is to this religion that we call you; the seal of all the previous religions. It is the religion of Unification of God, sincerity, the best of manners, righteousness, mercy, honor, purity, and piety. It is the religion of showing kindness to others, establishing justice between them, granting them their rights, and defending the oppressed and the persecuted. . . .

2) The second thing we call you to is cessation of the oppression, lies, immorality, and debauchery that have spread among you.

(a) We call you to be a people of manners, principles, honor, and purity; to reject the immoral acts of fornication, homosexuality, intoxicants, gambling, and trading with interest.

We call you to all of this that you may be freed from that which you have become caught up in; that you may be freed from the deceptive lies that you are a great nation, lies that your leaders spread among you to conceal from you the despicable state that you have attained.

(b) It is saddening to tell you that you are the worst civilization witnessed by the history of mankind:

(i) You are the nation who, rather than ruling by the Shari'ah of Allah in its Constitution and Laws, choose to invent your own laws as you will and desire. You separate religion from your policies, contradicting the pure nature that affirms Absolute Authority to the Lord and your Creator. You flee from the embarrassing question posed to you: How is it possible for Allah the Almighty to create His creation, grant them power over all the creatures and land, grant them all the amenities of life, and then deny them that which they are most in need of: knowledge of the laws which govern their lives?

(ii) You are the nation that permits usury, which has been forbidden by all the religions. Yet you build your economy and investments on usury. As a result of this, in all its different forms and guises, the Jews have taken control of your economy, through which they have then taken control of your media, and now control all aspects of your life, making you their servants and achieving their aims at your expense—precisely what Benjamin Franklin warned you against.

(iii) You are a nation that permits the production, trading, and usage of intoxicants. You also permit drugs, and only forbid the trade of them, even though your nation is the largest consumer of them.

(iv) You are a nation that permits acts of immorality, and you consider them to be pillars of personal freedom. You have continued to sink down this abyss from level to level until incest has spread amongst you, in the face of which neither your sense of honor nor your laws object.

Who can forget your President Clinton's immoral acts committed in the official Oval Office? After that you did not even bring him to account, other than to say that he "made a mistake," after which everything passed with no punishment. Is there a worse kind of event for which your name will go down in history and be remembered by nations?

(v) You are a nation that permits gambling in its all forms. The companies practice this as well, resulting in the investments becoming active and the criminals becoming rich.

293

(vi) You are a nation that exploits women like consumer products or advertising tools, calling upon customers to purchase them. You use women to serve passengers, visitors, and strangers to increase your profit margins. You then rant that you support the liberation of women.

(vii) You are a nation that practices the trade of sex in all its forms, directly and indirectly. Giant corporations and establishments are built on this, under the name of art, entertainment, tourism, freedom, and other deceptive names you attribute to it.

(viii) And because of all this, you have been described in history as a nation that spreads diseases that were unknown to man in the past. Go ahead and boast to the nations of man that you brought them AIDS as a Satanic American invention.

(ix) You have destroyed nature with your industrial waste and gases more than any other nation in history. Despite this, you refuse to sign the Kyoto Agreement because it threatens the profit of your greedy companies and industries.

(x) Your law is the law of the rich and wealthy people, who hold sway in their political parties and fund election campaigns with their gifts. Behind them stand the Jews, who control your policies, media, and economy.

(xi) That which you are singled out for in the history of mankind is the fact that you have used your force to destroy mankind more than any other nation in history; not to defend principles and values, but to hasten to secure your interests and profits. You who dropped a nuclear bomb on Japan, even though Japan was ready to negotiate an end to the war—how many acts of oppression, tyranny, and injustice have you carried out, O callers to freedom?

(xii) Let us not forget one of your major characteristics: your duality in both manners and values; your hypocrisy in manners and principles. All manners, principles, and values have two scales: one for you and one for the others.

(a) The freedom and democracy that you call to is for yourselves and for the white race only; as for the rest of the world, you impose upon them your monstrous, destructive policies and governments, which you call the "American friends." Yet you prevent them from establishing democracies. When the Islamic party in Algeria wanted to practice democracy and they won the election, you unleashed your agents in the Algerian army onto them, to attack them with tanks and guns, to imprison them and torture them—a new lesson from the "American book of democracy"!!

(b) Your policy on prohibiting and forcibly removing weapons of mass destruction to ensure world peace only applies to those countries which you do not permit to possess such weapons. As for the countries you consent to, such as Israel, then they are allowed to keep and use such weapons to defend their security. Anyone else whom you suspect might be manufacturing or keeping these kinds of weapons you call criminals and take military action against them.

(c) You are the last ones to respect the resolutions and policies of International Law, yet you claim to want to selectively punish anyone else who does the same. Israel has for more than fifty years been pushing U.N. resolutions and rules against the wall, with the full support of America.

(d) As for the war criminals which you censure and form criminal courts for—you shamelessly ask that your own be granted immunity! However, history will not forget the war crimes that you committed against the Muslims and the rest of the world; those you have killed in Japan, Afghanistan, Somalia, Lebanon, and Iraq will remain a shame that you will never be able to escape. It will suffice to remind you of your latest war crimes in Afghanistan, in which densely populated innocent civilian villages were destroyed; and where bombs were dropped on mosques, causing the roof to come crashing down on the heads of the Muslims praying inside. You are the ones who broke the agreement with the Mujahideen when they left Qunduz, bombing them in Jangi fort, and killing more than a thousand of your prisoners through suffocation and thirst. Allah alone knows how many people have died by torture at the hands of you and your agents. Your planes remain in the Afghan skies, looking for anyone remotely suspicious.

(e) You have claimed to be the vanguard of human rights, and your Ministry of Foreign Affairs issues annual reports containing statistics of those countries that violate any human rights. However, all

these things vanished when the Mujahideen hit you, and you then implemented the methods of the same documented governments that
you used to curse. In America, you captured thousands of Muslims
and Arabs, taking them into custody without reason or court trial, nor
even disclosing their names. You issued newer, harsher laws.

What happens in Guantánamo is a historical embarrassment to
America and its values, and it screams into your faces, you hypocrites: "What is the value of your signature on any agreement or
treaty?"

3) What we call you to thirdly is to take an honest stance with yourselves—and I doubt you will do so—to discover that you are a nation
without principles or manners, and that to you values and principles
are something to be merely demanded from others, not that which
you yourself must adhere to.

4) We also advise you to stop supporting Israel, and to end your support
of the Indians in Kashmir, the Russians against the Chechens, and to
also cease supporting the Manila government against the Muslims in
Southern Philippines.

5) We also advise you to pack your luggage and get out of our lands. We
desire for your goodness, guidance, and righteousness, so do not
force us to send you back as cargo in coffins.

6) Sixthly, we call upon you to end your support of the corrupt leaders in
our countries. Do not interfere in our politics and method of education.
Leave us alone, or else expect us in New York and Washington.

7) We also call you to deal with us and interact with us on the basis of
mutual interests and benefits, rather than the policies of subjugation,
theft, and occupation; and to end your policy of supporting the Jews
because this will result in more disasters for you.

If you fail to respond to all these conditions, then prepare for fight with the
Islamic Nation, the Nation of Monotheism that puts complete trust in
Allah and fears none other than Him. . . .

This Islamic Nation was able to dismiss and destroy the previous evil empires like yourself; this is the Nation that rejects your attacks, wishes to remove your evils, and is prepared to fight you. You are well aware that the Islamic Nation, from the very core of its soul, despises your haughtiness and arrogance.

If the Americans refuse to listen to our advice and the goodness, guidance, and righteousness that we call them to, then be aware that you will lose this Crusade Bush began, just like the other previous Crusades in which you were humiliated by the hands of the Mujahideen, fleeing to your home in great silence and disgrace. If the Americans do not respond, then their fate will be that of the Soviets who fled from Afghanistan to deal with their military defeat, political breakup, ideological downfall, and economic bankruptcy.

This is our message to the Americans, as an answer to theirs. Do they now know why we fight them and over which form of ignorance, by the permission of Allah, we shall be victorious?

QUESTION

1. What is al-Qa'eda's first demand of Americans?
2. What are the examples given of immorality?
3. How does bin Ladin feel about American separation of church and state? Constitutional law?
4. Toward the end, bin Ladin brings in several historical examples that resonate particularly with Islamic radicals. What are these examples and what purpose do they serve?